Builder's Guide to Change-of-Use Properties

Builder's Guide to Change-of-Use Properties

R. Dodge Woodson

McGraw-Hill, Inc.
New York San Francisco Washington, D.C. Auckland Bogotá
Caracas Lisbon London Madrid Mexico City Milan
Montreal New Delhi San Juan Singapore
Sydney Tokyo Toronto

hc   1 2 3 4 5 6 7 8 9 DOC/DOC 9 9 8 7 6 5

Library of Congress Cataloging-in-Publication Data
Woodson, R. Dodge (Roger Dodge), 1955–
    Builder's guide to change-of-use properties / by R. Dodge Woodson.
    p. cm.
    Includes index.
    ISBN 0-07-071789-3
    1. Construction industry—Management. 2. Buildings—Remodeling for other use—Management. I. Title.
    HD9715.A2W648 1995
    690'.24—dc20   95-17263
                                                              CIP

Acquisitions editor: April D. Nolan
Editorial team: Tom G. Begnal, Editor
               Susan W. Kagey, Managing Editor
               Joanne Slike, Executive Editor
               Jodi L. Tyler, Indexer
Production team: Katherine G. Brown, Director
               Rhonda E. Baker, Coding
               Rose McFarland, Desktop Opeator
               Linda M. Cramer, Proofreading
Design team: Jaclyn J. Boone, Designer   GEN1
               Katherine Stefanski, Associate Designer   0717893

To my new son, Adam,
my wonderful daughter, Afton,
and my lovely wife, Kimberley.

Acknowledgments

I would like to thank Brunswick Coal & Lumber, Andrews Building Supply, and Carol E. Bartlett, CKD, for their generous assistance in providing kitchen designs and drawings.

Contents

Introduction

If you are a contractor of any type and have not investigated the lucrative market of conversion projects, you are missing out on some great opportunities to make money. In my experience, conversion jobs present some of the best money-making ventures available, especially for people in the trades.

I started out as a plumber. This route took me to owning my own plumbing company. From there, I went into bath and kitchen remodeling. It was a natural tie-in. Then came full-scale remodeling. My next step was rehab work. My growth pattern expanded to the extent that I was building up to 60 single-family homes a year. From there, I became a real estate broker and property manager. Each step I took was along a well-planned path. Of all the work I've done, conversion projects have proved to be the best return on my investment.

What is conversion work? It is much like remodeling, except that there is some preliminary field work and research that must go into the project. Essentially, a conversion project changes the use of a building to take advantage of the building's potential as a profit maker. You might convert a house into a duplex or a quadplex. The job might entail changing a residential property into commercial office space. You might even convert an abandoned service station into a drive-through restaurant. Maybe you are going to take a deserted motel and convert it into condominiums. In the conversion business, the possibilities are limited only by your imagination.

Can a conversion contractor make good money? There's no doubt about it. A conversion job done properly can net you tens of thousands of dollars in profit in a very short period of time. I've helped people make upwards of $10,000 in less than a week by doing what I call quick-flips. Not only that, they never raised a hand to renovate the properties. Other people, myself included, have made even more money by seeing a conversion project through to its completion.

Regardless of your vocation, a commanding career is waiting for you in conversion work and change-of-use properties. How can you tap into this market of real estate money machines? You've taken the first step by picking up this book. The personal experiences I share are enough to get you up and running. Experience is going to come to you in time. Consider this an earn-while-you-learn program. I'm certain you are going to be captivated by the financial reward that awaits you in the world of conversion projects.

1

Selecting a suitable conversion project

The process of selecting a suitable conversion project shouldn't be done in haste. Proper selection is the cornerstone of a successful conversion project. It doesn't matter if you plan to sell or rent the building after the conversion; the selection process is crucial to the project. The choices you make at this stage can mean the difference between a highly profitable project and one that ends in bankruptcy.

What makes a sound selection decision? Many factors play important roles. One of the first considerations is determining the profit potential of a project. In addition, the durability of the building is important, especially if you plan to hold the property for a long period of time.

If you expect to rent the building, you must consider the difficulty of managing the property. Indeed, property management is something that you should carefully look at in any conversion project, even one that you plan to sell immediately. More factors that you must consider before you buy a building to convert are discussed later in this chapter.

Beginning the selection process

The selection process should begin before you look at any property. You must first start to assess your needs and desires. It is a time to make some major decisions. The selection process should start on paper.

How many rental units?

One of the first decisions to make is the number of rental units you want to gain from a conversion project. Your decision has a direct bearing on the type of building you buy. Let's say, for example, you want to convert a single-family home into a duplex. This is not a tall order to fill. However, if you hope to gain four rental units from a project, it can take a lot of looking to find a suitable house. I'll expand on this point with a few examples.

As a real estate broker, I once sold a duplex to a man who converted it to a four-unit building. Local zoning regulations allowed as many as five units, but creating a fifth unit would not have been cost effective. The buyer, with a little help from me, made a good decision. Why was his decision so good? He wanted at least four units, but he didn't want to get involved in extensive add-on construction. This particular buyer had good remodeling skills, yet he didn't feel qualified to add a new foundation and then build the entire addition from scratch. Not only that, the added cost of a fifth unit would take too long to pay for itself in rental income and tax advantages. So, even if the buyer wanted to build an addition, it would not have been financially feasible.

On a different occasion, I sold a rundown, old triplex to an investor. A large, old barn was attached to the back. The buyer saw the property as a great fixer-upper and was going to be satisfied with three rental units. After checking the local zoning ordinances, I discovered that the property could be converted to a maximum of five units. The attached barn made it possible to add two additional rental units at a reasonable cost. The owner took my advice and added the units. For the price of an old triplex, the buyer ended up with a money-making five-unit building. If the buyer had stopped at the obvious and stuck with the triplex plan, he would have lost out on some extra income.

You should be starting to see that there is more to conversion projects than meets the eye. They offer a great opportunity to anyone with the time, ability, and willingness to go out and find property that is suitable for conversion. In fact, conversion projects got me started as an owner of rental property. As a builder and remodeler, conversion projects provided winter work for me and my work crews. When the projects were complete, I had good rental property with a lot of equity in the buildings. I also had the option of either holding the buildings in my rental portfolio or selling them for a cash profit.

I'm a little better qualified than the average person when it comes to conversion projects. My many years of experience working as a builder, remodeler, master plumber, and real estate broker gives me some distinct advantages. This book shares my wealth of knowledge so that you, too, can become a competent conversion contractor.

Let's get back to the question at hand. How many rental units do you want to create? There is a broader sales market for duplexes, but four-unit buildings offer more investor advantages. Do you plan to live in the property? Is it likely that you are going to sell the property to an owner-occupant, or do you plan to hold it as a source of passive income? The questions just keep rolling at you. This is why the selection process begins before you inspect your first building.

The number of units you want has a direct effect on the type of building you buy, the amount of money needed, and the potential profit from the project. Typically, the more units you create, the more money you make. This, however, is not always true, just as it was not true for the investor in the first example. Let me give you a brief rundown of the advantages and disadvantages of different types of rental units.

Duplexes

Duplexes are often the easiest type of small multifamily property to sell. They generally sell for less than larger buildings, so they attract more potential buyers. Duplexes have only two units, so they cost less to rehab or create. A duplex can be an ideal property for some owner-occupants. The property owner can live in one unit and use the rental income from the other unit to offset the ownership costs.

There is a downside to owning duplexes. With only two rental incomes, duplexes don't offer great cash flow for aggressive investors. For that reason, most serious real estate investors won't buy duplexes. Unless you are an owner-occupant, it's difficult to make money renting duplexes. However, if you are planning to convert a building and then put it up for sale, a duplex might be just the ticket to a profitable project.

Triplexes

Triplexes fall into the middle ground. They can work great for an owner-occupant, and they sometimes pay their own way for an absentee owner. If you're looking for a good compromise, a triplex might be it. It has been my experience, however, that you should either deal in duplexes or concentrate on larger buildings that have no less than four units.

Quadplexes

I feel that quadplexes are ideal for a small-scale landlord. Under the right conditions, the income from the four units can pay all the ownership costs and associated expenses. Owner-occupants can often live in their four-unit buildings without having to allot ordinary income to the housing expense. Arm's-length investors can buy four-unit buildings that end up costing them nothing, since the tenants are paying the bills. In all of my experience, four-unit buildings have consistently proved to be winners.

Four-unit buildings are the largest multifamily properties you can finance with regular residential financing. Up to four units can be financed with the same types of loans used for single-family homes. This includes Federal Housing Administration (FHA) and Veterans Administration (VA) government financing. If a building contains more than four units, a commercial loan is normally required, especially if the loan is to be sold on the secondary mortgage market. The financing issue can be critically important.

When your conversion project is completed, you are going to need to target potential buyers. Buildings with two or three units are most often sold to owner-occupants. Four-unit buildings appeal to both owner-occupants and investors. If an owner-occupant is going to reside in the property, down-payment requirements are much lower when residential financing is available. A five-unit building requires commercial financing, so it might be much harder to sell. As a beginner in the conversion market, you should probably limit the building size to no more than four units.

Commercial buildings

Commercial buildings contain five or more rental units. Six-unit buildings are very popular with investors in my area. Properties with up to 10 units are usually a safe sell to investors, but larger buildings attract fewer buyers. Keep this in mind if you step up to larger rental properties.

One disadvantage to commercial buildings is the need for large down payments. Buyers are often required to put 20 to 30 percent of the purchase price as a down payment, which can be a lot of money.

On the other hand, since the building can be financed with a commercial loan, borrowers and lenders can get quite creative in their financing. I've been involved in the purchase of a number of large buildings where no cash was required for a down payment. I've even been involved in deals where purchasers of a big building not only didn't put any money down, they left the closing meeting with more cash than they had when they walked in the door.

The creative use of second mortgages and other financing maneuvers can get you into a building without the long-term use of any of your own money. I must warn you though, leveraging a building to the maximum can be very risky business. If anything major goes wrong, you could lose the building and your good credit rating.

Nonresidential properties

Nonresidential properties offer fantastic profit potential to some conversion contractors. These properties can start out as residential structures and end up as doctor's or real estate offices. If you can find residential homes that are located in commercial zones, you might be on a path to more money than you ever imagined.

Nonresidential projects are not for everyone, but they can produce the biggest bang for your buck. Converting an abandoned gas station into a fast-food restaurant can surely increase the value of the property. The market value of an old house is likely to grow considerably if it's converted into offices for medical professionals. Think about the increased value of the property in either of these cases. Without a doubt, sudden riches await those who are able to locate prime properties.

Living in the property

If you plan to live in the property, you are probably going to have more issues to deal with during the selection process than if you were buying it strictly on speculation. There are, however, some benefits to living in the property. For example, as an owner-occupant, you should have a lower down payment. Also, living in the property usually makes it easier to work on it in your spare time. It's cost effective to live in a building while you rehab it, although you might not like the unavoidable disarray that goes along with such a project.

If you plan to live in the property that you buy, concentrate on buying what I call a *keeper*. A keeper is a building with strong long-range potential. It is in a good neighborhood that is getting better. The property doesn't have any major structural defects, and it is purchased at a price that allows for a positive cash flow.

Buying for a quick sale

A conversion project is *quick-flipped* when it is sold as soon as possible for liquid capital. If you play the conversion game for quick profits, the rules change a bit. Your potential purchase options broaden because every building does not have to be a keeper. When you anticipate selling a property as soon as the conversion is completed, your only major requirement is to establish that there is a market for the property. That means you'll need to do some research, but it can be time well spent.

Don't get the wrong opinion from what I've just told you. Just because you are going to sell quickly doesn't mean that you should buy junk property. It is still important to choose your property carefully. "There's a dog for every dog house" is a saying my wife has that seems to apply to the world of real estate. There are buyers for all types of properties in all types of locations, but your profit and reputation can do better in some areas than in others.

Renting the property

If you plan to develop a rental portfolio for your retirement, you'll want to be looking for buildings that are keepers. The buildings should possess all the qualities needed for successful, long-term ownerships, even if they are properties you would not choose to live in.

Unfortunately, I don't have the space to discuss the many real estate issues that relate to rental properties. I can tell you this much—it's not always easy to be a landlord. Before you become one, I suggest you read a lot of books on the subject.

Profit potential

The profit potential of a conversion project is always an important concern. It doesn't matter if the project is a quick-flip or a keeper, you'll want to know how much profit stands to be made. As a conversion contractor, your primary interest is probably going to be with quick-flips.

If you are an experienced builder or remodeler, you already have the skills to determine the cost of conversion work. However, you might need some help determining the selling price of the property. Then it is wise to turn to other professionals.

Experienced real estate brokers and appraisers can be a great help in determining the market value of your property. Many brokers might talk to you free of charge, usually in hopes of getting the listing to sell the property. Free advice, however, is not always good advice. I recommend that you hire a qualified real estate appraiser to determine the current market value of your property. The few hundred dollars you pay to a licensed appraiser might be the best investment you'll make in a conversion project.

As you gain experience, you'll probably be able to come up with a reasonably close estimate of market values on your own. Indeed, if you take the time to check the recent property transfers and current property prices in your area, you can estimate prices pretty closely even when you are just starting your conversion business. Don't confuse the asking price with the selling price. It is not uncommon for a property to be sold for considerably less than the original asking price. To protect yourself, you must work only with closed sales and proven sales prices, which allows you to target the profit potential of various buildings.

Durability

A durable building is one that is not going to require any major repairs for at least 10 years. If the major mechanical systems are in good working order, and there are no structural defects, the building is solid. A durable building is a keeper. If the heating system must be replaced in five years, or if it needs a new roof in three years, the building should be considered for a quick-flip conversion. I would rate these problems against a keeper, but they shouldn't get in the way with a quick-flip. As you assess buildings, keep in mind what prospective buyers are likely to see and think. Take this into consideration when formulating your offer to purchase and your potential profit picture.

Management

The rental management of a building might be the furthest thing from your mind when you inspect potential conversion projects, but it shouldn't be. Management of a building can have much to do with the value of a property. If you plan to sell the property, you have no way of knowing if the new owner is going to manage the building personally or hire a management company. Either way, buyers want buildings that are not nightmares to manage. When you are checking out properties, think about management issues. A detailed discussion of management issues can be found in my book *Profitably Managing Your Rental Properties* (John Wiley & Sons, Inc., 1992).

Utilities

The availability and cost of utilities plays a part in selecting a building. Before you buy any property, you need to look carefully into all the utility factors. For example, a property that is too far out of town to be served by cable television can have a high vacancy rate. Buildings served by a private septic system could be troublesome. Explore previous costs for heating, cooling, water, and other expenses. If the property has a private well, confirm that the well produces enough water to satisfy the needs of all the tenants expected to live in the building. Do the same check on private sewage facilities. What works fine for a single family might create problems for multiple families.

Taxes

Real estate taxes are a fact of life in most communities, so it's important to check the tax rate that applies to your property. Keep in mind that the building is going to be reassessed once your conversion is completed. The value of the converted property is sure to go up and increase the tax payments. Higher taxes are a factor whether or not you plan to sell or hold the property.

Physical condition

The physical condition of a building might not be very important, as long as you buy the property for a good price. As a contractor, you shouldn't be afraid of what it takes to bring a building up to satisfactory standards. You should, however, spend enough time in the inspection process to make sure that you are not going to be faced with any surprises. As long as you are aware of what must be done, and at what cost, almost any property can be suitable for purchase.

Going into the field

Going into the field to look at potential properties can be very exciting. As long as you've done your homework first, seeking out properties to buy can be a lot of fun. By the time you begin site inspections, you should know the type of properties you want, where you want them located, and how they are going to be financed.

Seasoned contractors have little trouble evaluating the structural and mechanical aspects of properties. If you're new to the construction and remodeling business, you owe it to yourself to do some extra homework. Read books and learn what to look for when inspecting a potential property.

Take notes

Take scrupulous notes during your field work. Write down everything you can about the properties. As your search continues, you might soon forget key issues pertaining to particular properties without good notes. Your recorded thoughts can prove invaluable when the time comes to buy a building. A small tape recorder comes in handy, but a pad of paper and a pencil also can get the job done.

Tools of the trade

When you go into the field, you need to take a few important tools. They include a flashlight, tape measure, screwdriver, and perhaps a few other odds and ends. A good light is the most important part of your tool kit. A flat-blade screwdriver not only removes screws, it can be used to probe for rot in floor joists and sill plates. Your tape measure allows you to measure room sizes as well as the square footage of the building. In addition to your mechanical tools, don't forget your administrative needs, such as a tape recorder, pad of paper, pencil, and so forth. If you expect to be in unfamiliar territory, a good street map can come in handy.

Ask questions

Ask plenty of questions as you inspect a building. Talk to the owner whenever possible. If you can only talk to a real estate broker, confirm the broker's comments with the property owner before moving too far. If the building is being rented, make it a point to talk to the tenants. They can tell you things that you might not hear from the owner.

Location

Location is everything in real estate. Once you begin your hands-on search, spend some time investigating the area. Check the distances between the building and schools, shopping, medical facilities, and so forth. I can't stress enough how valuable location is to a real estate transaction, so please don't skimp on this phase of your shopping.

Post-inspection review

When you return from your field inspections, sit down and go over your findings. Make sure you won't be disturbed while you review the work. A minor mistake in evaluating a building can cost you major money. You might find it helpful to create simple checklists to use when comparing the buildings under consideration. The more thoroughly you assess the information, the more successful you are likely to be in the conversion business.

Be judicious

Be judicious in the selection process. Sometimes it pays to act quickly, but more often than not, a hasty decision is going to be a regrettable one. Until you are experienced enough to know a steal when you find it, take enough time to make sure you are seeing all angles of a deal. It is better to lose a good deal than to buy a bad building.

Fire jobs

A *fire job* is a property that has been damaged by fire. Fire jobs can look like wonderful opportunities, and they can be for people with the right experience—but they also can turn into disasters. Buildings damaged by fire can hold many secrets and surprises that can be quite costly. Your budget can be busted in the blink of an eye.

I have a fair amount of experience in fire restoration, yet I'm still leery of buying a fire-damaged building. While the prices can be very low, the value might be even lower with this type of building.

Don't be too creative

There is nothing wrong with getting creative when purchasing real estate, but be careful not to get too creative. Usually, the more complicated something is, the easier it is for something to go wrong. Be very careful if you have an owner that seems extremely anxious to sell and has an answer for your every objection. This owner might be looking to unload a bad building on some sucker. If the deal seems too good to be true, it probably is.

After the selection

Once you have made your selection, you have a lot of work to do, and much of it must be done before you ever own the property. Now is the time when you get to play detective. After finding what appears to be a suitable property, you must make sure that the property is everything you hope it is. This process is complicated and time consuming. Your journey down the road to acquiring your first conversion project begins in Chapter 2.

2

Preliminary legwork

You need to do some preliminary legwork before purchasing a property for conversion. The legwork costs time, but it could save you from a financial fiasco. Of course, all real estate purchases require that the buyer spend some serious time checking for potential problems, but conversion projects require added time and effort. There is much to be done before you commit yourself, and your money, to the acquisition of a conversion project.

Zoning is always a big issue in determining the viability of a conversion project. The physical condition of a building can also be very important when making a buying decision. Then there is the question of title work. If the title is clouded or encumbered in any way, the property might be worth only a fraction of its normal value. Other factors can also affect the value of a property. To expand, let's take a look at each step in the preliminary legwork process.

Zoning

Zoning is one of the key issues that affects the potential of a conversion project. It does no good to buy what looks like an ideal conversion project only to find out that zoning regulations limit the property to its present use.

The key to a super deal is to find property in an area that is zoned to accommodate a profitable conversion *and* where the owner chooses not to pursue a conversion or doesn't know one is possible.

Almost all communities have some type of zoning regulations. Some communities have regulations that are more stringent than others. It's your responsibility to dig into the zoning rules and regulations regarding the property you want to buy. If you fail to follow through on zoning requirements, you could be in for a very bad surprise and a costly lesson. Let's talk for awhile about how zoning can help or hinder your speculative efforts.

In Chapter 1, I told you how I helped a couple of investors pick up prime conversion projects. One property, the duplex that had zoning for five units, had been on the open market for over a year. It was priced too high considering the condition of the building.

When I came across the building, I was amazed at its size. There was plenty of interior room to create four units. A trip to the zoning office proved that the property was a prime pick. In less than a week, I had put the building under contract with my investor. If the listing broker had done the proper research, the seller might have gotten more money for the property and probably would have been able to sell it sooner. My investor profited from others not knowing the potential of the property.

If you go to the zoning office and beat the brush, you might just discover some hidden treasures. The zoning office is an ideal source of leads for properties that might not be for sale on the open market. If you check zoning records and find suitable properties, you can contact the owners directly and let them know you are an interested buyer. A lot of owners won't sell, but some might. The money you can make is well worth the effort, even when your offers are often declined. You only need a few owners willing to sell in order to keep busy and profitable.

Zoning requirements can cover a multitude of issues, one of which is the allowable uses for a piece of property. You might find that a single-family home can only be used as a house. Then again, you might discover that the house lies in a zone where professional office space is allowed. Bang! You've just hit the jackpot. The same can be true of finding a single-family home located in an area zoned for multifamily use. A trip to the zoning office should be considered mandatory procedure.

Covenants and restrictions

Covenants and restrictions in a deed can ruin your plans. It is not uncommon for developers to incorporate their own rules and regulations in property deeds before they are transferred to buyers. These restrictions can cover almost anything. For example, you might find that any commercial vehicle, like a plumbing van, cannot be parked in the driveway for more than a set period of time. The restrictions could limit the size, type, and color of any mailbox used on the property. It is not uncommon for deed restrictions to dictate the colors that can be used for exterior siding. The list of possibilities is almost endless, so check the property deeds very carefully before you buy.

Flood zones

Properties located in flood zones and flood plains can be a very poor investment. There are times when these properties are nearly worthless due to problems getting flood insurance. Buildings that appear to the untrained eye to be well away from any threat of flooding could be considered at risk. Federal flood maps are usually used to locate flood-risk areas. The best way to protect against buying a property that might be in a flood zone is to hire a professional land surveyor. The surveyor can do an elevation survey to determine if the property is safe to buy at normal market prices.

Title search

As you move closer to a closing, you should have an attorney or a title company perform a title search on the property that you have under contract. All contracts to purchase real estate should have some built-in escape clauses to protect you. These clauses can provide you with a reasonable time to check all conditions that might adversely affect your purchase. Once you complete your checks, the contingencies can be removed and the sale can be made.

When you are ready to have a title search done, go to a reputable real estate attorney or a good title company. Not all lawyers work with real estate on a daily basis. It's usually in your best interest to find an attorney who specializes in real estate. You can't afford to have anyone make a mistake when they are running the chain of title on the property you are buying.

Mechanic's and materialman liens

Mechanic's and materialman liens are dangerous. They can escape detection in a title search and pop up the next week. These liens cloud a title and can cause you financial pain. They occur when work has recently been done on a property. If the workers or the material suppliers haven't been properly paid, they have lien rights. These rights can extend for months, so you could buy a property and discover a month later that it's encumbered in liens.

If it's obvious that work was recently done to a building, don't purchase the property until you talk to the contractors and suppliers to make sure that they have been fully paid. You should require that the seller sign an affidavit at closing stating that no work has been done on the project for 90 days or that any work done in the last 90 days has been paid for. The affidavit provides a good legal basis for a lawsuit in the event that an unpaid subcontractor pops up later.

Liens run with the property, not the property owner, so you could inherit someone else's problems. If you don't think it can happen, consider the following story. I sold a multifamily building a few years ago. The building was owned by a real estate agent who had listed the property with a different real estate agency. My real estate company was the one to bring a buyer to the table. In fact, I was the broker who produced the buyer.

Many deficiencies were found during the inspection. The roof leaked in an apartment that the buyer had not been allowed to see until just a day or so before closing. Fortunately, I had written the purchase offer in a way to protect all parties, and the buyer was not hurt by the roof leak and other building-related problems. However, the buyer was not so lucky with another problem.

I noticed evidence of an underground oil tank. My suspicion turned out to be correct. Due to the local environmental rules and regulations, the tank had to be removed. By law, the broker, if he had knowledge of the tank, was required to disclose its presence. As real estate professionals, both the owner/broker and the listing brokers should have disclosed the oil tank, but neither of them did. Not wanting to get myself sued, I raised the question and got the answer I suspected. The seller agreed to have the tank removed, a job that was not cheap.

The buyer went to the closing table thinking all was well. So did I, and so did the listing broker. The seller sat through the closing, signed the papers and took his check. On his way out of the closing room, he looked back and told us, as a group, not to forget to pay the contractor for removing the oil tank. I was flabbergasted. The buyer has just taken possession of the property. A check for the full amount due to the seller had been issued by the bank, and now, some contractor had lien rights against the buyer's new building.

The listing broker and I split the cost of paying the contractor. This appeased the buyer and the seller walked free and clear. If we hadn't paid the contractor (and we didn't have to since we had not done anything wrong) the buyer would have been stuck with a big bill and a potential lien on his building. So, you see, it can happen. You must work hard to protect yourself.

Market demand

Whether you are converting an old motel into condominiums, a house into a duplex, or an abandoned warehouse into retail space, it's important to consider market demand when buying property for conversion. Market demand can change quickly, sometimes even before you can complete the conversion project. This adds a little risk to becoming a conversion contractor, but the risk can usually be managed. If you do enough research before you buy a property, the odds are good you won't get caught in a bind. Let me give you an example.

Assume that you are going to buy a duplex and convert it to a four-unit building. Can the area provide you with a steady stream of potential tenants? There are several ways to find out.

Check the newspaper to see what type of competition is presently on the market. This information might be useful, but not conclusive. A friendly banker might be able to obtain vacancy-rate statistics for the area, information that is helpful. Vacancy-rate statistics are based on historical data, so they should be dependable.

You can also go to a library and research advertisements in old newspapers. By tracking the past you can predict the future with startling accuracy. Look through the newspapers to see how long the rental ads run before they are canceled. They probably are not canceled until the rental unit is leased. This historical data can help you determine what to expect in rent-up time.

As you look through the newspaper, pay attention to the size of the units that are rented. Efficiency and one-bedroom units normally have a much higher turnover rate than larger units. Also check to see if units rent faster in a particular area of town. This information can tell you what part of town is the best place to buy. Collect as much information as possible from the old advertisements and create a written log. Use a computer or a pad of paper, but keep notes on your findings. These notes can help you now and later.

If you don't have the time or patience to do all the research, consult a licensed real estate appraiser. Appraisers have their fingers on the pulse of most real estate markets. After all, it's their job to know what's going on in the world of real estate. An appraiser might charge a few hundred dollars, but it is a great investment.

Companies that manage rental properties might be able to provide helpful information. If you talk with enough management companies, you can come up with some solid numbers for vacancy rates in almost any area. However, the companies might fluff over their vacancy rates a little. They don't like customers to believe they have high vacancy rates, so it's possible that the numbers they give you might not be completely accurate.

Check existing leases

Before you buy an existing rental property, you should check all the leases very closely. You might find a tenant with a long-term lease that doesn't allow for rent increases. It's possible that a tenant has a life estate in the property with provisions for no rental increases. Some investors use this tactic to buy buildings cheaply or to finance them creatively.

Security deposits are another issue to consider. Are there any? If there are, who has them and who gets them?

It could be financial suicide to buy a building when the tenants have leases that can tie your hands. You might want to have your attorney review the leases before you commit to buying a building.

When everything checks out

If all of your preliminary work checks out, you're ready to move on to the next step. Keep in mind that it is common for the property to be tied up with a contingency contract during many of the phases described in this chapter. You should not pay for title searches, surveys, and other such expenses until you have control of the property. Having control doesn't mean you own the property, it means you have a purchase option or a contingency contract.

What is the next step? Assuming that you have a property under contract, the next step should move you towards a successful closing. If you have not placed a property under contract, a stringent inspection of the premises is in order. Even if you have a property under contract, you should do a prepurchase inspection just before closing the deal. A building that was in good repair 60 days earlier might be trashed by the time you close the loan.

Your contract should make provisions for a last-minute inspection, with you retaining the right to withdraw from the purchase, without penalty, if the inspection goes poorly. Let's move to Chapter 3 and discuss how property inspections should be done.

3

The prepurchase inspection process

The prepurchase inspection process is vital to success as a conversion contractor. If you are a savvy buyer, you inspect a potential property at least three times. A first inspection takes place when you are looking for a property to buy. The second inspection should be done prior to making a commitment to purchase. A third inspection is in order just before finalizing the closing of your deal. Each of the three inspections is important, but the final inspection is the most crucial.

A first inspection determines if you are interested in the property. The second inspection is normally much more thorough than the first. Results from the second inspection are going to be the catalyst that moves you toward a final closing of your deal.

A lot can happen during the time it takes to close a real estate transaction. It is not uncommon for the closing process to take a couple of months. In two months, a heating system can fail, a roof can develop leaks, plumbing problems can crop up, and so on. Since a building can suffer serious problems between the time you sign a contract and the time you close your loan, it is essential to do a final inspection before closing the loan, while you still have time to back out of the deal.

Three options

When it's time to inspect the properties, you have a choice of three options:

1 Do the inspections yourself.
2 Call trade professionals to help you in certain areas of the inspections.
3 Hire an independent inspector to take care of the entire process.

Which option is best? The answer depends upon your knowledge, background and experience. To help bring it into focus, let's look at each of the three options more closely.

Personal inspection

Don't use a professional or an independent contractor to do the first-time inspection. You should do this one because much of this inspection hinges on your personal preferences. When you move to the second inspection, it might be time to call in professionals.

As a contractor, your knowledge of construction is probably strong in some areas and somewhat weak in many other areas. It is not enough, however, to possess only a little knowledge in various fields. Unless you are well versed in all aspects of construction, you should hire selected professionals to assist you in the second inspection.

Let's say that your trade strength is in carpentry. You are familiar with the mechanical trades because you have seen a lot of their work, but you are not a licensed electrician, plumber, or HVAC mechanic. It is likely that you could spot glaring problems in any of these fields, but it also likely that you could overlook some serious problems. For this reason, you should seriously consider having a plumber, electrician, and HVAC contractor inspect the property. You might also have other specialists take a look at the premises. By working together with these experts, you can limit your exposure to potentially serious problems.

Trade inspections

I've talked briefly about trade inspections and specialists, but let's go a little further on this subject. Many trades are involved in the construction of a home or office building. Some trades, such as plumbing and electrical, require special licenses. It is acceptable to have a representative from each trade perform a building inspection when you buy a property. This practice can be time consuming, and a little expensive, but it can be done. Do you need someone from every trade to walk through your planned purchase? Probably not. If you are entering the hands-on conversion business, you must possess some skills yourself.

Before you hire experts from each trade, decide which ones you really need. Plumbing, heating, and electrical contractors should normally be hired, but if you have considerable experience as a builder or remodeler, you might not need any other help. However, if you are a plumber, you might need a company to inspect the property for roofing and structural defects. You must match your needs to your own set of circumstances.

Most people know their limitations. For example, I'm a master plumber and I've been a builder and remodeler for more years than I care to talk about. Therefore, I have a broad base of experience. My knowledge of electrical work is good when it comes to new construction, but it's lacking in the area of service work. Heating systems are no stranger to me, but, on the other hand, I'm not as good with heating as I am with plumbing. My building experience doesn't include a lot of hands-on carpentry, so I might have trouble installing rafters or laying out a set of stairs, but I understand enough about those jobs to know when they are being done properly. Even with my 20 years of experience, there is still a lot that I don't know. For this reason, I sometimes rely on expert advice. There is no shame in this, it's just good business practice.

Professional inspections

Professional inspections can be expensive, but they can also prove to be a bargain in the long run. If you are not sure how to properly inspect a property, a professional inspection service can be the answer to your dilemma. Independent property inspectors are available to investigate all aspects of buildings, including the utilities and appurtenances. They can even check for such things as tainted water, lead paint, and radon gas.

I prefer to do my own property inspections, but I still use professionals in certain areas. Even if I hired a full-service inspector, I'd still go along on the inspection. Experience has taught me that things generally go better when I am directly involved in the activities.

However, my approach here might not be exactly right for you. If your time is valuable, you don't need to accompany the inspector on the project site. Most inspection firms provide clients with a detailed, written report of their findings and suggestions. It's possible for you to hire a professional inspector to take care of all the inspections. All you need to do is assess the information.

Surveys

Some buyers don't put much stock in a property survey, but it's as important as any inspection you have done. Many lenders require a full-blown survey before money changes hands, but that is not always the case. A survey should be done, even if your lender doesn't require one. I have quite a list of personal horror stories that could be shared with you on this subject. Here is one example.

Property lines

As a broker, I had a buyer who placed a four-unit building under contract. The building had a paved parking lot on two sides. It seemed safe to assume that the parking area was a part of the property. Ah, but the survey proved differently, and it wasn't discovered until the last minute at the closing table.

When I wrote the purchase offer for the buyer, I included some standard contingencies, one of which involved survey and engineering studies. The buyer was lucky this clause was in his contract. I'd repeatedly asked the listing broker for a copy of a survey, but I never got one.

On the day of the closing, as we all sat around the table, the listing agent passed me a copy of the survey. My eyes must have grown as wide as soup bowls when I looked it over. About one-half of the paved parking lot was on land that belonged to the city, not to the owner of the four-unit building.

I immediately interrupted the closing and took the buyer out of the meeting and into a hallway. After showing the buyer the survey, we discussed his two options. He could cancel the purchase or he could negotiate for better terms. To make a long story short, the buyer negotiated better terms and closed on the property. This situation, however, could have been quite a blow to the new buyer had he not been protected with a formal survey.

Flood zones

Flood zones and flood plains can really mess up your plans in the real estate business. Owning a building in a flood zone or flood plain can be very rough financially. A good survey can help you avoid buying property that requires expensive flood insurance. If you are unfortunate enough to stumble onto a piece of property in a flood hazard area, don't buy it until you know exactly how to deal with the potential problems.

Property setbacks

The distance from a property boundary that must remain as open space is called the *setback*. You can't build within the setback. Most localities have requirements for front, back, and side setbacks. Setbacks requirements provide another good reason for having a survey done. You are going to have a very costly experience if you buy a property that was built in violation of the setback ordinances.

Inspecting the grounds

Inspecting the grounds of a potential conversion project can be as important as inspecting the structure itself. Yet many novice investors ignore the grounds. Most buyers look for the obvious. They examine the exterior of the building, then move inside to look for interior problems. Few newcomers to the conversion business spend enough time outside. I'll explain this more fully.

Let's do a little role playing. Assume that I'm your real estate broker, a buyer's broker, and you're a prospective purchaser. We are riding together in my vehicle. We arrive at our first stop of the day, a large, rambling residential home lying in commercial zoning, and you are in awe of the building's size. You plan to convert the building into a dental clinic, and your mind races with ways to layout the interior of the building. You envision several dental offices in the building, some for general dentistry and some for specialists. As I look over at you, I can almost see dollar signs in your eyes. You are so taken with the size, and the potential for many rental units, that you are oblivious to anything else.

As a buyer's broker, I represent you, and it is my duty to bring you back down to earth by pointing out the potential problems with the building, as well as the positive features and benefits. Now, if I were a seller's broker, I wouldn't be obligated to give you my professional opinion, and I might be able to capitalize on your excitement and get you to sign on the dotted line. That's why, whenever possible, I feel it's best to deal with a buyer's broker, not a seller's broker. Since I don't have the room to detail all the reasons here, I suggest you do your own research to learn the benefits of using a buyer's broker.

Okay, we've parked in the driveway of this big house that you want to convert into a dental clinic. A number of questions immediately come to mind. Is there enough parking space for patients and staff? Does local zoning affect the size of the parking area? Can signs be erected? Is the building serviced by municipal utilities for water, sewer, and natural gas? How much land surrounds the building? Is the lot graded properly, or must you invest in extensive soil work? Do the neighboring properties detract from the building's value? I hope you are starting to see some of the potential problems that must be considered. The list goes go on and on. The use of checklists can be very helpful when inspecting potential properties (Figs. 3-1 and 3-2).

Property Information Sheet

Address _____

Style _____ Price _____

Exterior dimensions _____

Road frontage _____ Water frontage _____

Land area _____ Zoning _____

Number of rooms _____ Number of bedrooms _____

Number of bathrooms _____ Annual taxes _____

Deed book and page _____

Map/Lot/Block _____

Siding _____ Color _____

Electric service _____ Heat type _____

Type of hot water _____ Water (public/private) _____

Attic (yes/no) _____ Sewer (public/private) _____

Basement (yes/no) _____ Assumable loan (yes/no) _____

Floor Plan

	1st	2nd	3rd	Basement
Living room				
Dining room				
Family room				
Bedrooms				
Bathrooms				
Kitchen				
Comments				

_____

_____

3-1 *Property information sheet*

Seller's Disclosure Form

Owner _____

Owner's address _____

Property address _____

Age of structure _____

How long has the seller owned the property? _____

Water Supply Information

Public—Yes/no   Private—Yes/no   Drilled/Dug/Artesian

Other (Describe) _____

Location _____ Date installed _____

Installed by whom _____

Have any problems ever been experienced with the following:

Water quality _____ Quantity _____ Pump _____

Discoloration _____ Other _____

Has the water ever been tested? Yes/No   Date of test _____

Are test results available? Yes/No

Have any test results ever been unsatisfactory or satisfactory with notation? Yes/No   If yes, what steps were taken to remedy the problems

_____

Waste Disposal System

Public—Yes/No   Private—Yes/No   Quasi-public—Yes/No

Have there been any problems with waste disposal? Yes/No

If yes, explain _____

If system is private, circle the appropriate type of system:

Septic   Leach   Holding tank   Other _____

Tank size _____ Tank installation date _____

Type of tank: Concrete   Metal   Other _____

Tank location _____

Company providing service _____

Have you experienced any malfunctions? Yes/No

If yes, explain _____

3-2 *Seller's disclosure form*

Lead-Based Paint

Does the property contain lead-based paint? Yes/No/Unknown

Are you aware of any cracking, peeling, or flaking paint? Yes/No

Comments _____

Underground Storage Tanks

Are there now, or have there ever been, any underground storage tanks on your property? Yes/No/Unknown

If yes, are tanks in current use? Yes/No

What materials are or were stored in the tanks? _____

Age of tanks _____   Size of tanks _____

Location _____

Have you ever experienced any problems such as leakage? Yes/No

Are tanks registered with the authorities? Yes/No

If tanks are no longer in use, have tanks been abandoned according to the local authority's regulations? Yes/No

Additional items of disclosure are provided on the disclosure addendum, if any. Are there any? Yes/No

The Purchaser is encouraged to seek information from professionals regarding specific issues of concern involving hazardous materials or other concerns arising from this property.

_____		_____	
Seller	Date	Purchaser	Date
_____		_____	
Seller	Date	Purchaser	Date
_____			
Broker	Date		

3-2 *Continued*

Look below the surface when you inspect the grounds of a building. Parking and utilities are two primary considerations. Other aspects of the building lot come into play, depending on how you plan to use the property. For example, if you were planning an enterprise that required an additional access to a main road, you would likely need a permit for the new access. Depending on visibility, traffic, and other factors, you might not get approval for the additional access. This could destroy your conversion plan. Providing information like this makes a buyer's broker invaluable to you.

Get inside

There is plenty to look at once you get inside a building. You probably are going to look first at the existing layout to see if the premises are suitable for your needs. It might not matter much if you are planning to renovate the property completely. Under such conditions, only load-bearing walls can limit your creativity, and even those can be dealt with by using steel and other support materials.

Under the living space

Many buildings have some sort of space under the living area. The space could be a basement, cellar or crawl space. Start your inspection in this location. You can eliminate this step if the building is built on a slab foundation.

One of the first things to look for is dampness and standing water. Moisture can do a lot of damage in a building. Inspect the foundation walls to see if they are wet or have marks left by standing water. Water marks can be an indication that the basement leaks, even though no water is present during your inspection. Take a screwdriver and probe the sill plates and the floor joists to see if they are rotting.

Next, look over the mechanical equipment: plumbing, heating, electrical wiring, heating systems, water tanks and the like. Anything stored on an elevated platform might indicate a water problem. Assuming that the basement, cellar, or crawl space check out okay, you can move upstairs.

In the living space

A multitude of potential problems can hide in the living space. Some of the problems are not easy to detect—for example, uninsulated or poorly insulated walls. However, with a little effort you can find out if the walls are insulated. Remove the cover plates from the electrical switches and outlets on the outside walls (be careful not to come into contact with hot wires). Once the covers are removed, inspect the wall cavity to see if insulation is present. You can also determine the type of insulation. It is also helpful to ask the owner to provide you with the fuel and utility bills for the last year or two. The bills can help you determine if the building is costing more than normal to maintain climatic control.

Checking floor coverings, interior wall coverings, and assorted building components is not very difficult. Usually, if these items look good, they probably are okay. Check to make sure the windows and doors are of a good quality and properly installed. A quick check of the plumbing and light fixtures can tell you if everything appears to be in working order. If the lights work and the plumbing fixtures fill and drain, they are probably all right. Heating and air conditioning is easy enough to test. Just move the thermostat to desired levels and check to see that both systems are working.

A lot of interior cosmetic issues might not be of importance to you. As a conversion contractor, you probably are going to rip out much of the existing structure, so fancy wall coverings and little dings in the drywall won't have much impact on the property value. Concentrate on the structural issues and mechanical systems. That is where big money is spent, so inspect those areas very carefully. Don't leave anything to the imagination. Note your findings on an inspection log (Fig. 3-3).

Above the living space

Some attics provide a home for wood-infesting beetles, and those little insects can be a huge problem. In some areas, a building that has beetles, termites and other types of wood-infesting creatures must be tented and fumigated, an expensive procedure. Then you might incur added costs to repair the damage caused by the insects. Most pest control companies inspect properties without cost.

While you're in the attic, check the insulation and ventilation. Inspect ceiling joists, rafters, and roof sheathing. If the roof is leaking badly, you'll find evidence of it in the attic. Poke around a little. You might find that the insulation is hiding potential problems in the electrical or plumbing systems or in some other area.

Problems

Some problems can turn you away from a property very quickly. These problems can usually be solved, but they can get expensive. You must carefully examine the costs to determine if property with one of these problems can become a profitable conversion project.

Inspection Log

Item	Poor	Fair	Good	Excellent
Foyer				
Hall				
Kitchen				
Living room				
Dining room				
Master bedroom				
Family room				
Bedroom 2				
Bedroom 3				
Bedroom 4				
Bedroom 5				
Master bathroom				
Bathroom 2				
Bathroom 3				
Half bath				
Closet space				
Floor coverings				
Interior paint				
Plumbing system				
Heating system				
Electrical system				
Basement				
Attic				
Insulation				
Garage				
Deck				
Siding				
Exterior paint				
Lawn				
Roof				
Comments:				

3-3 *Inspection log*

Lead paint

If you buy an old building, there is a good chance that lead paint is present. Many communities have regulations that require the removal of all lead paint before the property can be rented. The cost can be quite expensive.

Asbestos

Asbestos is another issue of great concern. Asbestos is sometimes found in pipe insulation, floor tiles, or siding, among other things. A building that contains asbestos products can cost plenty in abatement fees. That means the purchase price must be extremely low in order for you to profit from the project.

Underground oil tanks

Underground oil tanks are a problem in some areas. You might recall that I related a story about such a tank in Chapter 2. If you buy property with underground oil tanks, you could be spending some very serious money to have them removed. Sellers and brokers who have knowledge of this type of problem are supposed to disclose the information to potential buyers, but that doesn't always happen. It's best to go into every deal with your eyes wide open.

Radon

Radon gas has become a big issue in recent years. Testing for the gas is relatively simple, and the test can be performed by nonprofessionals. However, I recommend that you have a professional screen potential projects for radon and other environmental hazards.

Radon can be found in private water supplies, as well as in the air within a home. In most cases, there are ways to overcome the presence of radon. For example, in some buildings, a special ventilation system can be installed to reduce the radon level. However, I'm not an expert on radon, so I can't say for certain what system is safest. Talk to the experts.

Toxic waste

You might not think about toxic waste very often, but if you buy a property that has this problem, you are going to think about it a lot. The cost of cleaning up a toxic waste site is almost unthinkable. It's possible you could get stuck with a huge clean-up bill, especially if you buy an old gas station or other such commercial building.

Take your time

Take your time when doing a prepurchase inspection. If you rush the job, you are more likely to make mistakes. Be methodical and patient. Spend enough time, and money if necessary, to get an accurate assessment of each property. Failure to do so can result in lost money and tarnished credit.

Once you're ready

Once you are ready to buy a property, you will have a lot of paperwork to deal with. You need to know the legal description of the property before you make an offer to purchase a building (Fig. 3-4).

It is a good idea to seek professional help when you are ready to buy a building. This help could come from a lawyer or real estate broker. There are many steps to take. The following forms will help you chart your progress through a real estate transaction (Figs. 3-5 through 3-19).

Legal Description

Address _____

Map _____

Block _____

Deed book _____

Deed book page _____

3-4 *Legal description checklist*

Seller's Information Sheet

Name _____

Address _____

Home phone _____

Work phone _____

Attorney's name _____

Inspector's name _____

Lender's name _____

Lender's phone _____

Loan officer's name _____

Loan number _____

Escrow agent's name _____

Escrow agent's address _____

Escrow agent's phone _____

Insurance agency's name _____

Insurance agency's address _____

Insurance agency's phone _____

3-5 *Seller's information sheet*

List of Professionals
Who Might Be Needed

Name	Address	Phone	Date

3-6 *List of professionals needed*

Earnest Money Deposit Receipt

This will serve as receipt for the earnest money deposit received of
_____, Purchasers of the real
estate commonly known as _____.

The Sellers of this property, _____, will
place this earnest money on deposit with the following lender
_____, of _____.

Any special arrangements for this deposit will be as follow:

_____

_____

_____

_____

_____   _____
Purchaser   Date   Seller   Date

_____   _____
Purchaser   Date   Seller   Date

3-7 *Deposit receipt*

Purchase Option

In consideration of the payment by _____,
hereinafter referred to as optionee, in the amount of _____
_____ ($_____) receipt of which is hereby acknowledged
by _____, optionor, agrees to grant
optionee the option to purchase the real estate described as _____
_____, and commonly known
as _____, in the city of _____, for a
purchase price of _____, ($_____)
under the following terms and conditions:

If option is exercised, said option will place into force the purchase and
sale agreement signed by all parties dated _____, that contains a
contingency allowing this option to purchase prior to the purchase and
sale contract being effective.

If not exercised by _____, this option shall expire and optionor
shall be released from all obligations from this agreement and from the
purchase and sale agreement. Optionee's rights shall cease and the
above named consideration shall be retained by the optionor.

Time is of the essence in this agreement.

To exercise this option, the optionee shall deliver written notice to the
optionor at the address of _____, prior
to the expiration of this option. An additional deposit in the amount of
_____ ($_____) shall be placed
with an escrow agent as detailed in the purchase and sale agreement.

If notice is mailed, the date indicated on the return receipt of the
certified mail shall be the date of notification.

_____ _____   _____ _____
Optionor   Date   Optionee   Date

_____ _____   _____ _____
Optionor   Date   Optionee   Date

3-8 *Purchase option*

Exercise of Option

To _____, Optionor, as
Optionee, it is my intent to exercise the option agreement dated
_____, between the Purchasers, _____
_____, and the Sellers _____
_____, for the sale of the real
estate commonly known as _____.

The escrow agent for this transaction is:

Name _____

Address _____

Phone _____

The amount deposited in escrow is _____

($_____) and this deposit was made on _____.

_____   _____
Optionor   Date   Optionee   Date

_____   _____
Optionor   Date   Optionee   Date

3-9 *Exercise of option*

Contract for Sale of Real Estate

Contract made this _____ day of _____, 19_____,
at _____, State of _____, by and
between _____(Seller)
and _____(Purchaser).
Seller hereby agrees to sell, and Purchaser hereby agrees to purchase, a
certain lot or parcel of land with any building or improvements thereon
(premises) situated in _____, State of _____,
and described as follows:

_____

_____

The following items to be included in this sale:

_____

_____

Said premises shall be conveyed within _____ days from the date of this
contract by a good and sufficient _____ deed or Seller conveying
good and merchantable title to the same free from all incumbrances,
except existing easements, restrictions, conditions, and covenants of
record, existing building and zoning laws, and usual and customary
public utility easements servicing the premises, however, should the title
prove defective, then the Seller shall have a reasonable time after due
notice of such defect or defects to remedy the title, after which time, if
such defect or defects are not corrected so that there is a merchantable
title, then the Purchaser may at their option, be relieved from all
obligations hereunder and withdraw earnest money or deposits, if any.

And for such deed and conveyance Purchaser shall pay the sum of
_____ dollars ($_____),
payment to be made as follows:

1. $_____ received of Purchaser as earnest money in
part payment on account for said lot or parcel of land with any buildings
or improvements thereon and items included, if any. That _____
_____ shall hold said earnest money or

(Page 1 of 3 initials _____)

3-10 *Real estate purchase contract*

deposit and act as escrow agent until transfer of title; that _____ days will be given for obtaining the Seller's acceptance; and in the event of the Seller's non-acceptance, this earnest money shall be promptly returned to Purchaser.

2. $_____ to be paid at the time of delivery of the transfer deed in cash, or by certified, cashier's, bank, or treasurer's check.

3. For a total purchase price of $_____
_____ ($_____).

This contract is subject to following conditions:

_____

_____

_____

_____

_____

_____.

Full possession of said premises shall be delivered to Purchaser at the time of the delivery of the transfer deed, said premises to be then in the same condition in which they now are, except in the case of new construction. New construction shall be completed according to attached plans and specifications and approved for occupancy by the local code enforcement officials. Reasonable use and wear of the buildings thereon are the only exception for existing buildings.

The following items will be pro-rated as of the date of the transfer of said deed:

Utilities, fuel, rents, real estate taxes for the current taxing period, for the town/city/county of _____.

The risk of loss or damage to said premises by fire or otherwise until the transfer of title hereunder is assumed by the Seller.

All covenants and agreements herein contained shall extend and be obligatory upon the heirs, personal representatives, and assigns of the respective parties. That in case of failure of Purchaser to make either of the payments, or any part thereof, or to perform any of the covenants on

(Page 2 of 3 initials _____)

3-10 *Continued*

its part made or entered into, this contract shall, at the option of the Seller, be terminated and Purchaser shall forfeit said earnest money; and the same shall be retained by Seller as liquidated damages and the escrow agent is hereby authorized by Purchaser to pay over to Seller the earnest money, if any.

This contract is also subject to a satisfactory water test, by a testing service approved by the State of _____.

The results of said inspection must be conveyed to all parties within _____ days of the final acceptance of this contract. Cost of this test to be paid by _____.

If a broker is involved, Purchaser acknowledges that _____ _____ represents the Seller and Seller acknowledges that _____ represents the Purchaser.

Witness our hands and seals on the day and year first above written.

I/we hereby agree to purchase the above described premises at the price and upon the terms and conditions above set forth.

_____	_____	_____	_____
Witness	Date	Purchaser	Date
_____	_____	_____	_____
Witness	Date	Purchaser	Date

I/we hereby accept the offer and agree to deliver the above described premises at the price and upon the terms and conditions above set forth.

I/we further agree to pay _____ a commission for his/her services herein, _____ percent of the sale price.

_____	_____	_____	_____
Witness	Date	Seller	Date
_____	_____	_____	_____
Witness	Date	Seller	Date

(Page 3 of 3 initials _____)

3-10 *Continued*

Contingency Purchase Clause

This contingency purchase clause shall become an integral part of the purchase and sale agreement dated _____, between _____, Purchasers and _____, Sellers of the real property commonly known as _____ _____. The Sellers retain the right to continue to market their property for sale and to accept offers subject to the rights of the Purchaser in this agreement. Sellers may accept such an offer subject to Purchaser's rights and after giving Purchasers 72 hours from the time of notification to remove this contingency and agree to a definite settlement date with the Sellers. If the Purchaser cannot perform to these specifications the seller may void the contract, return all deposit money held for Purchaser, and sell the property to another party. In the event the need for notification arises, the Purchaser may be notified by certified, return receipt mail at _____, and the Seller may be notified at _____. The date indicated on the return receipt as the day of receipt shall be the date of notification.

_____		_____	
Seller	Date	Purchaser	Date
_____		_____	
Seller	Date	Purchaser	Date

3-11 *Contingency purchase clause*

Real Esate Purchase-and-Sale Addendum

This addendum is an integral part of the purchase and sale agreement dated _____, between the Purchasers, _____ _____, and the Sellers, _____, for the real estate commonly known as _____. The undersigned parties hereby agree to the following:

_____

_____

_____

_____

_____

_____

_____

_____

_____

_____

_____

_____

Seller	Date	Purchaser	Date

Seller	Date	Purchaser	Date

3-12 *Purchase-and-sale addendum*

Inspection Addendum

This addendum shall become an integral part of the purchase and sale agreement dated _____, between _____, Purchasers and _____, Sellers of the real property commonly known as _____. Within _____ days of acceptance of the above mentioned contract, the Purchaser shall order an inspection of the property located at _____, from a qualified representative of the Purchaser's choice at the Purchaser's own expense. This inspection shall include the items indicated and checked below:

_____ Roof	_____ Appliances
_____ Heating system	_____ Chimney
_____ Cooling system	_____ Septic
_____ Foundation	_____ Well
_____ Plumbing	_____ Code violations
_____ Electrical	_____ Drainage systems

_____ Other: _____

In the event the Purchaser's are not satisfied with the inspection results they may void this contract if written notice is given to the Sellers by _____. Seller agrees to allow reasonable access to the property for the purpose of this inspection. Additional terms and conditions are as follows:

_____

_____

Purchaser	Date	Seller	Date

Purchaser	Date	Seller	Date

3-13 *Inspection addendum*

Disclosure Addendum

This addendum is an integral part of the property disclosure form dated
_____, by the sellers of the real estate commonly known as
_____.

The undersigned parties hereby disclose the following:

_____

_____

_____

_____

_____

_____

_____

_____

_____

_____

_____

_____

_____

_____		_____	
Seller	Date	Purchaser	Date
_____		_____	
Seller	Date	Purchaser	Date
_____			
Broker	Date		

3-14 *Disclosure addendum*

Contingency Release

This contingency release shall become an integral part of the purchase and sale agreement dated _____, between _____, Purchasers and _____, Sellers of the real property commonly known as _____.
The following contingencies are hereby removed from the above mentioned contract:

_____

_____

_____

_____

_____

_____

_____

_____   _____
Purchaser   Date   Seller   Date

_____   _____
Purchaser   Date   Seller   Date

3-15 *Contingency release*

Progress Chart

Events	Scheduled Date	Actual Date
Disclosure signed by Purchasers	_____	_____
Contract signed by all parties	_____	_____
Earnest money deposited	_____	_____
Purchaser's inspection	_____	_____
Contingencies removed	_____	_____
Loan application made	_____	_____
Rate and points locked in	_____	_____
Preliminary loan approval	_____	_____
Title work started	_____	_____
Title work completed	_____	_____
Appraisal ordered	_____	_____
On-site appraisal	_____	_____
Appraisal complete	_____	_____
Hazard insurance obtained	_____	_____
Loan sent to underwriting	_____	_____
Loan approval received	_____	_____
Commitment letter issued	_____	_____
Settlement scheduled	_____	_____
Earnest money taken to settlement	_____	_____
Signed closing statement received	_____	_____
Transaction complete	_____	_____

3-16 *Progress chart*

Contract Extension

The time for performance of the purchase and sale agreement dated
_____, between _____,
Purchaser and _____, Seller
for the sale of the real estate commonly known as _____
_____, is hereby
extended until _____.

Witness our hands and seals this _____ day of
_____, 19_____.

_____   _____
Purchaser   Seller

_____   _____
Purchaser   Seller

3-17 *Contract extension*

Purchaser Notification

To Purchaser:

_____ Purchaser

_____ Purchaser

In accordance with the contract of sale dated _____, and
the contingency purchase clause dated _____,
between you and _____ Seller, you
are hereby notified of the following:

The Sellers of the property commonly known as _____
_____ have accepted a written offer for the
purchase of the above real estate subject to your rights in the contingency
purchase clause. You are requested to respond within 72 hours by either
signing and returning the enclosed contract release form or providing
evidence of your ability to purchase the property with a settlement date
of _____.

Please respond to the Sellers at the following address:

_____

_____
Seller   Date

_____
Seller   Date

3-18 *Purchaser notification*

Contract Release

We hereby agree that the contract of sale dated _____ between _____, Sellers and _____ _____, Purchasers is null and void. Purchasers and Sellers shall have no rights, claims, or liabilities thereunder and each of them specifically waives any claims or rights he may have against any of the others. We further authorize _____ _____ to release earnest money deposited to the Purchasers in the amount of _____ _____, ($_____).

Seller	Date	Purchaser	Date
Seller	Date	Purchaser	Date
Broker	Date	Broker	Date

3-19 *Contract release*

4

Putting your plans on paper

By the time you reach the point of putting your construction plans on paper, you are very close to making your dreams come true. Now is when all the action begins. Up to now, you've been doing routine research and mundane investigations, holding back your creative juices. It is now time to break out and do some hands-on work. This work begins on paper and ends in a completed conversion project. Your equity gain or cash profits could be staggering. However, your success or failure depends heavily on your planning, so don't take the planning phase lightly.

Competition is not as great in the conversion business as it is in other forms of construction and remodeling, at least not in terms of the number of people doing it. Why? Fewer people have the knowledge of what a gold mine conversion projects can be. The number of participants in the conversion game is smaller than the number in other fields, such as new construction. This smaller pool can be to your advantage, but the people who endure in the conversion business are efficient, effective, and tough to beat. If you're going into the business for the long haul, you have to commit to doing it right.

You don't have to be an architect, engineer, or draftsperson to start putting your plans on paper. You might very well need these professionals to take your renderings and turn them into working plans before construction is started, but for now, you can let your imagination pour out onto paper. Simple line drawings suffice for this stage of your planning process. The drawings should be based on some consistent scale, but you don't even have to do that in the earliest stages. The drawings will, however, have to be drawn to scale prior to actual construction.

Notes

A lot of people don't believe in putting their thoughts down on paper. Many of these people believe that recording their thoughts and plans is a waste of time. For awhile, I even believed this way, but I found that I was wrong. Since I've been planning my work and working my plan, I've been much more productive. You can probably benefit from this practice as well.

When I talk about putting your plans on paper, I don't mean only blueprints and floor plans. My concept is to make notes on everything. This process should start with your first inspection of a property, and it shouldn't stop until the job is done. To be efficient at taking notes, you must have paper and pencil or a tape recorder available at all times. Good ideas often pop out of our heads as quickly as they pop in. If you record your thoughts immediately, you can go back and retrieve them later. If the plans never make it to paper or recording tape, they might be lost forever.

Written notes are instrumental to success in many types of businesses, and they are particularly valuable in the conversion business. Creative entrepreneurs like yourself have ideas flood over them at all times of the day and night. Have you ever been driving down the road and been besieged by a terrific idea? How many times have you been at a party or a seminar when a creative image flashed across your mind? You need to capture these moments, either on paper or on tape. For you to reach your maximum potential, you must take advantage of all the mental power you have.

As a writer, I get ideas all the time. Some are stupid, some are good. I write them all down. Sometimes I let the ideas simmer for a few weeks, even a few months, before I review them. If a thought still looks promising a month after its inception, I tend to think it probably is a good idea. You can do this same type of thing. When you first walk through a building and record the fact that you think the place would make an ideal location for the sale of arts and crafts, you can refer back to your notes before closing on the property to see if the idea still stands tall.

Drafting

Once you have consolidated your notes and are ready to proceed with a conversion project, you should begin some serious drafting for the project. Depending upon your skill levels, you might be able to do the drafting yourself. At this stage, I am talking about rough drawings, not working plans. The design and creation of working plans should normally be left in the capable hands of architects and engineers. It is an expensive stage of any conversion project, but it might be mandatory. Some jurisdictions do not issue a building permit until working plans stamped by an acceptable design professional are submitted and approved. I'll talk more about working plans a little later.

You need some type of sketch or rough drawing to determine how you want your conversion project to turn out. This sketch can be given to a professional draftsperson or engineer to create approved working plans. Since the conversion project is your venture, you are certainly entitled to put your own feelings into it. You can go to an architect and ask for a complete design service, from start to finish, but you might stifle your personal input. However, if you don't have the skill or experience to create a winning design, you probably need to rely on the advice of professionals.

I do a lot of my own design work. My credentials are in the trades, not in engineering, but my experience has shown me how to create layouts that people like. I couldn't begin to determine what size steel beam is needed for a specific span or when a footing has to be beefed up to accept new loads, but I know traffic patterns and floor plans that work. Armed with this information, I sketch out the way I want a project to look and hand the drawings over to a design professional.

You probably know very well what you are capable of. If you've never designed remodeling jobs, new houses, or conversion projects, you should consult experts for the design considerations in your first few projects. As you gain experience, you can take on more design responsibility. Never assume structural responsibilities unless you are trained specifically in this field.

Getting started

Getting started with your drawings doesn't require a lot of fancy equipment. If you have a computer and a computer-aided design (CAD) program, use it. If you don't have this type of equipment, you need a scale rule, some graph paper, and a pencil to get started.

Let's assume for the moment that you want to draw your own conversion plans in the rough-sketch stage. You have your drafting supplies, and you are ready to work. You should first create a drawing of the existing property. Let's say, for example, that you are buying a large single-family house and plan to make three rental units out of it. Go to the house with your drafting supplies, and create a drawing of the building. Measure the foundation and draw it to scale. A typical scale is ¼" to the foot, but you can use any scale you wish. You must, however, make the drawing to a consistent scale, or it will be worthless.

Once you have a scaled drawing of the foundation plan, you can move into the interior and scale out the existing rooms and partitions. Don't forget to draw in windows, doors, stairs, and other primary features. You are going to use this drawing later to determine your plan of attack, so the drawing must be accurate. After completing your on-site work, you can retreat to your home or office to finish the drawings.

Back in the office

Once you are back in the office, you can begin to make your design changes. You might want to use tracing paper to begin this process. By laying the tracing paper over your scaled drawing, you can shift walls, add walls, and remove walls on the paper. You don't have to use tracing paper, but some people find it easier to visualize the changes when looking through the tracing paper. I don't use the tracing method. I normally have a freehand sketch of what I want a building to be like. With this sketch and the scaled drawing, I am able to formulate a viable plan on graph paper or on my computer.

It is not really very important how you come up with your revised building, but it is essential that you keep the drawing to scale. I can't count the number of times that customers have come to me with a floor plan that was impossible to work with. If the plan is not drawn to scale, the artist can make almost anything fit in almost any space. Only by drawing the sketch to scale can you verify that certain objects, like refrigerators and laundry equipment, will fit in their allotted space.

Keep tinkering with your line drawing until you are happy with it. Once you have a rough idea of what you want, you can take your drawing to a drafting company, lumberyard, engineer, or architect, depending on the level of qualifications required in your region, to have working plans produced. Some lumberyards draw blueprints free of charge in exchange for your commitment to buy all your building materials from them. You can get a good deal this way, but it is only a bargain if the prices charged by the supplier are competitive with other suppliers.

Your working drawings

Your working drawings detail a lot of information about the conversion project. The plans include dimensions, details of cut sections for specific parts of the work, and possibly front, side, and rear elevations. A few professionals, mostly architects, draw in plumbing, heating, cooling, and electrical diagrams. Most plan preparers do not go to this extreme for residential plans. It is not unusual to find electrical diagrams on residential plans, but plumbing and heating layouts are not so common. Yet most code enforcement offices require riser diagrams for plumbing systems and layouts for heating systems before these types of permits are issued. The licensed subcontractors that you plan to use in these trades should be able to provide you with acceptable drawings pertaining to their trade work. If your working plans don't include layouts for mechanical equipment, you should contact licensed tradespeople, in the appropriate trades, to provide you with the needed drawings.

Local requirements

Local code requirements dictate the creation of your working plans. Some locations require that all plans submitted for approval be stamped by a licensed design professional. This is not at all uncommon. However, many regions don't maintain such rigid requirements. Let me give you some examples of what I'm talking about.

When I was building houses in Virginia, I never used an architect in the design or drafting of my house plans. My wife, Kimberley, designed a majority of the houses we built. She would create a scaled drawing on graph paper and revise it until we were satisfied with it. If we were building a custom home, she would work directly with the customer to lay out the house. Once she had a scaled drawing on paper, we delivered it to a drafting firm.

The drafting company we used would draw a full set of working plans from the sketches Kimberley provided. These plans included joist diagrams, roof structures, exterior elevations, floor plans, and so forth. The plans were far from simple line drawings. They were detailed working plans, but they were not created by architects. These plans, at that time, cost less than $1000. This price was a fraction of what similar plans would have cost if they were drawn by an architect.

Once the plans were completed, we submitted them to the local code officer for approval. I can't recall ever having any of the plans rejected. Not one of these plans carried the stamp of an engineer or architect. The drafting company relied on information from the building code for our area, and apparently the plan preparers knew what they were doing. I can't guarantee that a drafting firm can meet the criteria required for code approval in your area, but this approach worked well for us and saved us a lot of money.

Did I take additional risk by not using an engineer or architect to create my working plans? I might have. It never occurred to me at the time that there may be some liability for not using a specialized, licensed design expert to create my working drawings. I can't say whether I assumed risk in my decision to use a drafting firm or not. I recommend that you talk with your attorney before you have anyone other than an accredited architect draw your working plans.

I now live in Maine. The code requirements in this state are not nearly as restrictive as those I was used to in Virginia. In some jurisdictions in Maine, code inspections hardly exist. For example, I just finished building a new house for myself. The town required only a rough-in plumbing inspection and a septic-system inspection for the entire construction project. There was no footing inspection, no building inspection, no insulation inspection, no heating inspection, no town-required electrical inspection, and no final inspections. Personally, I think this situation is too lax. The only electrical inspection required was mandated by the power company, and it only required a letter from a master electrician. You might imagine that the requirement for architecturally drawn plans was not a big deal.

The two examples I've just given you might imply that the need for professionally drawn and stamped plans is not of much concern. This is not the impression that I wish to give you. I'm sure in some locations a building permit is not issued until a sophisticated, stamped set of working plans are submitted and approved. Check with your attorney in regards to any liability you might assume from not engaging an architect, and talk with your local code office to see what requirements pertain to the plans that you have prepared.

Drafting companies

Drafting companies can turn out some fine working plans, as I know from personal experience. If you are looking for a cost-effective alternative to an architect, a drafting company might be it. Quality and competence varies in all types of businesses, and drafting companies are no exception. Ask if the company assumes responsibility for their designs and if they are insured accordingly. If your local code office accepts plans drawn by drafting companies, you could save a lot of money by taking this route.

Lumberyards

I mentioned earlier that lumberyards and building suppliers frequently offer free drafting services to their customers. I have never taken this course before, but I have seen many sets of plans prepared by suppliers and lumberyards. Some of the drawings have been very good, and others have been a bit too simple. The fact that these sources provide plans free of charge is enticing. However, lumberyards and other suppliers usually require that you buy all of your materials from them if the plans are drawn free of charge. As long as the supplier is competitive in its pricing schedule, you don't have a problem. But if the prices of materials is considerably higher than those of another supplier, the free plans might not be such a good deal.

I want to stress that plans drafted by a building supplier might not meet the requirements for obtaining a permit in your area. It is also possible that some liability might be extended to you if you use these plans. Check your local requirements and legal standing closely before depending on these types of working plans.

You might or might not choose to have your working plans created by one of your material suppliers. Even if you choose some other route for your working plans, suppliers can give you a lot of help in the thinking process of your conversion project. They might also be able to provide you with plans and renderings that can help you to visualize what you want to do.

Almost all conversion projects involving rental units require the addition of a new kitchen (or kitchens). Since kitchens are a common denominator in residential conversion projects, I have chosen these rooms to illustrate some of the types of drawings that are available from building suppliers in my area. The drawings in this chapter were provided to me by one of my regular suppliers. This supplier offers a host of drafting services, and suppliers in your area probably do the same. Look at the type of drawings a building supplier can turn out on short notice (Figs. 4-1 to 4-18). All the figures in this chapter are courtesy of Brunswick Coal & Lumber/Andrews Building Supply/ Carol E. Bartlett, CKD.

Engineers and architects

Engineers and architects are by far the most reliable sources of working plans. These people have trained for years to draw plans that are safe, efficient, and dependable. There is a price to pay for this expert service, however, and it is usually steep.

Some jurisdictions require that any working plans submitted for approval in the application for a building permit be stamped by an architect or engineer. This requirement is common for plans used to build or remodel commercial buildings, even in Maine. Personally, I have never worked in a location where an architect's stamp was required for residential plans. My job locations have ranged from the very rural to big cities. My time working in northern Virginia, in the shadow of Washington, D.C., proved to be the most regulated. Still, I've never been required to use an architect to create residential building plans. I do, however, believe that an architect is the safest course of action to take when having plans drawn.

4-1 *Side elevation view of a custom-designed kitchen. This drawing (and all others in this chapter) was created by a certified kitchen designer and provided by a supplier of building materials.*

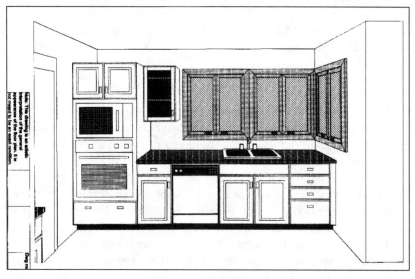

4-2 *Side elevation view of a custom-designed kitchen.*

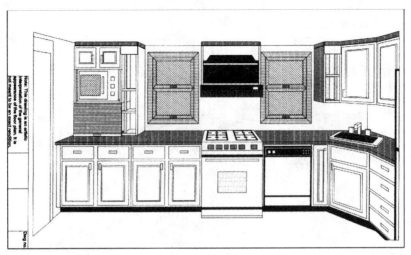

4-3 *Side elevation view of a custom-designed kitchen.*

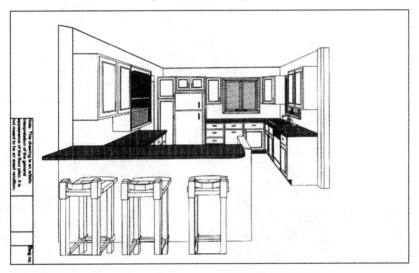

4-4 *Side elevation view of a custom-designed kitchen.*

4-5 *Side elevation view of a custom-designed work area in a kitchen.*

4-6 *Side elevation view of a custom-designed kitchen.*

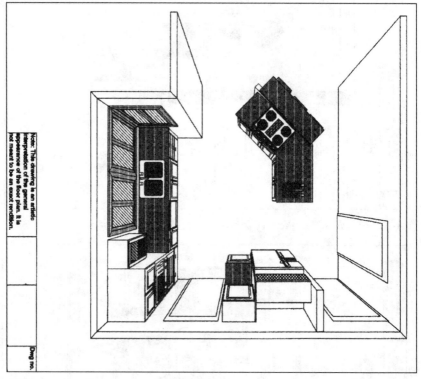

4-7 *Bird's-eye view of a custom-designed kitchen.*

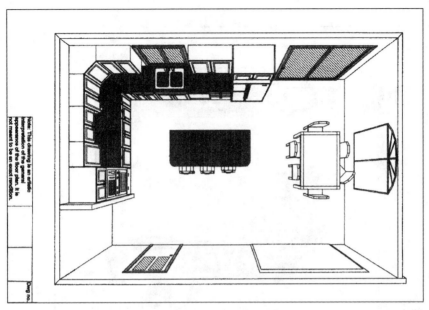

4-8 *Bird's-eye view of a custom-designed kitchen.*

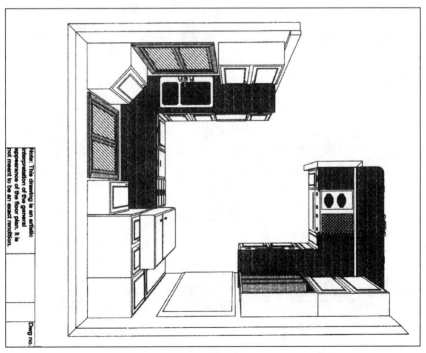

4-9 *Bird's-eye view of a custom-designed kitchen.*

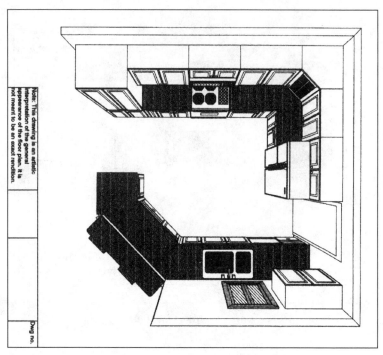

4-10 *Bird's-eye view of a custom-designed kitchen.*

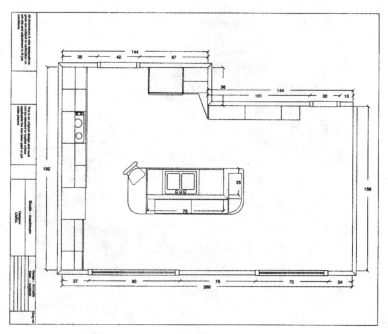

4-11 *A custom-drawn floor plan for a kitchen, dimensions given in inches.*

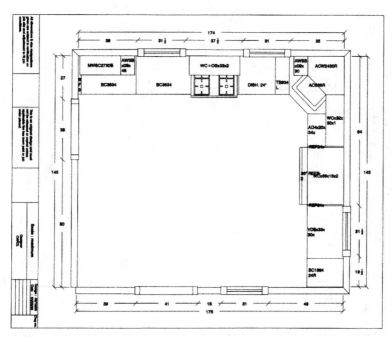

4-12 *A custom-drawn floor plan for a kitchen, including cabinet references, dimensions given in inches.*

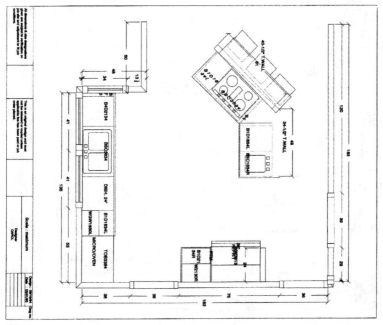

4-13 *A custom-drawn floor plan for a kitchen, including cabinet references, dimensions given in inches.*

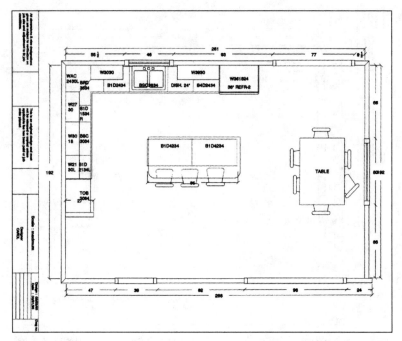

4-14 *A custom-drawn floor plan for a kitchen, including cabinet references, dimensions given in inches.*

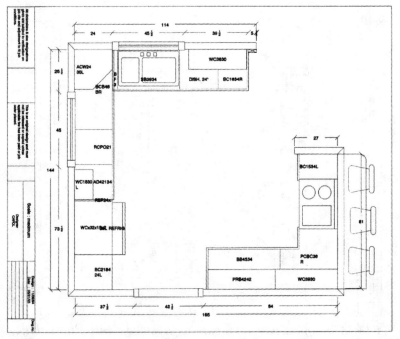

4-15 *A custom-drawn floor plan for a kitchen, including cabinet references, dimensions given in inches.*

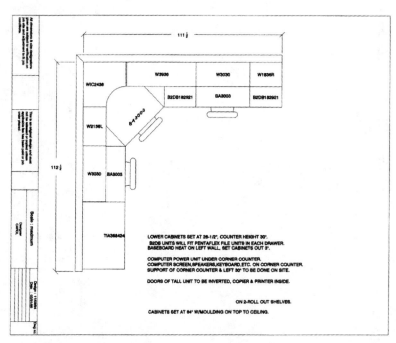

4-16 *A custom-drawn floor plan for a kitchen, including cabinet references, dimensions given in inches.*

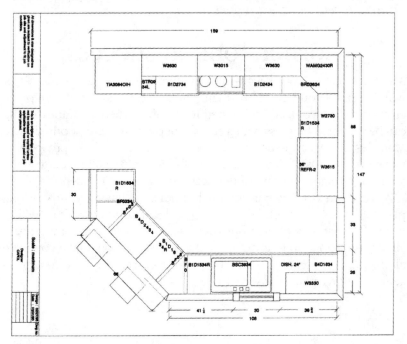

4-17 *A custom-drawn floor plan for a kitchen, including cabinet references, dimensions given in inches.*

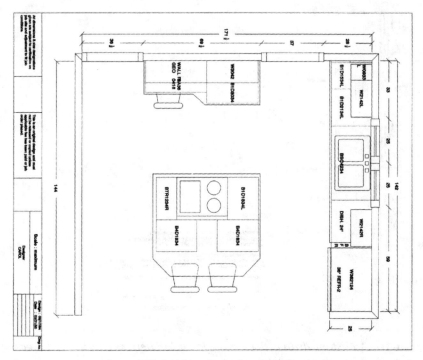

4-18 *A custom-drawn floor plan for a kitchen, including cabinet references, dimensions given in inches.*

Cornerstone to success

A cornerstone to your success in any conversion project is the set of working plans you have. If the plans are not designed and drawn properly, you leave yourself wide open for trouble. The best tradespeople can be rendered helpless with a set of blueprints that are poorly drawn. Money is always an issue in a conversion project, and the prospect of paying thousands of dollars for a set of blueprints can be hard to swallow. But it might be some of the best money you ever spend.

I've given you several potential options for having your working plans drawn. I can't tell you what your local conditions are. Neither can I say what type of plan preparer suits your needs best. Investigate all of your viable options before making any decision. Once you have all the facts, you can make an informed decision that leads to a good set of working plans for your project.

5

Soliciting bids

When you are ready to begin soliciting bids, you are getting close to seeing the project get off the ground. This is an exciting time, but it is also a period when you must be cautious. Bids received from suppliers and subcontractors are not always as they seem, something experienced contractors know very well. For those of you who are subcontractors or rookies to the conversion business, believe me when I tell you that bids are not all black and white.

I've been in the construction business for more than twenty years. Some of those years were spent as a subcontractor, and many of them were endured as a general contractor. I can tell you from experience that bids can burn you badly.

I started out as a plumber, then I got into bath and kitchen remodeling work. From there, I moved into full-scale remodeling. A few years later I started building houses. At the peak, I was building 60 houses a year. During this time, I also became a licensed real estate broker.

My career has followed a logical path and it has covered a lot of ground. I still dabble in real estate, and plumbing work continues to play a small role in my life. The home building work has slowed down, but I'm still active in the business. Having a couple of kids can tend to slow almost anyone down. And, of course, I'm writing books. What does any of this have to do with conversion projects? It shows I have paid my dues in a number of fields, yet I must confess, I still have a lot to learn.

I thought I knew it all when I was younger. Only now do I realize how much I didn't know at the time. Twenty years from now, I wonder if I'll look back at what I'm doing today and recognize mistakes caused by inexperience. My point is this, no matter how good you are, no matter how much you think you know, there is always room for improvement. Accepting bad bids is a harsh way to wake up to reality.

Those of you who are subcontractors have not been exposed to the type of bid-related problems that general contractors face. In fact, subcontractors are one of a general contractor's biggest problems. Getting quality subcontractors to show up on a job site on schedule can be like pulling teeth from a lion. If the subcontractors do show up, can they do acceptable work? This is a risk a general contractor must accept until the subcontractors have proven they can do quality work. You have big responsibilities if you are a general contractor, whether it's for your own account or for a customer.

Taking bids

Taking bids is a necessary part of most conversion projects. Few people can handle all aspects of a major conversion without some outside help. If you are a carpenter, you are probably going to need a licensed plumber, electrician, and heating contractor. You might need additional help, but these trades require special licensing that most carpenters cannot easily obtain. On the other hand, if you're an electrician, you are likely to need a plumber, heating mechanic, and carpenter. Indeed, the saying "no one is an island" applies to the work involved in a major conversion project.

Since you are likely to need help on your project, it is only natural that you put the work out to bid. This is the standard procedure for finding subcontractors who can take on a job within your budget. However, getting bids on a job is not as easy in the real world as it appears on paper. Theoretically, you should be able to call a few contractors, give them plans and specifications, and accept the lowest price. This, however, is not the way the game is played by successful conversion contractors.

When you line up prices for your project, you get two types of bids. One is from material suppliers and the second is from subcontractors. There is a great deal of difference between these two types of bids. For example, material suppliers should bid jobs in a way that make them easy to compare. If you ask for a price on a particular item, material suppliers should be able to give you a direct quote for the product you have specified.

Subcontractors, however, are not so easy to compare. Most of what you buy from a subcontractor is labor, quality in workmanship, and dependability, so it becomes more difficult to compare bids.

Material supplier bids

Supplier bids are the easiest to compare. Since you can specify makes, model numbers, brand names, and other detailed information, you can create a parallel relationship to each bid. This, at least, is the way it works in books. In reality, bids from suppliers can be as different as night and day.

If you're an experienced contractor, I'm sure you are familiar with the old contract clause known as the "or equal clause." Or equal clauses are basically a license to steal. This type of clause allows a bidder to substitute one brand (or make) of equipment for another. When this happens, it becomes impossible to check bids against each other in a way that's fair.

I have encountered a rather consistent problem with supplier quotes over the years. It seems that suppliers often forget to include the price of some items or they make mistakes when entering quantities of items. These mistakes make their quotes appear to be better than their competitors. If you choose a contractor that has missed some items, the job could be well underway before the problem is noticed, and by then it might be too late to correct. To avoid a headache like this, review all your quotes line by line, don't just scan the bottom line.

As a conversion contractor, you cannot afford to let suppliers play games. It is your responsibility to make sure that the prices you get are accurate and dependable. Many suppliers limit the length of time their prices remain valid. It is not unusual for a price to expire 30 days after it is quoted, sometimes even sooner. That does not allow you enough time to close on a property and complete the work. Therefore, you have to convince suppliers to guarantee prices for the duration of your job. Some suppliers are going to agree to your request, but not all of them.

I just completed the construction of a new home for myself. When I shopped the job I found a wide range in prices. The lowest bidder was willing to guarantee the prices for 14 days. Obviously, a house can't be built in 14 days, at least not under normal circumstances. The second lowest bidder, who was $700 higher, was willing to lock in the prices. Knowing that the materials market was somewhat volatile, I decided to deal with the second-lowest bidder. I knew up front that I might be spending an extra $700, but I also knew I was protected from escalating prices.

There are two ways to approach suppliers for prices. You can provide suppliers with your plans and specifications and let them do a take-off and give you a price. This is the easiest method, but not the best. I'll explain in a moment.

Another way to gather prices is to do your own take-off and provide each supplier with an itemized list of what needs to be quoted. This is, by far, the better way to do business.

It's risky to have a supplier do a take-off from your plans and specifications, and then bid on the job. The individual doing the take-off might make mistakes determining the sizes or quantities. That can have a considerable effect on the quote, and ultimately on the project budget. Even if the supplier does an accurate take-off, you are at the mercy of the supplier for brands, models, and grades of material.

It is always best to specify exactly what you want in a detailed list. Even if the supplier selects quality materials when doing a take-off, they probably are not going to match, item for item, the materials figured by competitive suppliers. If you get three bids and all three suppliers quote different brands, models, or grades of material, you are not going to be able to evaluate the bids in a way that is fair.

The only way to get good, solid competitive bids is to itemize a list and specify everything as much as possible. Even when you do this, you must check and compare the bids closely. I used an itemized list when I solicited material bids for my new house, but there were still problems with the quotes. One supplier listed interior doors on the quote, but failed to price them. My house is fairly large with many doors, so this little mistake threw the quote off by thousands of dollars. When I asked the supplier about the mistake, I was told that it must have been a computer error. The point is, this particular bid looked very good when looking only at the total price, but the quote wasn't accurate. If I had used the quote for my budget, the job would have gone way over budget and I might not have been prepared to cover the cost.

When I put my house out for bid, I was surprised by the lack of interest shown by some suppliers. I sent out six bid packages and only four of them were returned. One third of the suppliers didn't even bother to bid the job. I can't imagine why a building materials company wouldn't want to sell their products, but it seems that some just aren't all that interested in new business. With this in mind, you must solicit enough suppliers to ensure that you receive at least three bids.

Putting together a bid package generally helps get a quicker and more accurate response from suppliers. Bid packages can vary, but mine contain an itemized list of materials as I want them bid, a set of working plans (sometimes), a set of building specifications (sometimes), a self-addressed stamped envelope and a cover letter stating the date when the bids must be received in order to be considered. A bid package looks professional, and it provides a written timetable for the supplier to follow.

Price

Price is a key issue in the bidding process. After all, the purpose of bids is to find out how much suppliers are going to charge. However, price is not the only factor to consider. Earlier in this chapter, I told you how I paid $700 above the lowest bid to ensure a locked-in price with my regular supplier. There is more to this story, and I'll tell you about it now.

I had some concerns about the supplier who offered the lowest bid. Unlike my regular supplier, the lowest-bid supplier uses outside salespeople. If I'd use the lowest-bid supplier, all communications would have had a long channel to follow. That creates the risk of mis-communication and mistakes.

The deal with my regular supplier was made with the branch manager, so it was safe to assume that his word was good and enforceable. Had a salesperson told me that the quoted prices could be locked in, I would have been concerned that a higher authority could overrule the decision.

Although I agreed to buy almost all the material from my regular supplier, I reserved the right to buy siding and the garage door from the lowest-bid supplier. The reason was not so much price, but rather because the lowest-bid company had a machine that could stain the siding before it was delivered. The machine-staining saved me time and effort, and it provided better protection for the siding.

As it turned out, the lowest-bid supplier didn't perform well when I ordered my siding, and did even worse when it came time to get my garage door. I believe that had I used them for all the materials, the house might still be under construction. I'm sure glad that my intuition and experience came through for me when I had to chose between these two suppliers. This is just one example of why price isn't everything.

Availability

The availability of materials can have a huge impact on your project. If materials are not available when needed, the job can slow down while costs go up due to construction interest and other factors.

Suppliers sometimes quote on low-priced materials that are not kept in stock. For example, if you work off their quote, you might not know there is an eight-week lead time on the kitchen cabinets. The problem is discovered just before the cabinets are needed. You can't wait, so you have to buy a set of stock cabinets at a higher price. It keeps you on your production schedule, but it busts the budget. To avoid this, see to it that the quotes provide written information about availability of the materials, as well as the price.

Convenience

Convenience is another issue to be considered during the bid selection process. Most suppliers who cater to professionals are willing to deliver materials without adding a delivery charge. Some discount warehouses sell the same material for a little less, but won't deliver to the job site. It can be a real drag when you have to go pick up and haul all of the materials. You might have to pay a little more for free deliveries, but I think it's worth the extra price. When you get your quotes, ask if delivery is included in the prices.

Returns

Return policies vary from one supplier to another. Some sellers require a steep restocking fee. Others don't charge a fee for returned materials. It's best to deal with a company that won't charge you for the returns. Every job I've worked on had materials returned to suppliers.

Subcontractor bids

Getting bids from subcontractors can be a very frustrating process. It can also be a real eye-opener to see the vast differences in their prices.

Depending on the type of conversion project, you are likely to need subcontractors from many of the trades. General contractors probably have a stable of tried-and-true subcontractors. However, if you are just getting into the business, you are going to have to start from ground zero. It's a tough spot to begin, but there is no other way. You are going to need help in some areas of the conversion work, and subcontractors are usually the best way to get that help.

Making direct contact

Sometimes it seems impossible to get in contact with subcontractors. Many of the small contracting firms use answering machines or answering services. It can take days of phone tag before you actually talk to one. A lot of time is wasted.

If you start searching for subcontractors early, you can contact them by mail. Then, if you choose, you can follow-up with a phone call. This method isn't perfect, but it works pretty well.

One good thing about subcontractors—there is rarely any shortage of them. Good ones, however, could be booked up with work for weeks or even months, so start the bidding process early. In new construction it is standard procedure to give subcontractors a set of plans and specs so that they can bid on the job. In conversion work, however, subcontractors normally need to see the building before bidding. You are likely to waste time running to and from the project to meet the various subcontractors. There is, however, a good way to avoid this wasted time.

As soon as you are ready to have subcontractors bid your job, set aside specific times that you can be available for them at the job site. Have a telephone installed in the building and take along paperwork to keep you busy while you wait. If you don't already know this, many contractors are not always punctual. Some don't show up for appointments. This might bother you if you have nothing to do but twiddle your thumbs, because most entrepreneurs can't afford wasted time. But, if you take work along with you to the site, you can meet subcontractors without any lost time between meetings.

When the bids come in
When the bids come in from your subcontractors, you can begin to set your production budget. My guess is that you are going to see a wide range of prices. Don't automatically select the lowest price. Just as it was with suppliers, there is a lot more to selecting subcontractors than just getting the lowest price.

Most of what subcontractors sell is a bit intangible. If a plumber is selling you a length of type-L copper tubing, it is easy enough to compare the price you are given. But when the plumbing firm is selling you superior remodeling skills, based on years of experience, it is a lot harder to keep comparisons on an even keel.

Since subcontractors are selling labor, you are going to have to examine each one to find the cream of the crop. This is no easy task. Subcontractors who look great on paper can turn out to be nearly worthless, while questionable subcontractors might show you they can be the best in the business. It takes experience to figure out who's who. Even then, you can make a mistake.

Sorting out the subcontractors
Sorting out subcontractors is a big responsibility. You can check references, but this might not mean much. The best way to smoke out the bad guys is to take a look at the jobs they have in progress. Most professional subcontractors have more than one job in the works, so

there should be some project you can check. Proceed with caution if a subcontractor doesn't have a job in progress. Also, talk to their customers and find out if the subcontractors are meeting all the contract commitments.

Once you have narrowed down the list of potential subcontractors, you should arrange personal interviews to discuss contract issues, payment schedules, production schedules, and any other pertinent aspects of the job. It is often possible to learn a lot about contractors when you sit across a desk from them. Indeed, it could prove to be more beneficial than all other methods of inquiry. I am including a number of sample forms that should be helpful to you in the process of taking bids and sorting out subcontractors (Figs. 5-1 through 5-21).

Bid Request

Customer name: _____

Customer address: _____

Customer city/state/zip: _____

Customer phone number: _____

Job location: _____

Plans & specifications dated: _____

Bid requested from: _____

Type of work: _____

Description of material to be quoted: _____

All quotes to be based on attached plans and specifications. No substitutions allowed without written consent of customer.

Please provide quoted prices for the following:

All labor, materials, permits, and related fees to complete plumbing as per attached plans and specifications.

All bids must be submitted by: _____

5-1 *Bid request*

Your Company Name
Your Company Address

Dear Sir:

I am soliciting bids for the work listed below, and I would like to offer you the opportunity to participate in the bidding. If you are interested in giving quoted prices for the <u>Labor/Material</u> for this job, please let me hear from you at the above address.

The job will be started _____. Financing has been arranged and the job will be started on schedule. Your quote, if you choose to enter one, must be received no later than _____.

The proposed work is as follows:

_____

_____

_____

_____

Thank you for your time and consideration in this request.

Sincerely,

Your name and title

5-2 *Subcontractor bid solicitation letter*

Form Letter for Soliciting Material Quotes

Dear Sir:

I am soliciting bids for the work listed below, and I would like to offer you the opportunity to participate in the bidding. If you are interested in giving quoted prices on <u>material</u> for this job, please let me hear from you.

The job will be started in <u>four weeks</u>. Financing has been arranged and the job will be started on schedule. Your quote, if you choose to enter one, must be received no later than _____.

The proposed work is as follows:

_____

_____

_____

Plans and specifications for the work are available upon request.

Thank you for your time and consideration in this request.

Sincerely,

Your name and title

5-3 *Bid solicitation letter for materials*

Material Specifications

Phase	Item	Brand	Model	Color	Size
Plumbing	Lavatory	WXYA	497	White	19" × 17"
Plumbing	Toilet	ABC12	21	White	12" rough
Plumbing	Shower	KYTCY	41	White	36" × 36"
Electrical	Ceiling fan	SPARK	2345	Gold	30"
Electrical	Light kit	JFOR2	380	White	Standard
Flooring	Carpet	MISTY	32	Grey	14 yards

5-4 *Sample materials specifications*

Request for Substitutions

Customer name: _____

Customer address: _____

Customer city/state/zip: _____

Customer phone number: _____

Job location: _____

Plans & specifications dated: _____

Bid requested from: _____

Type of work: _____

The following items are being substituted for the items specified in the attached plans and specifications:

_____

_____

_____

_____

_____

Please indicate your acceptance of these substitutions by signing below.

_____   _____
Contractor   Date   Customer   Date

                                      _____
                                      Customer   Date

5-5 *Request for substitutions*

Work Estimate

Date: _____

Customer name: _____

Address: _____

Phone number: _____

Description of Work

ABC Contractors will supply all labor and material for the following work:

_____

_____

_____

_____

_____

_____

Payment for Work as Follows

Estimated price: _____, payable

as follows _____

_____

If you have any questions, please don't hesitate to call. Upon acceptance, a formal contract will be issued.

Respectfully submitted,

J. B. Williams
Owner

5-6 *Work estimate*

Subcontractor Questionnaire

Company name _____

Physical company address _____

Company mailing address _____

Company phone number _____

After-hours phone number _____

Company president/owner _____

President/owner address _____

President/owner phone number _____

How long has company been in business?_____

Name of insurance company _____

Insurance company phone number _____

Does company have liability insurance? _____

Amount of liability insurance coverage _____

Does company have Worker's Comp. insurance?_____

Type of work company is licensed to do _____

List business or other license numbers _____

Where are licenses held? _____

If applicable, are all workers licensed? _____

Are there any lawsuits pending against the company? _____

Has the company ever been sued? _____

Does the company use subcontractors? _____

Is the company bonded? _____

Who is the company bonded with? _____

Has the company had complaints filed against it? _____

Are there any judgments against the company?_____

5-7 *Subcontractor questionnaire*

Bid Comparisons

Phase	Vendor	Price

5-8 *Bid comparison chart*

Contractor Rating Sheet

Category	Contractor 1	Contractor 2	Contractor 3
Contractor name			
Returns calls			
Licensed			
Insured			
Bonded			
References			
Price			
Experience			
Years in business			
Work quality			
Availability			
Deposit required			
Detailed quote			
Personality			
Punctual			
Gut reaction			

Notes

_____

_____

_____

_____

_____

5-9 *Contractor rating sheet*

Material Take-Off

Item	Size	Quantity

5-10 *Material take-off form*

Material Order Log

Supplier: _____

Date order was placed: _____

Time order was placed: _____

Name of person taking order: _____

Promised delivery date: _____

Order number: _____

Quoted price: _____

Date of follow-up call: _____

Manager's name: _____

Time of call to manager: _____

Manager confirmed delivery date: _____

Manager confirmed price: _____

Notes and Comments

_____

_____

_____

_____

_____

_____

_____

_____

5-11 *Follow-up form for material orders*

Remodeling Contract

This agreement, made this _____ day of _____,
19____, shall set forth the whole agreement, in its entirety, between
Contractor and Customer.

Contractor: Your Name, referred to herein as Contractor.

Customer: _____, referred
to herein as Customer.

Job name: _____

Job location: _____

The Customer and Contractor agree to the following:

Scope of Work

Contractor shall perform all work as described below and provide all
material to complete the work described below: All work is to be
completed by Contractor in accordance with the attached plans and
specifications. All material is to be supplied by Contractor in accordance
with attached plans and specifications. Said attached plans and
specifications have been acknowledged and signed by Contractor and
Customer.

A brief outline of the work is as follows, and all work referenced in the
attached plans and specifications will be completed to the Customer's
reasonable satisfaction. The following is only a basic outline of the
overall work to be performed:

_____

_____

_____

_____

_____

Commencement and Completion Schedule

The work described above shall be started within three days of verbal
notice from Customer; the projected start date is _____. The
Contractor shall complete the above work in a professional and

(Page 1 of 3 initials _____)

5-12 *Remodeling contract*

expedient manner, by no later than twenty days from the start date. Time is of the essence regarding this contract. No extension of time will be valid, without the Customer's written consent. If Contractor does not complete the work in the time allowed, and if the lack of completion is not caused by the Customer, the Contractor will be charged one-hundred dollars ($100) per day, for every day work is not finished beyond the completion date. This charge will be deducted from any payments due to the Contractor for work performed.

Contract Sum

The Customer shall pay the Contractor for the performance of completed work, subject to additions and deductions, as authorized by this agreement or attached addendum. The contract sum is

_____, ($_____).

Progress Payments

The Customer shall pay the Contractor installments as detailed below, once an acceptable insurance certificate has been filed by the Contractor, with the Customer:

Customer will pay Contractor a deposit of _____
_____, ($_____), when work is started.
Customer will pay _____,
($_____), when all rough-in work is complete.
Customer will pay _____,
($_____) when work is _____ percent complete.
Customer will pay _____,
($_____) when all work is complete and accepted.

All payments are subject to a site inspection and approval of work by the Customer. Before final payment, the Contractor, if required, shall submit satisfactory evidence to the Customer, that all expenses related to this work have been paid and no lien risk exists on the subject property.

Working Conditions

Working hours will be 8:00 a.m. through 4:30 p.m., Monday through Friday. Contractor is required to clean work debris from the job site on a daily basis and to leave the site in a clean and neat condition. Contractor shall be responsible for removal and disposal of all debris related to their job description.

Contract Assignment

Contractor shall not assign this contract or further subcontract the whole of this subcontract without the written consent of the Customer.

(Page 2 of 3 initials _____)

5-12 *Continued*

Laws, Permits, Fees, and Notices

Contractor is responsible for all required laws, permits, fees, or notices required to perform the work stated herein.

Work of Others

Contractor shall be responsible for any damage caused to existing conditions. This shall include work performed on the project by other contractors. If the Contractor damages existing conditions or work performed by other contractors, said Contractor shall be responsible for the repair of said damages. These repairs may be made by the Contractor responsible for the damages or another contractor, at the sole discretion of Customer.

The damaging Contractor shall have the opportunity to quote a price for the repairs. The Customer is under no obligation to engage the damaging Contractor to make the repairs. If a different contractor repairs the damage, the Contractor causing the damage may be back-charged for the cost of the repairs. These charges may be deducted from any monies owed to the damaging Contractor.

If no money is owed to the damaging Contractor, said Contractor shall pay the invoiced amount within seven business days. If prompt payment is not made, the Customer may exercise all legal means to collect the requested monies. The damaging Contractor shall have no rights to lien the Customer's property for money retained to cover the repair of damages caused by the Contractor. The Customer may have the repairs made to his satisfaction.

Warranty

Contractor warrants to the Customer all work and materials, for one year from the final day of work performed.

Indemnification

To the fullest extent allowed by law, the Contractor shall indemnify and hold harmless the Customer and all of their agents and employees from and against all claims, damages, losses and expenses.

This Agreement entered into on _____, 19_____
shall constitute the whole agreement between Customer and Contractor.

_____   _____
Customer   Date   Contractor   Date

_____
Customer   Date

(Page 3 of 3 initials _____)

5-12 *Continued*

Subcontract Agreement

This agreement, made this ____ day of _____, 19___, shall set forth the whole agreement, in its entirety, between Contractor and Subcontractor.

Contractor: _____,
referred to herein as Contractor.

Job location: _____

Subcontractor: _____, referred to herein as Subcontractor.

The Contractor and Subcontractor agree to the following:

Scope of Work

Subcontractor shall perform all work as described below and provide all material to complete the work described below.

Subcontractor shall supply all labor and material to complete the work according to the attached plans and specifications. These attached plans and specifications have been initialed and signed by all parties. The work shall include, but is not limited to, the following:

_____

_____

_____

_____

_____

_____

_____

_____

Commencement and Completion Schedule

The work described above shall be started within three days of verbal notice from Contractor, the projected start date is _____.

The Subcontractor shall complete the above work in a professional and expedient manner no later than _____ days from the start date. Time is of the essence in this contract. No extension of time will be valid without

(Page 1 of 3 initials _____)

5-13 *Subcontract agreement*

the Contractor's written consent. If Subcontractor does not complete the work in the time allowed, and if the lack of completion is not caused by the Contractor, the Subcontractor will be charged fifty dollars ($50) per day, for every day work extends beyond the completion date. This charge will be deducted from any payments due to the Subcontractor for work performed.

Contract Sum

The Contractor shall pay the Subcontractor for the performance of completed work subject to additions and deductions as authorized by this agreement or attached addendum. The contract sum is
_____($_____).

Progress Payments

The Contractor shall pay the Subcontractor installments as detailed below, once an acceptable insurance certificate has been filed by the Subcontractor with the Contractor:
Contractor shall pay the Subcontractor as described:

_____

_____

_____

_____

_____

_____

_____

_____

_____

    All payments are subject to a site inspection and approval of work by the Contractor. Before final payment, the Subcontractor shall submit satisfactory evidence to the Contractor that no lien risk exists on the subject property.

Working Conditions

Working hours will be 8:00 a.m. through 4:30 p.m., Monday through Friday. Subcontractor is required to clean his work debris from the job

(Page 2 of 3 initials _____)

5-13 *Continued*

site on a daily basis and leave the site in a clean and neat condition. Subcontractor shall be responsible for removal and disposal of all debris related to his job description.

Contract Assignment

Subcontractor shall not assign this contract or further subcontract the whole of this subcontract, without the written consent of the Contractor.

Laws, Permits, Fees, and Notices

Subcontractor shall be responsible for all required laws, permits, fees, or notices, required to perform the work stated herein.

Work of Others

Subcontractor shall be responsible for any damage caused to existing conditions or other contractor's work. This damage will be repaired, and the Subcontractor charged for the expense and supervision of this work. The Subcontractor shall have the opportunity to quote a price for said repairs, but the Contractor is under no obligation to engage the Subcontractor to make said repairs. If a different subcontractor repairs the damage, the Subcontractor may be back-charged for the cost of the repairs. Any repair costs will be deducted from any payments due to the Subcontractor. If no payments are due the Subcontractor, the Subcontractor shall pay the invoiced amount within ten days.

Warranty

Subcontractor warrants to the Contractor, all work and materials for one year from the final day of work performed.

Indemnification

To the fullest extent allowed by law, the Subcontractor shall indemnify and hold harmless the Owner, the Contractor, and all of their agents and employees from and against all claims, damages, losses and expenses.

This agreement, entered into on _____, 19_____, shall constitute the whole agreement between Contractor and Subcontractor.

_____   _____
Contractor   Date   Subcontractor   Date

(Page 3 of 3 initials _____)

5-13 *Continued*

Quote

This agreement, made this _____ day of _____, 19___, shall set forth the whole agreement, in its entirety, by and between YOUR COMPANY NAME, herein called Contractor and _____, herein called Owners.

Job name: _____

Job location: _____

    The Contractor and Owners agree to the following:

Contractor shall perform all work as described below and provide all material to complete the work described below. Contractor shall supply all labor and material to complete the work according to the attached plans and specifications. The work shall include the following:

_____

_____

_____

_____

Schedule

The work described above shall begin within three days of notice from Owner, with an estimated start date of _____. The Contractor shall complete the above work in a professional and expedient manner within _____ days from the start date.

Payment Schedule

Payments shall be made as follows:

_____

_____

This agreement, entered into on _____, shall constitute the whole agreement between Contractor and Owner.

_____   _____
Contractor   Date   Owner   Date

_____
Owner   Date

5-14 *Quote*

Proposal

Date: _____

Customer name: _____

Address: _____

Phone number: _____

Job location: _____

Description of Work

(Your Company Name) will supply, and or coordinate, all labor and material for the above referenced job as follows:

_____

_____

_____

Payment Schedule

Price: _____($_____),

Payments to be made as follows:

_____

_____

_____

All payments shall be made in full, upon presentation of each completed invoice. If payment is not made according to the terms above, (Your Company Name) will have the following rights and remedies. (Your Company Name) may charge a monthly service charge of one-and-one-half percent (1.5%), eighteen percent (18%) per year, from the first day default is made. (Your Company Name) may lien the property where the work has been done. (Your Company Name) may use all legal methods in the collection of monies owed to it. (Your Company Name) may seek compensation, at the rate of $30 per hour, for attempts made to collect unpaid monies.

(Your Company Name) may seek payment for legal fees and other costs of collection, to the full extent the law allows.

(Page 1 of 2 initials _____)

5-15 *Proposal*

If the job is not ready for the service or materials requested, as scheduled, and the delay is not due to (Your Company Name) actions, (Your Company Name) may charge the customer for lost time. This charge will be at a rate of $30 per hour, per man, including travel time.

If you have any questions or don't understand this proposal, seek professional advice. Upon acceptance, this proposal becomes a binding contract between both parties.

Respectfully submitted,

Your name and title
Owner

Acceptance

We the undersigned do hereby agree to, and accept, all the terms and conditions of this proposal. We fully understand the terms and conditions, and hereby consent to enter into this contract.

Your Company Name   Customer

By _____   _____

Title _____   Date _____

Date _____

Proposal expires in 30 days, if not accepted by all parties.

(Page 2 of 2 initials _____)

5-15 *Continued*

Progress Payments

The contractor shall pay the subcontractor once an acceptable insurance certificate has been filled by the subcontractor with the contractor and the contractor approves the finished work. Payment schedule will be as follows:

_____

_____

All payments are subject to a site inspection and approval of work by the contractor.

Before final payment, the subcontractor, if required, shall submit satisfactory evidence to the contractor, that all expenses related to this work have been paid and no lien risk exists on the subject property.

Working Conditions

Working hours will be 8:00 a.m. through 4:30 p.m., Monday through Friday. Subcontractor may work additional hours if desired.

Subcontractor is required to clean his work debris from the job site on a daily basis and leave the site in a clean and neat condition. Subcontractor shall be responsible for the removal and disposal of all related debris from his job description.

Contract Assignment

Subcontractor shall not assign this contract or further subcontract the whole of this subcontract without the written consent of the contractor.

Laws, Permits, Fees and Notices

Subcontractor shall be responsible for all required laws, permits, fees, or notices, required to perform the work stated herein.

Work of Others

Subcontractor shall be responsible for any damage caused to existing conditions or other trade's work. This damage will be repaired and the subcontractor charged for the expense and supervision of this work. The amount charged will be deducted from any payments due to the subcontractor, if any exist.

5-16 *Sample contractual clauses*

Subcontractor Liability for Damages

Subcontractor shall be responsible for any damage caused to existing conditions. This shall include new work performed on the project by other contractors. If the subcontractor damages existing conditions or work performed by other contractors, said subcontractor shall be responsible for the repair of said damages. These repairs may be made by the subcontractor responsible for the damages or another contractor, at the discretion of the general contractor.

If a different contractor repairs the damage, the subcontractor causing the damage may be back-charged for the cost of the repairs. These charges may be deducted from any monies owed to the damaging subcontractor, by the general contractor. The choice for a contractor to repair the damages shall be at the sole discretion of the general contractor.

If no money is owed to the damaging subcontractor, said contractor shall pay the invoiced amount, to the general contractor, within seven business days. If prompt payment is not made, the general contractor may exercise all legal means to collect the requested monies.

The damaging subcontractor shall have no rights to lien the property where work is done for money retained to cover the repair of damages caused by the subcontractor. The general contractor may have the repairs made to his satisfaction.

The damaging subcontractor shall have the opportunity to quote a price for the repairs. The general contractor is under no obligation to engage the damaging subcontractor to make the repairs.

5-17 *Damage clause*

Commencement and Completion Schedule

The work described above shall be started within 3 days of verbal notice from the customer, the projected start date is _____.
The subcontractor shall complete the above work in a professional and expedient manner by no later than _____ days from the start date. Time is of the essence with this subcontract. No extension of time will be valid without the general contractor's written consent. If subcontractor does not complete the work in the time allowed and if the lack of completion is not caused by the general contractor, the subcontractor will be charged one-hundred dollars ($100) for every day work is not finished after the completion date. This charge will be deducted from any payments due to the subcontractor for work performed.

5-18 *Completion clause*

Subcontractor Contract Addendum

This addendum is an integral part of the contract dated _____,
between the Contractor, _____,
and the Customer(s), _____,
for the work being done on real estate commonly known as _____
_____. The undersigned parties hereby
agree to the following:

_____

_____

_____

_____

_____

_____

_____

_____

The above constitutes the only additions to the above-mentioned
contract, no verbal agreements or other changes shall be valid unless
made in writing and signed by all parties.

_____   _____
Contractor   Date   Customer   Date

_____
Customer   Date

5-19 *Subcontractor contract addendum*

Warranty

Subcontractor warrants to the contractor all work and materials for one year from the day work is completed.

Indemnification

To the fullest extent allowed by law, the subcontractor shall indemnify and hold harmless the owner, the contractor and all of their agents and employees from and against all claims, damages, losses, and expenses.

This Agreement entered into on _____ shall constitute the whole agreement between contractor and subcontractor.

_____   _____

Contractor   Subcontractor

5-20 *Warranty form*

Conversion Contractors, Inc.
P. O. Box 555
Kanton, Maine 55555
107-555-5555

I understand that as an Independent Contractor, I am solely responsible for my health, actions, taxes, insurance, transportation and any other responsibilities that may be involved with the work I will be doing as an Independent Contractor.

I will not hold anyone else responsible for any claims or liabilities that may arise from this work or from any cause related to this work. I waive any rights I have or may have to hold anyone liable for any reason as a result of this work.

Independent Contractor _____

Date _____

Witness _____

Date _____

5-21 *Independent contractor agreement*

Cutting your best deal

It takes some finesse to be able to cut your best deal with suppliers and subcontractors. Suppliers normally give you a better break if you agree to buy all of your materials from them. That's okay as long as you are truly getting a better deal. But it is often hard for a single supplier to offer the best prices on every item you need. One supplier might have the best price for siding, another might have the lowest price on dimensional lumber. Assess all your quotes and determine how you would like the deal to be worked out. Then it is just a matter of seeing if the suppliers can accommodate you.

There are a couple of other ways to get a price break from subcontractors. You might see some savings if you allow the contractor to use your conversion project as a reference. Another great way to save some money, if time is not a big factor, is to let the subcontractors use your job as fill-in work. This gives them a place to work when other jobs are stalled by weather or other circumstances. While this can save you substantial money, it is likely to take longer to complete the project. Unfortunately, there isn't enough space here to cover all the details from an administrative point of view. This book is geared to conversions, not business management. However, my earlier book *Building Contractor: Start and Run a Money-Making Business*, also published by McGraw-Hill, can help you in all aspects of your business operation.

6

Creating a budget and production schedule

Creating a budget and production schedule that you can adhere to is not as easy as it might seem. The budget is often easier to control than the production schedule, and staying on budget is no piece of cake. Experienced subcontractors and general contractors are already familiar with budgets and work schedules. But until you get into a full-blown conversion project, you might not understand how much time and attention it takes to stay on time and within the budget.

Experienced remodelers have the biggest edge in this part of the job. In a conversion project, most of the work involves remodeling rather than a lot of new construction. Sometimes the project is a combination of remodeling and new construction. For this reason, it takes a contractor with a well-rounded background to stay on track.

The first budget

Your first budget is probably going to be based on a lot of guesswork. A rough budget like this is often done as a part of a feasibility study to see if a property is worth pursuing. A budget filled with guesswork won't be accurate enough to hang your hat on, but it can serve as a starting point. Only experienced contractors have a good enough feel for prices to compile an off-the-cuff budget that is close to accurate.

Most first budgets are quickly replaced as soon as bids are received from suppliers and subcontractors, therefore I won't dwell the subject of "guesstimates." It's more important to learn how to arrange bids and draft a solid working budget.

The working budget

It's pretty easy to create a budget by arranging the prices from the bids. Start by creating categories for each phase of work on the project. Once all the phases have been listed, review your bid prices and plug them into the budget. Use either the low bid, the high bid, or an average of the two. I usually use either an average or the high bid, depending on the project.

You are not likely to exceed the budget if you use the high bids on paper and the low bids on the job. However, when you use only the low bids to create your budget, you might find yourself in trouble if the low-bidder is not available when you need work done. You'll be forced to use a different subcontractor who is going to charge a price that exceeds your budget. I like to plan high and work low.

I believe the best way to design your budget is to have it arranged in chronological order. Listing various phases of work in the order they are going to be done makes it easy to assess your cash flow needs as the job progresses. For example, if your job requires site work, that would be a logical starting point. Foundation work, if required, would be the second category on your budget. The checklist would continue in this fashion. Since heating is usually done before plumbing, and plumbing is usually done before electrical, the chronological order of work would be listed as heating, plumbing, and then electrical. The use of forms and checklists can be very valuable in building a budget (Figs. 6-1 and 6-2).

When I build a budget, I include three columns for prices. I put headings above each column to represent the best case, the probable case, and the worst case. This allows me to list low bids, mid-range bids, and high bids on the same budget. I can immediately see the range of total costs. You don't have to go to this extreme, but I find this system works quite well.

Hard and soft costs

Hard costs are normally the first category of prices to be considered. These costs consist of the materials and labor. Hard costs are the expenses that most people think of when they compute a construction budget.

Other expenses, called soft costs, must also be taken into account. Soft costs elude some inexperienced contractors, but you can't afford to let that happen. Any number of items can be considered as soft costs. They include survey fees, bank fees, interest on loans, permit fees, administrative costs, and other similar expenses.

Cost Projections

Item/Phase	Labor	Material	Total
Plans			
Specifications			
Permits			
Trash container deposit			
Trash container delivery			
Demolition			
Dump fees			
Rough plumbing			
Rough electrical			
Rough heating/ac			
Subfloor			
Insulation			
Drywall			
Ceramic tile			
Linen closet			
Baseboard trim			
Window trim			
Door trim			
Paint/wallpaper			
Underlayment			
Finish floor covering			
Linen closet shelves			
Closet door & hardware			
Main door hardware			
Wall cabinets			
Base cabinets			
Counter tops			
Plumbing fixtures			
Trim plumbing material			
Subtotal			

6-1 *Cost projections*

Item/Phase	Labor	Material	Total
Final plumbing			
Shower enclosure			
Light fixtures			
Trim electrical material			
Final electrical			
Trim heating/ac material			
Final heating/ac			
Bathroom accessories			
Clean-up			
Trash container removal			
Window treatments			
Personal touches			
Financing expenses			
Miscellaneous expenses			
Unexpected expenses			
Margin of error			
Total estimated expense			

6-1 *Continued*

Job Budget

Phase	Cost
Plans	
Permits	
Demolition	
Framing	
Stairs	
Dormers	
Plumbing	
Heating	
Electrical	
Insulation	
Drywall	
Paint	
Doors	
Hardware	
Underlayment	
Floor coverings	
Cabinets	
Counters	
Cleanup	
Other	
Other	
Total Cost	

6-2 *Job budget*

Soft costs can add up to a lot of money. You could run thousands of dollars over your anticipated expenses if you don't include all of them. You must include all costs, both hard and soft, if your budget is to be accurate. Creating an outline of the work you will be doing is one way to reduce the risk of error. Following are some examples for you to consider (Figs. 6-3 through 6-21).

Outline of Work when Building an Addition (before Physical Work Begins)

Choose style of addition to be built.

Review requirements of space; closets, additional baths, windows, door sizes, etc.

Draw a rough draft of addition plans.

Make a list of required materials for the job.

Price materials.

Make a list of subcontractors or general contractors for selection.

Contact contractors for price quotes.

Evaluate your budget and the affordability of the addition.

Make financing arrangements.

Make a final decision on the plans for the addition.

Obtain blueprints.

Apply for the necessary permits.

Choose your contractors and check their references.

Meet with your attorney to draft contracts and other documents.

Schedule work.

Schedule material deliveries.

Schedule contractors.

6-3 *Outline for building a room addition*

Outline of Work when Building an Addition (when Physical Work Begins)

Start work.

Inspect work.

Obtain copies of all code enforcement inspections.

Make payments as scheduled in the contracts and obtain signed lien waivers from contractors and suppliers.

Inspect completed job.

Make punch-lists, as necessary.

Make absolute final inspection and approval.

Make final payments, except for retainages.

Make retainage payments.

6-4 *Outline for building a room addition*

Possible Work when Building an Addition

Survey	Roofing	Interior trim
Plans	Exterior trim	Finish floor covering
Specifications	Exterior hardware	Wall cabinets
Permits	Windows	Base cabinets
Site preparation	Doors	Countertops
Footings	Plumbing	Window treatments
Foundation	Heating/ac	Landscaping
Pest control treatment	Electrical	Trash container
Backfill labor, if applicable	Insulation	Dump fees
Demolition	Drywall	Cleanup
Repairs to existing wall	Paint	Personal touches
Framing	Interior doors	Gutters
Siding	Interior hardware	Decks

6-5 *Typical work involved with building a room addition*

Budget Estimates for
Building a Room Addition

Item/Phase	Labor	Material	Total
Survey			
Plans			
Specifications			
Permits			
Site preparation			
Dig footings			
Concrete for footings			
Pour footings			
Foundation wall material			
Foundation wall labor			
Pest control treatment			
Foundation backfill labor			
Demolition			
Repairs to existing wall			
Framing lumber			
Roof trusses			
Attic vents			
Sheathing			
Framing labor			
Siding			
Siding labor			
Shingles			
Roof labor			
Exterior trim material			
Exterior hardware			

6-6 _Budge projection form for building a room addition_

Item/Phase	Labor	Material	Total
Windows			
Doors			
Nails & misc. material			
Shelving			
Pull-down attic stairs			
Misc. carpentry labor			
Rough plumbing material			
Rough plumbing labor			
Plumbing fixtures			
Final plumbing labor			
Rough heating/ac material			
Rough heating/ac labor			
Heating/ac equipment			
Final heating/ac labor			
Rough electrical material			
Rough electrical labor			
Light fixtures			
Final electrical labor			
Insulation			
Insulation labor			
Drywall			
Drywall labor			
Paint			
Paint labor			
Interior doors			
Interior hardware			
Interior trim			
Interior trim labor			

6-6 *Continued*

Item/Phase	Labor	Material	Total
Underlayment			
Finish floor covering			
Wall cabinets			
Base cabinets			
Countertops			
Window treatments			
Landscaping			
Trash container deposit			
Trash container delivery			
Dump fees			
Cleanup			
Trash container removal			
Personal touches			
Financing expenses			
Miscellaneous expenses			
Options:			
Concrete for slab			
Wire mesh			
Gravel			
Plastic ground cover			
Pour slab			
Finish slab			
Gutters			
Decks			
Unexpected expenses			
Margin of error			
Total projected expenses			

6-6 *Continued*

Outline of Work for Kitchen Remodeling
(before Physical Work Begins)

Review requirements of space; additional windows or appliances, eat-in area, built-in seating or storage, lighting, etc.

Draw a rough draft of kitchen plans.

Make a list of required materials for the job.

Price materials.

Make a list of subcontractors or general contractors for selection.

Contact contractors for price quotes.

Evaluate your budget and the affordability of the kitchen project.

Make financing arrangements.

Make a final decision on the plans for the kitchen.

Obtain blueprints, if necessary.

Apply for the necessary permits.

Choose your contractors and check their references.

Meet with your attorney to draft contracts and other documents.

Schedule work.

Schedule material deliveries.

Schedule contractors.

6-7 *Outline for kitchen remodeling*

Outline of Work to be Done for Kitchen Remodeling (when Physical Work Begins)

Start work.

Inspect work.

Obtain copies of all code enforcement inspections.

Make payments as scheduled in the contracts and obtain signed lien waivers from contractors and suppliers.

Inspect completed job.

Make punch-list, if necessary.

Make absolute final inspection and approval.

Make final payments, except for retainages.

Make retainage payments.

6-8 *Outline for kitchen remodeling*

Possible Work for Kitchen Remodeling

Plans	Subfloor	Hardware
Specifications	Insulation	Wall cabinets
Permits	Drywall	Base cabinets
Trash container	Trim	Countertops
Demolition	Windows	Appliances
Dump fees	Doors	Kitchen accessories
Plumbing	Paint/wallpaper	Cleanup
Electrical	Underlayment	Window treatments
Heating/ac	Finish floor covering	Personal touches

6-9 *Typical work required during kitchen remodeling*

Budget Projections for Kitchen Remodeling

Item/Phase	Labor	Material	Total
Plans			
Specifications			
Permits			
Trash container deposit			
Trash container delivery			
Demolition			
Dump fees			
Rough plumbing			
Rough electrical			
Rough heating/ac			
Subfloor			
Insulation			
Drywall			
Baseboard trim			
Window trim			
Door trim			
Paint/wallpaper			
Underlayment			
Finish floor covering			
Hardware			
Wall cabinets			
Base cabinets			
Countertops			
Plumbing fixtures			
Trim plumbing material			
Final plumbing			
Light fixtures			
Trim electrical material			
Final electrical			
Trim heating/ac material			
Final heating/ac			

6-10 *Budget projection form for kitchen remodeling*

Item/Phase	Labor	Material	Total
Appliances			
Kitchen accessories			
Cleanup			
Trash container removal			
Window treatments			
Personal touches			
Financing expenses			
Miscellaneous expenses			
Unexpected expenses			
Margin of error			
Total projected expenses			

6-10 *Continued*

Outline of Work for Bathroom Remodeling (before Physical Work Begins)

Obtain various product information.

Review requirements of space; linen closet, door sizes, windows, additional electrical outlets (GFI), fans, etc.

Draw a rough draft of bathroom plans.

Make a list of required materials for the job.

Price materials.

Make a list of subcontractors or general contractors for selection.

Contact contractors for price quotes.

Evaluate budget and the affordability of the bathroom remodeling.

Make financing arrangements.

Make a final decision on the plans for the bathroom.

Obtain blueprints, if necessary.

Apply for the necessary permits.

Choose your contractors and check their references.

Meet with your attorney to draft contracts and other documents.

Schedule work.

Schedule material deliveries.

Schedule contractors.

6-11 *Bathroom remodeling outline*

Outline of Work for Bathroom Remodeling (when Physical Work Begins)

Start work.

Inspect work.

Obtain copies of all code enforcement inspections.

Make payments as scheduled in the contracts and obtain signed lien waivers from contractors and suppliers.

Inspect completed job.

Make punch-list, if necessary.

Make absolute final inspection and approval.

Make final payments, except for retainages.

Make retainage payments.

6-12 *Bathroom remodeling outline*

Possible Work for Bathroom Remodeling

Plans	Subfloor	Finish floor covering
Specifications	Insulation	Hardware
Permits	Drywall	Wall cabinets
Trash container	Ceramic tile	Base cabinets
Demolition	Linen closet	Countertops
Dump fees	Trim	Shower enclosure
Plumbing	Windows	Bath accessories
Fixture installation	Doors	Cleanup
Electrical	Paint/wallpaper	Window treatments
Heating/ac	Underlayment	Personal touches

6-13 *Typical phases of bathroom remodeling*

Outline of Work for an Attic Conversion (before Physical Work Begins)

Review requirements of space; stairs, built-in storage, closets, windows, new attic space ventilation, etc.

Draw a rough draft of conversion plans.

Make a list of required materials for the job.

Price materials.

Make a list of subcontractors or general contractors for selection.

Contact contractors for price quotes.

Evaluate your budget and the affordability of the conversion.

Make financing arrangements.

Make a final decision on the plans for the conversion.

Obtain blueprints, if necessary.

Apply for the necessary permits.

Choose your contractors and check their references.

Meet with your attorney to draft contracts and other documents.

Schedule work.

Schedule material deliveries.

Schedule contractors.

6-14 *Outline for attic conversions*

Outline of Work to Be Done for an Attic Conversion (when Physical Work Begins)

Start work.

Inspect work.

Obtain copies of all code enforcement inspections.

Make payments as scheduled in the contracts and obtain signed lien waivers from contractors and suppliers.

Inspect completed job.

Make punch-list, if necessary.

Make absolute final inspection and approval.

Make final payments, except for retainages.

Make retainage payments.

6-15 *Outline for attic conversions*

Possible Types of Work
for an Attic Conversion

Plans

Specifications

Permits

Demolition

Repairs to existing ceiling

Framing

Stairs

Dormer work, if required

Plumbing

Heating/ac

Electrical

Insulation

Drywall

Paint

Interior doors & hardware

Interior trim

Underlayment

Finish floor covering

Wall cabinets

Base cabinets

Countertops

Window treatments

Trash container

Dump fees

Cleanup

Personal touches

6-16 *Types of work involved with attic conversions*

Budget Projections for an Attic Conversion

Item/Phase	Labor	Material	Total
Plans			
Specifications			
Permits			
Demolition			
Repairs to existing ceiling			
Framing lumber			
Framing labor			
Dormer material			
Dormer labor			
Nails & misc. material			
Misc. carpentry labor			
Rough plumbing material			
Rough plumbing labor			
Plumbing fixtures			
Final plumbing labor			
Rough heating/ac material			
Rough heating/ac labor			
Heating/ac equipment			
Final heating/ac labor			
Rough electrical material			
Rough electrical labor			
Light fixtures			
Final electrical labor			
Insulation			
Insulation labor			
Drywall			

6-17 *Budget projection form for an attic conversion*

Item/Phase	Labor	Material	Total
Drywall labor			
Paint			
Paint labor			
Interior doors & hardware			
Interior trim			
Interior trim labor			
Underlayment			
Finish floor covering			
Wall cabinets			
Base cabinets			
Countertops			
Window treatments			
Trash container deposit			
Trash container delivery			
Dump fees			
Cleanup			
Trash container removal			
Personal touches			
Financing expenses			
Miscellaneous expenses			
Unexpected expenses			
Margin of error			
Total projected expenses			

6-17 *Continued*

Outline of Work for Garage Construction (before Physical Work Begins)

Choose style of garage to be built.

Draw a rough draft of garage plans or obtain pre-drawn plans.

Make, or obtain, a list of required materials for the job.

Price materials

Make a list of subcontractors or general contractors for selection.

Contact contractors for price quotes.

Evaluate budget and the affordability of the garage.

Make financing arrangements.

Make a final decision on the plans for the garage.

Obtain blueprints.

Apply for the necessary permits.

Choose your contractors and check their references.

Meet with your attorney to draft contracts and other documents.

Schedule work.

Schedule material deliveries.

Schedule contractors.

6-18 *Outline for garage construction*

Outline of Work for Garage Construction (when Physical Work Begins)

Start work.

Inspect work.

Obtain copies of all code enforcement inspections.

Make payments as scheduled in the contracts and obtain signed lien waivers from contractors and suppliers.

Inspect completed job.

Make punch-list, if necessary.

Make absolute final inspection and approval.

Make final payments, except for retainages.

Make retainage payments.

6-19 *Outline for garage construction*

Possible Work for Garage Construction

Survey	Trim	Hardware
Plans	Windows	Landscaping
Specifications	Small door	Cleanup
Permits	Garage doors	Personal touches
Site preparation	Garage door openers	*Options:*
Footings	Electrical	Heating/ac
Pest control	Insulation	Plumbing
Slab floor	Drywall	Interior trim
Framing	Paint	Floor sealant
Siding	Trash container	Apron
Roofing	Dump fees	Driveway repair or extension

6-20 *Typical phases of garage construction*

Budget Projections
for the Construction of a Garage

Item/Phase	Labor	Material	Total
Survey			
Plans			
Specifications			
Permits			
Site preparation			
Dig footings			
Concrete for footings			
Pour footings			
Concrete for slab			
Wire mesh			
Gravel			
Plastic ground cover			
Pest control			
Pour slab			
Pour apron			
Finish slab			
Framing lumber			
Roof trusses			
Attic vents			
Sheathing			
Framing labor			
Siding			
Siding labor			
Shingles			
Roof labor			
Trim material			
Windows			
Small door			
Garage doors			
Garage door openers			
Overhead door labor			
Nails & misc. material			

6-21 *Budget projection form for garage construction*

Item/Phase	Labor	Material	Total
Pegboard			
Shelving			
Pull-down attic stairs			
Misc. carpentry labor			
Rough electrical material			
Rough electrical labor			
Light fixtures			
Final electrical labor			
Insulation			
Insulation labor			
Drywall			
Drywall labor			
Paint			
Paint labor			
Trash container deposit			
Trash container delivery			
Dump fees			
Hardware			
Landscaping			
Cleanup			
Trash container removal			
Personal touches			
Financing expenses			
Miscellaneous expenses			
Options:			
Heating/ac			
Plumbing			
Interior trim			
Floor sealant			
Driveway repair or extension			
Unexpected expenses			
Margin of error			
Total projected expenses			

6-21 *Continued*

Adding up

After adding all the expected costs, you should have a reasonably accurate picture of your expenses. However, some unexpected costs usually pop up during a project. For example, you might discover that one of the material take-offs is not completely accurate. The job you thought needed only a new floor covering might actually need an entirely new subfloor. Some of these surprises can be quite costly.

As a hedge against unexpected costs, it's important to add a certain percentage to the overall costs. The added percentage acts as a built-in safety factor. If you are doing your first conversion job, this float figure for unexpected expenditures should be high. As you gain experience, you can gradually reduce the built-in safety margin.

Although there isn't a rule-of-thumb percentage used as a safety factor, I normally factor in from 3 to 10 percent of the total job cost. This often leaves me with extra money in the budget at the end of a job, but I'd rather have money left over than need to go searching for cash at the last minute.

You'll be able to refine the safety factor percentage if you keep detailed records of each job you do. If, after a few jobs, you see that the cost overages are consistently running 3 percent of the job's anticipated cost, you might decide to use a 5-percent safety factor.

Keeping tabs

Be sure to keep tabs on your spending as the job progresses (Figs. 6-22 through 6-27). It is a good way to avoid the kind of trouble that can get you in over your head. If you lay out your budget chronologically, as I have advised, you can track and predict your spending on a phase-by-phase basis. You know early on if you start to creep outside the boundaries of your budget.

Contractors who fail to keep track of spending often wind up in a big mess near the end of their projects. All of a sudden they find they have depleted their allocated funds, yet the job isn't finished. This can cause plenty of stress, and it can also lead to bankruptcy.

When a budget is designed to allow the tracking of each phase of construction, you can catch cost overruns before they consume you. For example, you might discover that the rough plumbing cost $500 more than you had planned. Or, if the project is progressing slowly, you can see that you are going to exceed the amount budgeted for construction interest. As you find these problems, you can begin to counteract them. This might be done by altering your plans or talking to your lender about a higher loan amount. In either case, you are better off catching the overages early in the project.

Job Cost Log		
Item	*Quantity*	*Size*

6-22 *Job cost log*

Materials Log	
Supplier's name	
Contact person	
Order number	
Date of order	
Delivery date	
Cost of order	

6-23 *Materials log*

Cash Receipts

Date	Account Description	Amount Paid	Date Received

6-24 *Cash receipts log*

Cash Receipt

Date _____

Time _____

Received of _____

Address _____

Account number _____

Amount received _____

Payment for _____

Form of payment _____

Signed _____

6-25 *Cash receipt*

Petty-Cash Records

Month_____

Year_____

Vendor	Amount	Item	Date	Job

6-26 *Petty-cash records*

Accounts Payable

Vendor	Job	Amount due	Date due	Date paid

6-27 *Accounts payable log*

The production schedule

Your production schedule is easy to establish, but adhering to it might not be so easy. Subcontractors have ways of destroying the best-laid plans of general contractors. If one subcontractor messes up your schedule, the ripple effect can create havoc with the work schedule of the other trades. It can leave you shaking your head and staring blankly at what once was your work schedule.

You can reduce scheduling problems like this, but you can't entirely eliminate them. Before we discuss how you can attempt to keep your job on track, let's talk about the proper ways to create a production schedule (Figs. 6-28 and 6-29).

Layout

The layout of your production schedule can be similar to that of your budget. Draft a checklist that contains all phases of work to be done on your project. Chronological order is again the best structure for this form. A common way of doing this is to list the work phases in a column on the left side of a piece of paper. The next column over might contain the subcontractor's name for that phase of work. A third column can list your intended start date for that work. A fourth column can provide space for the expected completion date. You can create a few additional columns for changes or make sure the columns you are using allow room for changes. You can bet the farm that there are going to be changes in any major conversion job.

After completing your form, you can begin to fill in the scheduling information. To do this, you are going to have to talk with your subcontractors. You can create your own schedule, but until you get confirmation from subcontractors, your tentative schedule is not going to mean much. You probably won't be able to get all your subcontractors to cooperate enough to meet your ideal production schedule.

When you begin getting commitments from the subcontractors, you can start charting your promised dates. However, don't depend too heavily on the dates you are given. I can't stress enough that some subcontractors won't show up on schedule. The same contractors can also have trouble meeting the promised completion dates. Set up your production schedule as best you can, but allow extra time for all phases of the work. That way you'll be covered if you run into the types of problems inherent in the construction business.

Ask the subcontractors when they can be available and when they are going to complete their part of the job. The dates you are given should be included in the contract agreement between you and

Subcontractor Schedule

Type of service	Vendor name	Phone number	Date scheduled
Site work			
Footings			
Concrete			
Foundation			
Waterproofing			
Masonry			
Framing			
Roofing			
Siding			
Exterior trim			
Gutters			
Pest control			
Plumbing/R-I			
HVAC/R-I			
Electrical/R-I			
Insulation			
Drywall			
Painter			
Wallpaper			
Tile			
Cabinets			
Countertops			
Interior trim			
Floor covering			
Plumbing/final			
HVAC/final			
Electrical/final			
Cleaning			
Paving			
Landscaping			

Notes/Changes

6-28 *Subcontractor schedule*

Job Schedule		
Phase	*Start date*	*Completion date*

6-29 *Job schedule*

the subcontractor. I have a clause in my subcontract agreement that allows me to charge a cash penalty for each day a subcontractor runs past the promised completion date. When subcontractors lose $100 every day a project extends past its deadline, they are more likely to get the work done on time, even if it means letting someone else's job suffer. A general contractor that includes a penalty clause in contracts is probably going to get the most attention from subcontractors. However, not all states allow penalty clauses, so check with an attorney before adding it to your contract.

Some trades must have their work inspected and approved by local code officials before other trades can do their work. For example, most cities and towns require inspections for footings, foundations, framing, plumbing, heating, electrical work, and insulation. If your plumber has finished the rough plumbing, it must be inspected before it can be covered by the walls or ceilings. Your drywall crew can't do much until the plumbing has been inspected and approved. The same applies to heating, electrical work, and insulation.

You'll need to allow extra time for these inspections, and you should not assume that the work is going to be approved the first time around. If you are using quality subcontractors, the work should pass the first inspection, but there are times when it won't. If the work is rejected, the subcontractor must make the required changes and get it inspected a second time. This can take days, and during that time your project is falling further behind schedule. As I said earlier, it's easy to make the first draft of a production schedule, but meeting and maintaining that schedule can present some real challenges.

Staying on schedule

It can be extremely difficult to stay on schedule, especially if you are working with subcontractors who are new to you. What can be done to prevent the problems? I believe it is impossible to eliminate all delays, but they can be reduced with proper management. After all, management is the primary duty of a general contractor. Let's discuss a few ways that can help keep your conversion project on schedule.

Completion clauses

We've already talked about completion and penalty clauses, so there is not much need to rehash them. These clauses, however, can be a big help keeping your job up to speed. You should consult an attorney on all of your contract issues. What's legal for me to do in Maine might violate the statutes in your state, so check with an attorney before creating any legal agreements.

Money

Most people work to earn money. If you control the money, you generally control the subcontractor. When you pay out a large deposit before the work is done, a subcontractor might not be as motivated to finish the job. Making payments only after the work is complete and inspected can give you an edge in making contractors move to the beat of your drum.

Bonus money

Bonus money is another way to get top production out of subcontractors. Let's say an electrical contractor has given you a price of $2300 and promises to complete the work in four days. If you need the work completed sooner, consider offering the subcontractor a 10-percent bonus for getting the job done in three days. Money can be a strong motivator.

You must be prudent with bonuses. If every contractor picked up an extra 10 percent, your job cost could turn out to be too high. Use bonuses sparingly, but know that they might just bail you out of a tough spot.

Additional work

The promise of additional work can create plenty of motivation for hungry subcontractors. When I was building 60 houses a year, I had considerable leverage on my subcontractors. I got priority treatment because I was a big contractor who could offer them a lot of future work.

When your conversion business is in the start-up stage, you can't offer subcontractors much future work, so you'll probably lack the leverage that's needed to keep your first few jobs on schedule. However, it doesn't hurt to explain to the subcontractors that your project is not a one-time shot. As long as they respect you as an up-and-coming conversion contractor, you might get a little better service than the average homeowner.

Stack them up

Subcontractors don't like it, but they do respect the power you have when you stack them up. What am I talking about? I mean that you should have three subcontractors available for each trade. In other words, you should have three plumbing firms, three electrical firms, three insulation crews, and so on.

Once you have this depth of talent, evaluate all the subcontractors and rate them as first, second, or third choices in each trade. Let the subcontractors know about each other. Explain the rules and tell them what actions you'll take if they stray from the game plan. Make provisions in your contract to void the agreement and bring in a replacement if the present subcontractor violates the agreement.

Stacking up the subcontractors puts you in a much stronger position. Conversion work is not usually a high-volume business, but it can be. The more work you do, the better a stacking plan works. For example, when my building activity was at a peak, I would start constructing ten houses almost simultaneously. My first-choice subcontractor got five of the jobs, my second choice got three, and my third choice got two. All of them wanted more work.

If my first choice failed to meet the contract obligations, the subcontractor was dropped to the third-place position. The other two contractors each moved up a level. This created competition, causing them to try and prove their worth to me as a first-choice subcontractor. Having three subcontractors in each trade allowed me the luxury of having back-ups that I knew first hand. The subcontractors might not have liked the arrangement, but they all accepted it and played by the rules most of the time. This has proved to be my most successful approach to maintaining control over subcontractors. Unfortunately, it doesn't work very well until you are well established and have plenty of work.

Good communication

Good communication can help you stay on schedule. Too many general contractors are deficient in this area. You'll be less likely to suffer delays if you develop a good relationship with your subcontractors and talk with them frequently. It's a good idea to log phone calls so that you can remember and document your phone arrangements (Fig. 6-30).

Call your subcontractors several days before they are scheduled to start and remind them about the project. Don't be surprised if some have forgotten all about the start date on your job. During the time they are working on your project, contact the subcontractors every day, preferably at the job site. If you can't get to the job site, at least call them on the phone. You might resent having to hold the hands of professionals, but sometimes a little babysitting is needed. Your direct attention and clear communication can solve problems before they happen.

Weather

The weather is one part of your production schedule that you can't control. While it is true that you can't change the weather, you can change the effect it has on your projects. Unlike new construction, much of the work on conversion projects can be done even when the weather is poor. Cold temperatures might affect some of your work, such as roofing, but most of your activity can remain at good production levels in almost any weather. You might have to rent heaters for temporary use, or make some other on-site adjustments to overcome bad weather, but you can do a lot to keep the ball rolling. The key to success here is to have a plan to deal with anticipated weather problems.

Material deliveries

When materials don't arrive at the job site on time, it can wreak havoc with your schedule. It is not wise to overstock a job or stock materials too far in advance. But it is important to place your orders early enough to ensure that the materials are going to be at the job site when they are needed.

Phone Log

Date/Time	Company Name	Contact Person	Remarks

6-30 *Phone log*

I've seen seasoned contractors order materials the day before they are needed. Sometimes these deliveries arrive in time, sometimes they don't. When they don't, work crews stand idle at the job site. Don't let this happen to you.

Suppliers are not too different from subcontractors. Sometimes orders get misplaced. Call your supplier two days before the scheduled delivery date and give them a friendly reminder of your order. Stay on top of all the orders. Don't let the suppliers brush you off in order to tend to larger accounts. Let them know that you are a larger account in the making, and that you can take your business elsewhere if it is not appreciated. Sometimes you have to play hard ball.

Personal supervision

Personal supervision of your project is paramount to success. You need to be at the job site at least once a day, and you should spend as much time there as you can. If possible, set up a temporary office on the site. It can enable you to do your paperwork and other administrative duties, yet you are immediately available to check on the subcontractors and answer any questions. You don't have to do the job to get it done right, but you do have to provide supervision and management (Fig. 6-31).

Pay your subcontractors promptly

If you pay your subcontractors promptly, they are going to want to work for you again because you'll be recognized as a prime contractor. You might also find that they are more likely to oblige your needs. A lot of generals contractors "jerk around" their subcontractors when it comes time to pay the bills. This is a big mistake. General contractors who are slow to pay have trouble finding good subcontractors. Word travels fast in the trades. Make sure the word on your business is a good one.

Experience

Experience is something you can't buy; it must be earned. The learning process can be expensive. Making mistakes is a part of life, and what might seem at the time to be a major headache can turn into a good learning experience.

Pay attention to your mistakes and don't make the same ones twice. After you survive in the conversion business a few years, you gain strength through your hard-earned experience. Some of the lessons are tough, but they can all be used to your advantage in future deals. Don't look at mistakes as setbacks, view them as opportunities for the future.

Inspection Log

Phase	Ordered	Approved
Rough plumbing		
Finish plumbing		
Rough electrical		
Finish electrical		
Rough heating		
Finish heating		
Framing		
Insulation		
Final		

6-31 *Inspection log*

7

Financing
a project

The process of financing a project can be simple or difficult; it all depends on a number of circumstances. Rarely are any two conversion projects exactly alike, so each one can require different approaches to financing. Many of the basic elements for obtaining a loan are going to remain the same, but some key elements of the deal might have to be altered. The changes can be quite minor and still have a major impact on your overall project if they are not made.

You can look at financing several ways. You can take the simple approach and live with the consequences, or you can invest the extra time it takes to arrange the kind of attractive financing that makes deals more profitable. I prefer the latter.

Many people take the simple approach out of ignorance. They don't know how to improve upon what they consider to be standard financing. Profits are often lost because they don't understand the financing process. You don't want to be in this crowd. Instead, you want to rub elbows with the savvy investors and contractors who know how to maximize their profits and comfort with the right financing. This chapter gives you all the knowledge you need to begin your journey toward more profitable financing.

Most conversion projects won't get off the ground without some type of financing. As you have probably already gathered, some financing programs are better than others. There is even free money available for certain types of projects. If you play your cards right, you might be able to tap into money sources where you never have to repay the money you obtain, and it's all legal. I'll detail these programs a little later in the chapter. Before we discuss how you can improve your odds of obtaining financing, let's discuss the various types of loans that you might find interesting.

When you start to talk about financing, there is a lot of information to cover. To be successful as a conversion contractor, you must learn to tailor your financing to each project. Loans that are great for some properties are not always good for other types of real estate. The first step in securing the right financing is learning what is the best financing for your project.

Most conversion projects require at least two different types of loans, sometimes more. The first type of loan you are going to be interested in obtaining is an acquisition loan. It is similar, in some ways, to the loan you might have on your home. It is financing that allows you to acquire a property. After all, getting a property you can convert is the first step. This doesn't mean, however, that you should run out and apply for an acquisition loan without some further thought.

Acquisition loans only allow you to purchase a property. They don't provide extra money for converting the property, unless you structure a combination acquisition and improvement loan. As another option, you could get one loan to buy a property and another loan to fix it, but this normally costs more than a combination loan. If you don't know how to ask the right questions, you are going to probably pay extra for your financing. This chapter is going to help you understand the process.

Straight acquisition loans

Straight acquisition loans are fine for anyone buying real estate that is going to be maintained in its present condition. However, conversion contractors are in the business of modifying property, so straight acquisition loans are not ideal financing options. An acquisition loan only allows you to acquire a property. This step is necessary, but much more money is needed when you are going to convert a building. If you end up with a straight acquisition loan, you are also going to need a short-term construction or improvement loan.

Short-term financing

Short-term financing is available in many forms. There are loans that can be obtained on one's signature for 90 days. Construction loans are considered short-term financing, even though some have terms up to one year. Improvement loans are similar to construction loans in that they provide money for conversion and improvement for up to a year, and perhaps longer. Interest rates on short-term financing are usually higher than the rates charged for long-term mortgage loans. Promissory notes (Figs. 7-1 and 7-2) are often used for short-term financing in construction.

Promissory Note

City _____

State _____

Date _____

Face amount of note $_____

For value received and/or services rendered, the undersigned promises to pay to the order of _____ at _____ the principal sum of $_____ ($_____) with interest thereon at the rate of _____ percent per annum, said interest to be paid in monthly payments of $_____, ($_____) for _____ months. The balance is due in full and payable on _____. This note shall be secured by the personal guarantee of the undersigned and their heirs. Further security for this note shall be as follows:

_____

_____

_____

_____   _____

Debtor   Date   Debtor   Date

_____

Witness   Date

7-1 *Promissory note*

Balloon Promissory Note

City _____

State _____

Date _____

Face amount of note $_____

For value received and/or services rendered, the undersigned promises to pay to the order of _____ at _____
_____ the principal sum of
$_____ ($_____)
with interest thereon at the rate of _____ percent per annum, said principal and interest to be paid in full on _____
_____. This note shall be secured by the personal guarantee of the undersigned and their heirs. This note is not assignable without written permission by _____. Further security for this note shall be as follows:

_____

_____

_____   _____

Debtor   Date   Debtor   Date

_____

Witness   Date

7-2 *Balloon promissory note*

Permanent financing

Permanent financing can be compared to acquisition financing. The two loans are often identical in structure. However, permanent or acquisition financing for an investor is likely to be a little different (at least in down-payment requirements), than the financing for a buyer who lives in the property.

Permanent financing can take on many faces. Some loans have 15-year terms. Loans with 20-year terms are common with investors. Most long-term loans for real estate, with the exception of raw land and commercial property, have 30-year terms.

With a long-term loan, the choice of how long the loan runs is up to you. Depending on your borrowing conditions, the lender might set some limits, such as a 20-year term, but basically the decision is yours.

Many people go for a 15-year loan so the financing can be paid off earlier. A 15-year loan results in higher monthly payments, which can be bothersome if the property has a high vacancy rate. I prefer to get a 30-year loan and pay it off early if I choose. I can make payments as if the loan was a 15-year loan and achieve the same benefits of a 15-year loan, without being firmly committed to the higher payment. If I have a bad month, I can pay the amount due on the 30-year loan. This arrangement allows me flexibility without losing any real advantage.

With a conversion project, you might not be able to get permanent financing until the project is completed. If you're working on speculation and plan to sell the project when it's completed, permanent financing might not even be a part of your plans. It should be, though, because you never know when you are going to find yourself in a bad real estate market. If that happens, you might not be able to sell the building for enough money to make the deal worthwhile. For this reason, you should line up permanent financing for every project, even if it's never used. It's a good safety net.

Operating capital

Operating capital is needed to fund your conversion project until enough work is done to qualify for a bank draw from your construction or improvement loan. Perhaps you have enough of your own money to bridge this gap, but a lot of contractors don't. They need some short-term, interim financing to see them through different phases of a job.

Sometimes subcontractors and suppliers provide this interim money. They don't actually give you cash, but it's effectively the same thing. They help you by not requesting payment for their labor and materials until the project is far enough along to qualify for a bank disbursement. If you're short on cash, working out a deal like this with your suppliers and subcontractors can be the easiest and least-expensive way to get over the hump.

However, if your conversion team can't wait for their money, you might need to apply for some additional short-term financing. Of the various loans we have discussed, this particular type of loan is normally the hardest to get approved. Lenders don't like to see 100-percent financing in a deal. If you don't have enough of your own money to keep a job rolling between draw disbursements, you might be out of luck. You should require all suppliers and contractors to sign lien waivers (Figs. 7-3 and 7-4) at the time they are paid.

Short-Form Lien Waiver

Customer name: _____

Customer address: _____

Customer city/state/zip: _____

Customer phone number: _____

Job location: _____

Date: _____

Type of work: _____

Contractor: _____

Contractor address: _____

Subcontractor: _____

Subcontractor address: _____

Description of work completed to date: _____

_____

Payments received to date: _____

Payment received on this date: _____

Total amount paid, including this payment: _____

The contractor/subcontractor signing below acknowledges receipt of all payments stated above. These payments are in compliance with the written contract between the parties above. The contractor/subcontractor signing below hereby states payment for all work done to this date has been paid in full.

The contractor/subcontractor signing below releases and relinquishes any and all rights available to place a mechanic or materialman lien against the subject property for the above described work. All parties agree that all work performed to date has been paid for in full and in compliance with their written contract.

The undersigned contractor/subcontractor releases the general contractor/customer from any liability for non-payment of material or services extended through this date. The undersigned contractor/subcontractor has read this entire agreement and understands the agreement.

_____
Contractor/Subcontractor   Date

7-3 *Short-form lien waiver*

Long-Form Lien Waiver

Customer name: _____

Customer address: _____

Customer city/state/zip: _____

Customer phone number: _____

Job location: _____

Date: _____

Type of work: _____

The vendor acknowledges receipt of all payments stated below. These payments are in compliance with the written contract between the vendor and the customer. The vendor hereby states that payment for all work done to this date has been paid in full.

The vendor releases and relinquishes any and all rights available to said vendor to place a mechanic or materialman lien against the subject property for the described work. Both parties agree that all work performed to date has been paid for, in full and in compliance with their written contract.

The undersigned vendor releases the customer and the customer's property from any liability for non-payment of material or services extended through this date. The undersigned contractor has read this entire agreement and understands the agreement.

Vendor	Services	Date Paid	Amount Paid
Plumber	(Rough-in)		
Plumber	(Final)		
Electrician	(Rough-in)		
Electrician	(Final)		
Supplier	(Framing lumber)		

NOTE: This list should include all contractors and suppliers. All vendors are listed on the same lien waiver, and sign above their trade name for each service rendered, at the time of payment.

7-4 *Long-form lien waiver*

A broad-brush definition

Now you have a broad-brush definition of the four primary types of financing you might need as a conversion contractor. Do you know where or how you are going to seek this financing? If you are a bit taken aback by all of this, don't feel alone. Many contractors are not aware of what is involved when financing conversion projects. Now that you have an overview of the various types of loans, let's put your new knowledge to use in some real-world examples. I always feel that it is easier to learn from examples and stories than it is from old-school textbooks.

I found it

If you are a serious conversion contractor hunting for a perfect project, there is going to come a day when you yell, "I found it." That is, indeed, a great day. It is also when you must put all of your thought, training, and experience into cutting the best deal.

Financing can have a substantial effect on the profit or loss of your project. Let's assume you have found a property that's just perfect. How are you going to finance it? To help with the explanation, we are going to look at two different scenarios. In the first one, you are going to take the same steps that a lot of contractors do. In the second scenario, you are going to play by my rules. We can see which scenario makes the most money. Before starting, I want to mention that I'm holding an ace in my vest, the free-money angle. I am going to expose it a little later in the chapter.

An average deal

This first example involves an average deal between a seller and a novice conversion contractor. Let's assume that a buyer is purchasing a duplex to convert into a four-unit building. The building's interior is not in very good shape, but it is structurally sound and zoning laws allow the conversion. This buyer has no obstacles, except for financing.

The buyer is a husband-wife team. The man is a plumber and the wife is an electrician. Their combined skills and construction experience gives them an edge in the conversion side of the deal. Unfortunately, neither party has much experience when it comes to financing real estate, let alone real estate conversions. The couple has some money in the bank and good credit, so this is going to help.

The couple begins their search for financing by going to their regular bank, the one where they have their checking and savings accounts and their car loans. They talk to a friendly loan officer about their plans and they present their proposal for the purchase, conversion, and sale of the property.

The banker is skeptical. This particular bank likes to make car loans and home mortgages, but it is not so keen on making speculation loans and investor loans. Our couple, we'll call them Bob and Betty, made their first mistake by going to their own bank. The mistake is not predicated on the fact that it was their bank, but on the fact that their bank doesn't like to make the type of loans Bob and Betty want. Lack of planning puts the couple off on the wrong foot. Their loan officer is not encouraging, although the borrowers are not given a definitive answer right away.

After paying a $300 loan-application fee and waiting for nearly two weeks, Bob and Betty receive a denial letter in the mail. Their loan has been rejected due to their lack of experience as conversion/general contractors and landlords.

Stung, but undaunted, Bob and Betty prepare to visit other lenders. After considerable effort, they find a commercial bank who is willing to give them an acquisition loan. Bob and Betty are ecstatic. They pay the fees, the points, the closing costs, and revel in their success. It is not until they have possession of their new property that they realize they don't have enough money to convert the building.

Bob and Betty arrange to meet with their friendly banker who so willingly gave them their acquisition loan. However, the banker wants no part of a construction or improvement loan. Bob and Betty are in another bind. The property is not profitable with only two units, but they cannot afford to convert it to four units. Bob and Betty are devastated, but they refuse to give up.

Our conversion couple spends hours on the telephone, seeking possible lenders. Fortunately, they find three potential lenders for their short-term loan. After meeting with each lender, Bob and Betty do a deal with Ms. Banker of We Do Them Right Savings and Loan. The improvement loan has a short fuse, only six months to get the work done, but it is better than nothing. Bob and Betty are a little nervous, but happy.

Bob and Betty now have their acquisition and improvement loan. The only element missing is a take-out, or permanent loan. Bob and Betty decide to gamble on not needing a take-out loan, so they proceed onward with their conversion plans. Are Betty and Bob setting themselves up for destruction? What mistakes have they made so far? What is your opinion? Well, let's dissect what they have done and evaluate it.

Betty and Bob lost time when they went to their regular bank. Time is money. If the conversion couple had done a little legwork up front, they wouldn't have wasted time during a critical aspect of their deal. A quick phone call could have saved days of lost time, not to mention the fee they paid for loan application. Not all lenders are prime prospects for conversion projects. You must ferret out the proper lenders before you start.

Bob and Betty felt they succeeded at the second bank. Did they? They won, but at their own expense. It costs money each time a loan is originated, money that a conversion contractor can pocket if it isn't spent. Since our conversion couple got an acquisition loan from one lender and an improvement loan from another lender, they paid much more than they should have in loan fees. Their extra costs might not have been double what they needed to spend, but it wasn't far from it. Loan closing costs frequently amount to 5 percent of the loan amount. On a $200,000 deal, this amounts to ten grand. Do you want to give away $10,000 of your profit?

Betty and Bob might have been able to better their circumstances if they could have arranged a combination (combo) loan. With a combo loan, the acquisition and improvement loan is one and the same. Many commercial banks are willing to combine acquisition loans with improvement loans. By using a combo loan, you can reduce your time, effort, and costs. I've used this type of loan many times, and so have many of the investors I've advised.

I can't give you exact figures, but you save a considerable amount of money using a combo loan. The savings result because you pay for only one survey, one title search, one appraisal, and one set of points and application fees. The savings can easily amount to thousands of dollars. Not all lenders make combination loans, but many do. Spend enough time to find lenders who are going to loan you money the way you want it.

A better deal

There might not be free rides in life, but there are ways to obtain free money for conversion projects. As long as you meet proper guidelines, you can have the use of other people's money without ever having to pay it back. Even if you don't qualify for free money, many programs are available that offer conversion money at interest rates way below market rates. Where can you find this special money? Well, you have to check with your uncle—Uncle Sam, that is.

The following programs can all offer grants or low-interest loans:
- Community development block grants
- Community development block grants for states and small cities
- Urban development action grants
- Rental rehabilitation
- Rehabilitation loans
- Condominium housing
- Multifamily housing
- Multifamily rental housing for moderate-income families

With all of these programs available, you are probably going to find one that fits your needs. Each program is a little different, but they all can be beneficial by increasing a contractor's profit margin while helping other people.

Community development block grants

Community development block grants are intended to help low- and moderate-income families. The grants are made to communities. Once communities receive these grants, they can create their own local programs. Your local housing authority should be able to provide complete details on this and other programs. If you strike out on the local level, write to: Assistant Secretary for Community Planning and Development, Department of Housing and Urban Development, Washington, D.C. 20410-7000.

Community development block grants for states and small cities

This program is similar to the one just discussed. The two programs differ in that this one picks up where the community development block grants leave off. In most cases, recipients of this program are in areas with a population of less than 50,000.

Urban development action grants

Urban development action grants are designed to stimulate economic recovery in some cities and urban areas. The grant money is provided to local governments. They, in turn, loan the money to private developers and builders for both commercial and residential projects. Conversion contractors can benefit from these loans. You must meet special guidelines in order to take advantage of these loans, but they are well within the reach of most conversion contractors. This program is well worth checking out.

Rental rehabilitation

If your conversion projects include residential rental properties, you won't want to ignore the rental rehabilitation program. This program gives grants to cities and states for the purpose of rental revitalization. As a conversion contractor, you might be able to receive from $5000 to $8500 for each rental unit you provide.

Guidelines govern the disbursement of the funds, but they are not difficult to meet. Basically, the amount of money available is based on one-half of the total eligible improvement costs. In other words, if you are spending $10,000 per unit in improvement money, you might be eligible for a $5000 advance from the program. However, some additional requirements must be met.

Money from the rental rehabilitation program is intended to correct substandard living conditions. Another use for the money is the essential improvement of rental real estate, which includes major repairs and energy-related improvements. Conversions to meet disability guidelines are also worthy of funding. At least 70 percent of the rental tenants must be low-income families. There are other restrictions and guidelines, so check this program against your plans to see if it is right for you.

Rehabilitation loans

Rehabilitation loans can be used for single-family, multifamily, and nonresidential properties. It is possible to obtain loans for more than $33,000 per dwelling unit for residential properties, or up to $100,000 for nonresidential properties. Building demolition is not covered by this program, but most rehab and conversion work qualifies for funding. You should have up to 20 years to repay the loan, and the interest rates are extremely low. This is one program you owe it to yourself to explore in depth.

Condominium housing

The condominium housing program is targeted at properties with at least four units that are going to be sold. If you think this program can be advantageous, you should check into it.

Multifamily housing

The multifamily housing program is aimed at buildings that have five or more rental units. These units should be set up to accommodate families. If you're playing in the big league, it's worth investigating this program because it might have some strong benefits for you.

Multifamily rental housing
for moderate-income families

The multifamily rental housing for moderate-income families program is meant for investors who are working with buildings that have five or more units. This is another good opportunity for players in the commercial side of residential rental property. Call your local housing authority for details on how this program can help your business.

Applying for a loan

Applying for a loan can be a traumatic experience. It shouldn't be, but sometimes it is. Arranging financing is a task that most adults have done at one time or another, but every loan application can be different.

For conversion contractors, there is no cookie-cutter answer to the financing question. If you think your project might qualify for grants or low-interest loans, you should check them out. Plenty of local lenders should be willing to work with you on combination loans.

Regardless of the type of loan you decide to use, you should apply some fundamental procedures to all of your loan applications, which I'll discuss now (Fig. 7-5).

The basics

It's easy to complete the basic loan application process. Typically, you receive a loan application to fill out. The application spells out all the information you must provide. A basic loan application requires a ton of information. For example, self-employed individuals are usually required to provide their tax returns for the past two years and a financial statement (Fig. 7-6 on page 148). This requirement doesn't apply to people with regular jobs. Social security numbers are always required, and so are bank account numbers and loan amounts.

The loan application is the least of your responsibilities and worries. It is an essential part of getting a loan, but the application alone is normally not enough to persuade a lender to give you a loan. You must present an irresistible proposal to make a lender take a chance on your conversion project.

Setting the stage to win over your banker is not a game, but it is something like one. You might compare it to walking a tight rope. One wrong step can send you falling into a net of despair. This tragedy can be avoided. If you do your homework and present a powerful proposal, you can win more often than you lose. There can be times when things don't work out to your satisfaction, but much of your financing is within your control.

Checklist of Loan Application Needs

❑ Home address for the last five years

❑ Divorce agreements

❑ Child support agreements

❑ Social security numbers

❑ Two years tax returns, if self-employed

❑ Paycheck stubs, if available

❑ Employee's tax statements (i.e., W-2, W-4)

❑ Gross income amount of household

❑ All bank account numbers, balances, names, and addresses

❑ All credit card numbers, balances, and monthly payments

❑ Employment history for last four years

❑ Information on all stocks or bonds owned

❑ Life insurance face-amount and cash value

❑ Details of all real estate owned

❑ Rental income and expenses of investment property owned

❑ List of credit references with account numbers

❑ Financial statement of net worth

❑ Checkbook for loan application fees

7-5 *Loan-application needs*

Executives who are responsible for approving loans like to cover themselves. They don't want to make bad loans, because that could cost them their jobs. They also don't want to approve loan proposals that appear weak. However, if you give a loan officer a solid proposal, one that just can't lose, you are almost guaranteed approval.

Convincing loan proposals

A convincing loan proposal is just that, convincing. When you go to a lender in search of a loan, your proposal must be bulletproof. You must remove every objection and fear that a loan officer can imagine. If you can do that, all your loan applications should be approved.

Traditional lenders are conservative by nature. They don't like risk. To win over this type of person, you must make the risk seem so insignificant that it is not a factor. This is not always easy to do in the con-

Financial Statement

Date of statement: _____

Statement prepared by: _____

Assets

Cash on hand	$ 8,543.89
Securities	$ 0.00
Equipment	
1992 Ford F-250 pick-up truck	$14,523.00
Pipe rack for truck	$ 250.00
40' Extension ladder (2)	$ 375.00
Hand tools	$ 800.00
Real estate	$ 0.00
Accounts receivable	$ 5,349.36
Total assets	$29,841.25

Liabilities

Equipment	
1992 Ford F-250 truck, note payoff	$11,687.92
Accounts payable	$ 1,249.56
Total liabilities	$12,937.48
Net worth	$16,903.77

7-6 *Financial statement*

version business. It is, however, possible under most circumstances. In order to make a conversion deal palatable for a starched-shirt banker, you have to spend a few days taking the rough edges off of it.

When you sit down to prepare your loan proposal, you should attempt to assume the personality of a tight-fisted lender. Pretend it is your own money that you are lending to some investor off the street. Would you lend your hard-earned cash to a stranger who wants to start on a potentially risky remodeling job? My guess is that you wouldn't part with your money. If you feel this way, you can't hold it against a loan officer for wanting clear documentation on how you plan to make good on a loan.

Loan officers like to see facts, statistics, written documents, and anything else that can fill out a file folder. The more paper that loan officers put in a file, the safer their jobs are. Loan officers have rather tenuous job security. During my career, I've seen countless bankers and loan officers come and go. From my perspective, the job stability of a loan officer is not good, so loan officers who plan to survive must protect themselves with reams of paperwork. This is the jelly spot that you can attack. If you give a loan officer enough documentation, you can get almost anything you want. This might mean spending a day or two doing nothing except preparing a loan proposal, but if you want a loan, it is time well spent.

Beyond the basics

To increase your odds of having a conversion loan approved, you must go beyond the basics. All lenders are going to expect the normal information for a loan application. The contractors who go above and beyond the minimum requirements have a higher success ratio with their loans. To slant the odds for approval in your favor, you must make a strong case for the project.

I don't know how many loan applications an average processor runs into in any given week, but I'm sure it is plenty. My experience as a broker has shown me that most people don't provide enough data to convince a loan officer to put a stamp of approval on an application. I tend to go to the other extreme, providing more details than many loan officers care to sift through. My loans always seem to get approval. There is probably some place in the middle of the two extremes that works, but why take chances? If you want a loan, build your case and then sell it to the lender. Sell it? Yes, sell it. Contractors who consistently win are more than just good construction managers. They possess a number of varied skills, including sales ability.

Unless you enjoy financial pain, you are not going to take on a project that you don't believe in. If you believe the job can produce a profit, you must be basing your opinion on some facts, such as rental rates, market values, and so forth. Put this information into an easy-to-understand narrative to present with your loan proposal. You have to get the lender to have as much faith in you and your project as you do.

A standard loan application for a conversion project requires documentation on the changes that are going to be made to the building, how they affect the value of a building, and what the borrower's plans are for repaying the loan. But don't stop with just what a lender requires. You should have done a lot of homework prior to tackling the project. Condense your research into a few pages. Show this prospectus to your loan officer. If you do this properly, the loan is almost certain to be approved. Let me give you a few examples of what I mean.

Hold it

Let's assume you are going to do a conversion project on a rental property and you plan to hold it for a long-term investment. Show your banker exactly what improvements you are going to make. Then, build a case that shows why the neighborhood can support a new multifamily property. Use census reports, classified advertisements for rental property, and supporting documentation you might have received from real estate brokers or appraisers.

After you establish that the conversion is viable and that there is a market for additional rental units in the area, you must lay out your plans for profit. Show the equity gain you expect to have in the property once the conversion work is done. Project a clear picture of local rental rates, vacancy rates, and management costs. Even if you plan to manage the building, most lenders take away a portion of the gross income for management expenses when they run your qualifying numbers. They don't actually escrow an amount of money, but they factor in what it would cost to have a property managed by a professional firm. It is not unusual for a commercial bank to factor in a management fee of 10 percent of the building's gross rental income. It is also common to use a 5 percent factor for vacancy rates. These figures can put a dramatic dent in your cash-flow picture, at least on paper, and bankers like to work from paper.

It is possible to overcome big hits for management and vacancy rates. If you gather enough evidence to prove that the local vacancy rate rarely exceeds 2 percent, you might be able to compromise with your lender. The same holds true for management fees, especially if you have past experience in managing rental properties.

Bankers tend to look for the worst in a project, so you should show them the best. Build a spreadsheet that shows how much your building's rental income is going to rise in five years based on logical annual increases. You can establish a local rental increase rate by researching old newspaper classified ads in the local library. Pull as much information together as you can before sitting down for the formal loan application, and make sure you present it in a way that lenders can appreciate.

If your loan will be based on government financing, you must complete a financing addendum. Veteran's use a VA addendum (Fig. 7-7). Most people are more likely to use FHA financing (Fig. 7-8). To help you project monthly payments, I've included an amortization chart (Table 7-1). Also, become familiar with the closing statements (Figs. 7-9 and 7-10).

VA Addendum

This addendum is an integral part of the purchase and sale agreement
dated _____, between the Purchasers, _____
_____, and the Sellers,
_____, for the sale of the real estate
commonly known as _____.

It is expressly agreed that, notwithstanding any other provisions of this
contract, the Purchaser shall not incur any penalty by forfeiture of
earnest money or otherwise be obligated to complete the purchase of the
property described herein, if the contract purchase price or cost exceeds
the reasonable value of the property established by the Veterans
Administration. The Purchaser shall, however, have the privilege and
option of proceeding with the consummation of this contract without
regard to the amount of the reasonable value established by the Veterans
Administration.

_____   _____

Purchaser   Date   Seller   Date

_____   _____

Seller   Date   Seller   Date

7-7 *VA addendum*

Flip it

If you plan to convert a building and then flip it for a quick profit, put
your plans on paper. Show your lender the conversion costs, the present market conditions, the expected selling price of property and the
expected profit. Build your proposal one step at a time, and do it with
facts and figures that can stand up to attack. A few hours spent with a
licensed appraiser can pay big dividends in this type of project. Bankers
like to see official reports from recognized real estate appraisers.

Before closing the chapter, I want to again impress upon you
how much of a difference you can make in your success ratio just by
collecting pertinent information and presenting it properly to a loan
officer. This work might not be your favorite part of being a conversion contractor, but it can be essential to reaching your goals.

FHA Addendum

This addendum is an integral part of the purchase and sale agreement dated _____, between the Purchasers, _____ _____, and the Sellers, _____ _____, for the sale of the real estate commonly known as _____.

It is expressly agreed that, notwithstanding any other provisions of this contract, the Purchaser shall not be obligated to complete the purchase of the property described herein or to incur any penalty by forfeiture of earnest money deposits or otherwise unless the Seller has delivered to the Purchaser a written statement issued by the Federal Housing Commissioner setting forth the appraised value of the property for mortgage insurance purposes of not less than $_____ ($_____), which statement the Seller hereby agrees to deliver to the Purchaser promptly after such appraised value statement is made available to the seller.

The Purchaser shall, however, have the privilege and option of proceeding with the consummation of this contract without regard to the amount of the appraised valuation made by the Federal Housing Commissioner.

_____   _____
Purchaser   Date   Seller   Date

_____   _____
Purchaser   Date   Seller   Date

7-8 *FHA addendum*

Estimate of Seller's Proceeds

Sales price _____(A)

Amount of first mortgage _____

Amount of second mortgage _____

Amount of other liens _____

Total of loans and liens _____ (B)

Gross equity (subtract B from A) _____(C)

Estimated costs:

Escrow fees _____

Document preparation fees _____

Broker commission _____

Legal fees _____

Prepayment penalty _____

Transfer tax _____

Pest control fees _____

Repairs _____

Recording fees _____

Discount points _____

Origination points _____

Trustee fees _____

Notary fees _____

Prorated taxes _____

Interest _____

Loan payments in arrears _____

Prorated rents _____

Security deposits _____

Prepaid rents _____

Other: _____

Total costs _____ (D)

Credits

Prorated prepaid taxes _____

Other credits: _____

Total credits _____ (E)

Estimated net cash proceeds (C minus D plus E) _____

7-9 *Sample seller's closing statement*

Estimate of Purchaser's Closing Costs

Sales price _____ (A)

Estimated costs:

Escrow fees _____

Document preparation fees _____

Loan origination fee _____

Legal fees _____

Loan assumption fee _____

Transfer tax _____

Pest control fee _____

Loan application fee _____

Recording fees _____

Points _____

Trustee's fees _____

Notary fees _____

Prorated taxes _____

Interest _____

FHA/MIP (mortgage insurance) _____

Inspection fees _____

Credit report fee _____

Hazard insurance _____

Title insurance _____

Down payment _____

Other fees _____

Total costs _____ (B)

Credits _____

_____

_____

Total credits _____ (C)

Total estimated closing costs (B minus C) $ _____

7-10 *Sample purchaser's closing statement*

Table 7-1. Amortization chart

ESTIMATED MORTGAGE LOAN CALCULATION TABLE

To obtain payment amount, multiply the amount in the table by the amount of loan in thousands.

EXAMPLE: If the interest rate of your proposed loan is 10%, find 10% in the Interest rate % column. Read across into the column with 15- or 30-year terms. Use the multiplier in these columns to determine the approximate monthly payment. (i.e., with a 10% rate, a $100,000 loan amount, and a 30-year term, you would multiply $1000 × 8.78 to arrive at a monthly payment of $878.

Interest rate %	15 years	30 years
7	8.99	6.66
7.25	9.13	6.83
7.50	9.28	7.00
7.75	9.42	7.17
8	9.56	7.34
8.25	9.71	7.52
8.50	9.85	7.69
8.75	10.00	7.87
9	10.15	8.05
9.25	10.30	8.23
9.50	10.45	8.41
9.75	10.60	8.60
10	10.75	8.78
10.25	10.90	8.96
10.50	11.06	9.15
10.75	11.21	9.34
11	11.37	9.53
11.25	11.52	9.71
11.50	11.69	9.90
11.75	11.84	10.09
12	12.01	10.29
12.25	12.16	10.48
12.50	12.33	10.67
12.75	12.49	10.87
13	12.66	11.06
13.25	12.82	11.26
13.50	12.99	11.45
13.75	13.15	11.65
14	13.32	11.85

8

Site work

Many contractors fail to think about site work when assessing the value of a potential project, but that can be an expensive mistake. Site work isn't an issue in many projects, but it can be a major expense in some jobs. You cannot afford to overlook the cost of earth moving, paving, utilities, and other expenses that might be necessary to make your conversion dream a reality.

Site work can involve any number of jobs on the outside of a property. This type of work for new construction is generally somewhat different than it is for remodeling and conversion projects. However, if you are making a substantial change of use in a property, you could be looking at thousands of dollars in site work. The most common forms of site work include:

- Grading
- Utilities
- Driveways
- Trees
- Drainage
- Demolition
- Seeding, sodding, and landscaping

Converting into office space

When you are converting a residential property into office space, you are probably going to need some site work. You might have to increase the size of the water and sewer mains. There almost certainly is going to be a need for additional parking space. This work alone can cost a lot more than you might think.

You might also need entrance permits and site work to install additional entrances and exits to the parking areas. You might need to haul in fill dirt to raise existing elevations to make access easier for those who are physically disadvantaged. Anytime you are converting from a residential property to an office building, you should be alert to the site needs.

Enlarging residential space

Enlarging residential space is common in the conversion business. Let's say that you are taking a rambling single-family home and converting it into a four-unit building. Is the existing driveway and parking area going to accommodate four families? Probably not. You are going to need a site contractor to enlarge these areas. Don't forget to get quotes for this work and add it into your conversion budget.

If you are enlarging a residential property that is not served by a public sewer, you might have to enlarge the septic system. This job can be quite expensive. If the property is served by a water well, you could run into problems if the well can't produce enough water for all the tenants. Septic systems, wells, and other hidden costs can cut heavily into your profits. A lot of potential problems can arise around site work.

What to look for

Knowing what to look for is half the battle with site work. Many contractors lose profit to site work because they don't notice a need for it until they are committed to a project and its budget. If a phase of work is omitted from a budget, it is obviously going to put stress on any profit picture. General contractors who do a lot of new construction work have an advantage here because they are involved with site work on every job.

Remodelers and single-trade people are more likely to get caught off guard. Not accustomed to dealing with bulldozers and backhoes, they don't focus on site work when estimating the cost of a job.

Grading

Let's say that you are planning to convert a single-family residence into a multifamily property. What conditions might cause you to spend money on grading?

If you add additional exterior space to the property, you are likely to have to do some grading. Building an addition to an existing structure normally requires some minor grading. Parking facilities could also force you into additional grading, and the grading work for this type of a situation could get complicated. You might need to haul fill dirt to the site. Then the dirt must be leveled. The job could take a couple of days and a sizable chunk of change.

Grading might be needed to solve drainage problems. If the existing house has moisture problems or standing water, grading could be necessary. Even if rough grading isn't required, you might find a need for some finish grading. If the lawn around the property is not presentable, you might find it necessary to haul in some topsoil and have it graded out for seeding.

I've covered most of the reasons why a conversion property can require grading, but not all of them. Therefore, it is wise to have your site contractor visit prospective projects before you make purchasing commitments. The experienced eye of a professional site contractor can often catch things that you miss.

Utilities

Utilities are not normally a problem when converting houses into small multifamily buildings, but they can be. If the property is connected to a municipal sewer and water main, the chances of having to upgrade the utilities are minor. They do, however, exist.

For example, most plumbing codes allow a 3-inch sewer pipe for houses that do not contain more than two toilets. If the property has a 3-inch sewer and you plan to have four toilets, you have a problem. The sewer is too small for the number of toilets in the building. That means you might be forced to either replace the existing sewer or add a new sewer. In either case, you are going to incur both plumbing and site work expenses. The municipality could also charge a tap fee if you must connect a second sewer to the main sewer line. This work can cost thousands of dollars. This kind of grief can be avoided simply by checking the size of the sewer pipe when you first inspect the building.

It is also a good idea to check the size of the incoming water service. It is less likely that the water service is going to have to be upgraded to a larger size, but why take a chance on an unwanted surprise?

Electrical service is another issue to consider. When you expand a property to house more families, it is normal to install electrical services to each individual unit. The job could require site work if the supply cables are run underground. If the service is installed overhead, you might have to remove tree limbs or trees.

Septic systems can create a lot of problems when converting houses to accommodate multiple families. When a single-family home is built, its septic system is usually designed to handle the needs of one family. Adding a second, third, or fourth family to a building can make it impractical, not to mention illegal, to use the existing septic system. A larger septic tank is probably needed and the drain field normally requires additional drainage lines. Enlarging an existing septic system or adding a new septic system can run into many thousands of dollars. In the worst case, you might not have enough land to suitably enlarge the septic system. Then you're really in trouble.

Site contractors often do septic field work. A reputable site contractor should be able to offer professional advice before you buy a property. It can be well worth talking to one or two experts in the field of site work. If you are considering the purchase of a property where a public sewer hookup is not available, be very thorough in your research.

A water well can cause problems, especially if the well doesn't have a large reservoir of water and a fast recovery rate. You can have a major expense from a well contractor if a new well must be dug or drilled. Also, a site contractor is needed to dig a ditch, which then must be covered, graded, and seeded.

Gas piping is normally run underground. Guess who is going to be needed if the building's gas supply pipe must be enlarged? That's right, the site contractor. Beefing up a gas line is not likely to be required for most residential projects, but it could become a big issue in commercial conversions.

Driveways

Conversion projects often require that you enlarge driveways and parking areas, which involves site work. The extent of the work varies from project to project. If you are converting a building into professional offices, parking space could be a major cost. If you need to only rough out a few additional parking spots at a residential rental property, the cost is not going to be so steep. In either case, expenses can be significant enough to taint your budget if they are not covered. Remember that almost all conversion projects require some provisions for additional parking.

Trees

You might need to remove trees when enlarging driveways, adding parking spaces or for any number of other reasons. You can hire tree-removal specialists, but in many cases your site contractor can do the work. The fewer people involved in your project, the better it is likely to go. Every subcontractor is a potential risk in time and cost overruns, so try to keep the number of contractors to a minimum.

Drainage

Drainage work is a part of a site contractor's duty. Drainage work can mean sloping existing land to divert water, hauling in fill to build up an existing elevation, or installing sub-soil drains.

Drainage work can result from other aspects of site work. A property that you look at today, in its present condition, might not show a need for drainage work. However, as you convert the property to another use, your drainage requirements can change.

For example, by adding a large, paved parking area, you could create a problem with runoff water. Unlike the ground, a paved parking area can't absorb rain water. The rain that falls on the parking area has to go somewhere. You might need to install underground piping to remove the water, which falls under the category of site work.

Demolition

Conversion projects sometimes require demolition work. You might need to bulldoze an old outbuilding or haul away debris. Your site contractor can help you with such problems, but it's going to cost money. Any demolition work must be done in accordance with the Occupational Safety and Health Act (OSHA). Demolition work should be done safely and be preplanned. One accident can ruin a project, a company, and possibly a career.

Seeding, sodding, and landscaping

Seeding, sodding, and landscaping a conversion project can transform a marginal property into a grand one. Almost all conversion projects can benefit from landscaping. This part of the site work can also get expensive. Whether you plant trees or shrubs, or simply fill in bare spots in a lawn, it's going to cost you money. Many rookies in the conversion game fail to account for these costs.

Avoid surprises

Site work is not normally a major part of a conversion project, but sometimes the work can be extensive as well as expensive. If you plan to convert a property from residential to commercial use, you could find that zoning and other code requirements are stiffer for commercial property than for residential real estate. Such code requirements can force you into unexpected costs.

I have a little saying, "Before you buy, verify." I believe that it applies to all conversion projects. Check all angles of all trades and make sure you know what you are getting into before signing on any dotted lines.

9

Foundation work

Foundation work is the first step to improving the physical condition of a building targeted for conversion. It is also a phase of work that can cost a lot of money. The foundation is important because it supports the building. Unfortunately, a lot of contractors don't spend much time checking a foundation.

In the conversion business, it is not uncommon to buy buildings that are old. In some parts of the country, you might find shaky foundation walls made from old fieldstone. In other areas, a building might simply sit on rotting wood sills. Even modern foundations can have significant structural problems.

Buying a building with a shaky foundation might be okay, as long as you know what it takes to correct the structural deficiencies. It can spoil all your plans if you buy a building and then find out that it has a serious foundation problem.

Ideal circumstances

Ideally, when you are seriously considering buying a building, it should be inspected by every subcontractor, in all the trades, that you might use. This is the best way to buy a building, but it is not always practical. The next best option is to have an experienced, well-rounded, professional property inspector look at the building.

You can take it upon yourself to do some or all of the inspections, but you risk losing money if you make a mistake in judgment or fail to see a problem. Unless you have a strong background in all aspects of building and are very comfortable with your abilities, have the trade professionals or an experienced professional property inspector look over any buildings you plan to buy.

Obvious problems

Some foundations have obvious problems that almost anyone can see. For those not accustomed to working with foundations, they can also harbor some hidden surprises. I'll talk first about some of the obvious foundation problems.

No foundation

The most obvious foundation problem is one where no foundation exists. Many old buildings do not sit on solid foundations. These properties are often found resting on wood sills that can be partially or completely rotted. A property like this is probably not worth the risk. However, you can overcome almost any problem with enough money, so a conversion might make sense if you can buy the building at a cheap price.

What can you do for a building that doesn't have a foundation? It is not a simple process, but you can raise the structure and install a foundation underneath. Contractors who have the special equipment and talent to do this type of work are available. If you ask them for a price quote, you'd be well advised to sit down before reading the estimate. The costs are staggering. Still, it might be worthwhile for some buildings.

Let's say that you've found a residential property for sale and you know it can be transformed into commercial space without jumping through a lot of hoops. The building is in good shape, but it doesn't have a foundation.

You might be able to purchase the building at a good price by making an issue of the fact that it is not sitting on a foundation. If a contractor has quoted you a price to replace the foundation, you might use it as a bargaining chip. Show the quote to the seller and ask that the price be lowered to accommodate the cost of the foundation work. The seller might not agree to your request, but it never hurts to ask.

Even if you can't get the seller to absorb the cost of a new foundation, the change of use you have planned might be more than profitable enough to allow you to install the foundation at your own expense. This situation must be assessed with each property on an individual basis. In general, however, it is not wise to buy a building that needs a new foundation.

Cracked foundation

Cracked foundations are fairly common, even in new buildings. Sometimes the cracks are cause for concern, and sometimes they are just an eyesore. If you can find the kind that are only a cosmetic blemish, you might be able to use the cracks to your advantage. Point out the damaged foundation to the seller when you are negotiating a selling price. Even if the cracks don't pose a major problem, you might be able to convince the seller to lower the asking price because of them. After you acquire the property, you can fill in the cracks and go about your business.

Should you happen upon a cracked foundation that could put the structural integrity at risk, call an expert for an evaluation. If the cracks are not too far advanced, filling them with hydraulic cement and sealing them might be all that is needed. However, if the cracks are large and have been there for a while, the foundation might have suffered more damage than you can see. If water invades the cracks and then freezes, the ice can push on the foundation, causing the cracks to expand and the foundation to weaken. Cracked foundations are also prone to leaking.

If water has been seeping through a foundation for very long, you should find some evidence of the problem. Usually there are water stains on the foundation walls. The same is true of basements that fill with water. A quick visual scan around the foundation walls can turn up high-water marks that indicate a problem. Most cracked foundations can be repaired and made nearly waterproof with minimal effort and expense. However, your main concern is to be sure that the cracks have not weakened the foundation.

Leaking foundation

Foundations that leak a lot require some action on your part. Perimeter drains and sump pumps are normally used to overcome wet basements. If a basement doesn't flood, but stays damp most of the time, a dehumidifier can solve your problem.

One way or another, you must get rid of the water and moisture. Mold and mildew can form in damp basements. Tenants might complain about musty odors or allergies associated with the mold and mildew. Wood structural members can be adversely affected by a high moisture content. In time, the building can rot, paint can peel, and the repair can far exceed what you would have paid to properly fix the water problems in the beginning.

How you go about fixing a wet basement depends largely on the type of problem you have. It is best to waterproof foundation walls on the outside of a building, but products are available for use on interior basement walls. For example, damp walls might be corrected with a simple waterproof coating that is applied much like paint. This product works reasonably well. If the walls are only damp, the waterproofing has a good chance of solving the problem. If water is running through the walls, I wouldn't hold my breath waiting for the coating to stop the leak.

Larger water problems call for more extensive work. A lot of basements take on water during certain times of the year. The groundwater can rise to levels that are not only a nuisance, but dangerous as well. Mechanical equipment can become flooded, and if electrical connections become submerged, the water could become a death trap.

To solve this more serious problem, you probably have to break up some of the basement floor and install slotted drain piping to carry the water to a sump. A trench is made all the way around the foundation walls. Crushed stone is added to the trench and slotted drain pipe (with the slots facing up) is installed on the stone. The entire length of pipe is pitched towards the sump, then more stone is added to cover the pipe. To complete the installation, a special pump, called a sump pump, is placed in the sump.

In use, the pipe takes in water through the slots and carries it to the waiting sump. The sump pump evacuates the water as the sump fills. This job is not complicated in technical terms, but it can get expensive. If you suspect a building has water problems in the basement, try using your knowledge to lower the sales price.

Sinking foundation

A sinking foundation can cause a lot of problems. Fortunately, they are not very common. Foundations sink when they are not installed on a solid base. If footings for a foundation are poured on ground that was filled in and not properly compacted, the foundation is going to gradually sink. The sinking causes the main structure to shift, which adds to the problem. Doors begin to stick, windows don't operate properly, walls develop nail pops and ceilings begin to crack where they meet walls. These are just some of the side effects of a sinking foundation.

Foundations don't normally sink in a uniform manner. Usually, one corner begins to sink, essentially pulling the main structure apart. This type of problem is not easy or inexpensive to fix. You should normally avoid any building that does not have a solid foundation.

How can you spot a sinking foundation? You might see some sway in the roof line. Doors and windows that don't operate smoothly might be a tip-off. Cracks and nail pops in the walls and ceilings are another clue. Short of using a transit, it's best to use a line level to check any foundation you suspect might be sinking. You or your inspector should look closely to make sure that the building you plan to buy has a solid foundation.

Disintegrating foundation

Disintegrating foundations are common in older homes. Have you ever seen mortar that has been reduced to little more than sand? It happens a lot. Many old buildings rely on brick foundations. When the mortar between the bricks turns to sand, bigger problems are not far behind. This situation also occurs with chimneys. As the mortar deteriorates, bricks can become loose. I don't think you want a foundation where the bricks might pop out at any time.

A disintegrating foundation is a serious problem, but it doesn't mean that you have to run in the opposite direction. When mortar turns to sand, the problem might be concentrated in just one area of a foundation, or it might be widespread. Check this condition carefully. Filling the voids between bricks is a job that is best left to an experienced professional. A good brick mason can remove the bad mortar and replace it with new, stable mortar. It's not a cheap proposition, but it can be done.

Open foundation

Open foundations can cause various problems. Any time there is a pier or open foundation, there is a risk of trouble. One of the most common problems is frozen plumbing pipes.

Fortunately, pier foundations can be enclosed. The expense can vary considerably, depending on how you do the enclosing. A brick facade is expensive. A wood skirt won't be cheap, but it is not as costly as masonry work. Unfortunately, a wood skirt won't look as good as masonry.

Open foundations do not normally present enough problems to kill a deal, but you should be prepared to enclose the foundation. If your budget doesn't allow you to enclose the foundation, you should at least add insulation between the floor joists and cover them with plywood.

Stone foundation

Stone foundations can be, pardon the pun, solid as a rock. Just because a building is sitting on rocks doesn't mean that the foundation is no good. One frequent problem with a stone foundation is the invasion of groundwater, which can be a problem even when a building is sitting over only a crawl space. Any excess moisture in or under a building can cause severe damage.

To get an idea of how serious any moisture problems are, you can inspect for mold, mildew, plant life, mud, and other indicators of water. A good ground cover used as a vapor barrier can greatly reduce any minor moisture risk.

Hidden defects

Hidden defects can be present in any foundation. Some imperfections can look innocent while posing serious complications. An untrained eye might not notice a foundation that is being heaved by frost. A small crack could represent a more serious problem. Because of the possibility of hidden defects, you should depend on professional help when inspecting a foundation. After all, the foundation supports your entire investment.

Can't handle it

If you want to add a second or third story to a building, you might find that the existing foundation can't handle it. If the foundation is not wide enough, deep enough, or strong enough, it might not be able to support the added weight of one or two more stories. This situation is another that calls for a professional. Chances are good that the foundation is going to be fine, but it is better to be safe than sorry.

Expanding

Expanding the size of a foundation to accommodate more ground-level floor space is not a job that is difficult. You must, however, be careful not to dig too closely to an existing foundation, at least not without the proper precautions.

How you connect the new foundation to an old one depends on the two foundations. The connection point is a cold joint, but the foundation contractor can lay out your attachment options. This part of the job shouldn't set you back with surprises.

10

Framing

Framing work generally accounts for much of the labor that goes into a conversion project. When buildings are converted to multifamily status or office status, you normally must build a lot of interior partitions. If you have framing skills, you're in luck. Framing labor is required for practically every conversion job.

A lot of the framing that goes into a conversion project doesn't affect the structure of a property. Most of the work deals with interior partition walls. Since the walls do not bear any load, they don't have to be engineered. They are basically just separators and can be added anywhere in the property.

It is likely, however, that a certain amount of structural work will be required in the framing process. This part of the job can require the services of an architect or engineer.

Framing carpenters

Framing carpenters normally do their own framing work. If you are not an experienced framer, you are going to either have to hire subcontractors or your own framing crew.

When you look at the numbers on paper, hiring your own framing crew can appear to be the least-expensive approach. But, in reality, subcontractors are probably a better value. Since this issue stymies a lot of general contractors, I'll discuss the pros and cons of hourly carpenters versus independent subcontractors.

Hiring your own crew

Hiring your own crew of carpenters can look appealing. It appeals to the ego and, at least on paper, to the wallet. Is it wise to put together your own crew of carpenters? It might be, but you can probably do just as well, or better, using independent subcontractors.

I don't have space to go into all of the issues surrounding employees and subcontractors, but I would like to touch on some of the key issues. If you'd like more information on this subject, you can refer to another of my books, *Building Contractor: Start and Run a Money-Making Business,* also published by McGraw-Hill.

One key to the decision is your volume of work. A framing crew can save you money if you have enough work to keep them busy most of every week. However, if you do one job here and one job there, without continuity, subcontractors make more sense.

The first problem associated with hiring a framing crew is the task of finding qualified help. My experience has shown that the best people either have their own business or they are securely employed and don't want to change jobs. A help-wanted ad might turn up a good carpenter, but many of the respondents are not going to be the type of person you want to hire. While it is not always true, it does seem that all of the good people already have jobs. Of course, you could get lucky, so don't give up. Even if you have to interview 20 people to find one good person, you are better off than if you hire the first so-called carpenter who walks through your door.

Before deciding which option is best, you must look carefully at all the costs. Perhaps you can hire a crew of framers for $10 per hour while a subcontractor gets $30 per hour. If all the carpenters are equally productive, it would appear that hiring a crew cuts your cost by two-thirds. However, this isn't a true picture of all the costs.

When you hire employees, you have overhead expenses that go along with them. You might have to provide a truck, tools, benefits, and a lot more. After factoring in tax contributions that must be made for employees, you are deeper in a hole. Also, figure in the money you pay the employee for lost time. When all these expenses are tacked onto the hourly rate, you are paying a lot more than $10 per hour for the carpenter you hired. For this reason, employees are often a bad idea.

Subcontractors cost more on an hourly basis when you compare only hourly wages. But if you assess all the costs, on an annual basis, for both subcontractors and employees, you might discover that subcontractors are the real bargain.

Subcontractors

The great thing about independent subcontractors is that they are independent. All you have to do is pay them the agreed-upon contract price. You don't have to bother with tools, trucks, employee benefits, lost time, or mistakes in estimating labor requirements for a job. Once you have a firm contract, you pay one price, the price on the contract. If the job runs several days over the estimated labor time, you still pay only the fixed price in the contract. If a subcontractor goofs off for a couple of hours, you don't pay for the wasted time. Granted, you indirectly pay for slow work in the form of construction interest and other fees, but you are not paying when the subcontractor sits around reading magazines and drinking coffee.

There is another big advantage to using subcontractors. If a subcontractor makes a mistake on your project, you are not responsible. The added costs fall on the shoulders of the subcontractor. However, if a carpenter from your crew wastes materials by making inaccurate cuts or other mistakes, you must absorb the extra costs.

When a wall gets framed improperly, and this happens from time to time, subcontractors must rebuild the wall to the standards specified in their contract. If this same mistake is made by your own hourly crew, you have to eat the loss of reframing the wall. All in all, subcontractors are usually a great bargain.

Removing existing walls

In the conversion business, it is common to remove existing walls in a building. In a major remodeling job, you normally tear out a few walls. This isn't much of a job in most cases, but some circumstances can make the removal of walls a bit more challenging.

Bees, bats, snakes, and rats

Finding that a colony of honey bees has taken up residence in a wall you are tearing out can really get your attention. It's happened to me, so I know. I've also been dive-bombed by a bat when I ripped open a wall.

Then, too, snakes sometimes find a cozy home in the walls of a house. Pulling off a piece of drywall only to come eyeball to eyeball with a snake is not much fun. Yes, I've had this happen, too.

Rats can also give you a few surprises when tearing out walls. I once worked in a house where Norway rats had taken up squatter's rights. Let me tell you, Norway rats are nothing to mess around with. These rats are big, very big, and they can be extremely aggressive. Animals are only one of the complications that can await you in your conversion project.

Electrical wires

Electrical wires are usually located in interior walls. **Warning!** These wires can present a dangerous situation for a remodeling conversion contractor. If you rip into a wall with a reciprocating saw, you might wind up with a shocking experience. I've always found it safer to open walls with a hammer prior to using a saw. Hitting a wire with the face of a hammer is not likely to electrocute you. Chewing through a wire with a saw blade is a whole other story. In reality, you must be very careful not to have a bad encounter with electrical wires.

Plumbing

Plumbing pipes can be hidden in existing walls. Cutting through a water pipe can really make life interesting. You might not have a problem with plumbing pipes, but if you do encounter them, you could have a sizable obstacle in front of you. If a drain or vent pipe runs through a wall you want to remove, the pipe must be relocated. Plumbers aren't cheap. Again, I recommend using a hammer to open existing walls. A hammer is a lot safer than a saw when working around plumbing pipes and electrical wires.

HVAC

Heating, ventilation, and air-conditioning (HVAC) ducts can present some pretty formidable challenges in the conversion and remodeling of buildings. Electrical wires are fairly easy to relocate. Plumbing is tougher to move than electrical wires. But it's easier to relocate plumbing than the heating and air-conditioning ducts. However, when you are doing a big-league rehab job, you probably are going to be rearranging all of the mechanical systems. This is a real plus.

Removing interior partitions

The job of removing interior partitions is a basic procedure. Once you get around the mechanical obstacles, ripping out non-load-bearing walls is easy. A reciprocating saw, a hammer, and a nail puller make the job simple.

Be sure you do not remove load-bearing walls. When your plans call for the removal of walls that support key elements of a structure, you are going to have to invest more time, and probably more money, in research.

Removing load-bearing walls

Load-bearing walls present more complications than simple partition walls. Structural walls can be removed, but some concessions must be made. You might have to install a flitch plate, an I-beam, or some other form of beefed-up support.

Before you start removing support walls, talk with an engineer or architect. I know many contractors skip this part of the job and jump right in with their own opinions of what to do. Experienced carpenters can frequently to a good job designing support systems, but this approach is risky. If a problem crops up down the road, the individual who made the call on what to use as a replacement for a bearing wall can be held responsible. While it is likely that such a decision is going to be made by someone other than an engineer or architect, I can't recommend such an act.

Cutting in new windows

Cutting in new windows is a routine chore with conversion projects. As the interior of a building is modified, it often becomes necessary to add new windows.

The decision to add new windows is not always an elective choice, sometimes it is required by code. For example, if you are making a multifamily building, each bedroom needs a means of egress. This could be an exterior door, but it normally is a large window. Without a means of egress, a room cannot be used as a bedroom without violating the building code. Also, all the model building codes require that each room have a certain amount of window area for exterior light and a certain amount of ventilation available.

How difficult is it to add new windows to an existing structure? It normally is not very difficult for a competent framing crew, but the process can get tricky at times. You might find ductwork, a plumbing vent, or a chaseway for electrical wires located in the same place you want to put a new window. Any of these situations can complicate matters.

I recommend starting on the inside of the building when you prepare to cut in a new window. If you work from the inside and discover an obstacle that prevents the window installation, you need only patch the interior wall. But, if you start the work from the outside, you have to repair the siding and sheathing, a much bigger job.

Once the window hole has been cut out on the inside wall, you can see if there are going to be any problems installing the window in the desired location. If there is no reason to change your plans, you can move ahead with the process. This entails the alteration of existing framing to accommodate a header, jack studs, and cripple studs. As mentioned earlier, you also have to cut away some of the exterior siding and wall sheathing.

When the rough opening is completed, the window can be installed. This is the last step, and it usually goes smoothly. It is the early stages of this job that present you with the most problems, but if you work from the inside out, you can keep the risk to a minimum.

Existing floor and ceiling structural members

Existing floor and ceiling structural members can present problems during a conversion. Floor joists and subflooring could be rotted. Most remodelers have dealt with this problem from time to time. As a rule, repairing damaged framing is no big deal. But what are you going do if you find that the existing joists are not strong enough to handle the live load of your converted space? A problem like this is much more difficult to solve.

First-floor conversions don't normally present any problems with joists that are too weak. Attic conversions are another story, and attic conversions are one way to get a lot of cheap space in some houses. Assuming that the project has adequate headroom in the attic, you might be able to tuck a few extra bedrooms or offices up there. Buildings with roof trusses, unless they are attic or room trusses, don't allow much opportunity for an affordable attic conversion. Stick-built roofs, if the pitch is enough, can provide a host of opportunities for an alert conversion contractor. However, the ceiling joists, or bottom cords, are not normally big enough to support living space. Don't despair, there are ways to solve this problem.

Let's assume that you've bought a building that has substantial attic space and a steep roof pitch. There is plenty of room to get a full apartment in the attic. However, there is a problem, the building has 2-by-6 ceiling joists. Based on calculations made for this property, 2-by-8 joists must be used in order for the attic to be used as living space. Additionally, the existing joists are set on 24-inch centers, but the 2-by-8 joists must be set on 16-inch centers.

What can be done? I can remember similar jobs where professional contractors recommended removing all the old 2-by-6 joists before installing the new 2-by-8 joists. Of course, this is ludicrous. You need only add new 2-by-8 joists to the existing framing. The 2-by-6 joists can stay put.

It's no harder to frame conversion projects than it is to frame remodeling jobs. Essentially, conversion jobs are remodeling work. If you are used to doing large-scale remodeling jobs, you shouldn't have any problem in the conversion business.

However, if all of your experience has been gained through new construction, there is a learning curve to overcome as you move into conversions. A major part of success in conversion projects is having the ability to think creatively. If you can do this, you can prosper. If conversion projects were simple and presented you with all the answers, everyone would be cashing in on them. It might take a while for you to figure all the ins and outs of conversion work, but the effort should be rewarded in time.

The layout

The layout that you come up with for your conversion project is one of the most important aspects of the job. I bring this up now since framing is a key component in making a layout work. It's easy to draw lines on paper, but turning those lines into walls can be difficult. Getting the maximum use out of a building is what the conversion business is all about. With that in mind, let's spend some time talking about different framing scenarios that can help you achieve higher profits.

A duplex

My first conversion project was an old, single-family home that I wanted to convert to a duplex. It was a two-story house with a long, narrow shape. When I inspected the house for the first time, I saw an excellent conversion opportunity. I bought the house and got to work.

The house already had two bathrooms, one upstairs and one downstairs, so I didn't need to add another one. There was only one kitchen, but that was not problem. I used one of the rooms adjoining the upper bathroom as a kitchen. This gave me easy access to plumbing and I didn't need to do any major wall construction or removal.

Both levels of the house had bedrooms. Also, there was space to provide a living room in each duplex unit. I still had to separate the living spaces, but the layout of the house made that easy.

The front door opened to a hall that had steps to the upper level. I had outside access and the rooms off the lower hall had doors that could be locked. The end of the hall led to the lower level living room, so that was the only place left to close off. Sealing this opening only took a few studs and a little drywall work.

The amount of framing required for this project was so minimal that it is hardly worth mentioning. Some properties lend themselves to nearly effortless conversions. Shop for just the right building and you might be able to avoid major framing altogether.

This project did require some additional work, such as the addition of a fire escape for the upstairs apartment and a lot of cosmetic work. But, all in all, this conversion project was very simple.

Going from two to four

An investor buddy of mine had similar luck converting a property from two units to four units. I had found a nice duplex that could be built out to accommodate four units. Since my plate was full when the deal came along, I showed the property to an investor I worked with frequently. The investor jumped on the property with both feet, signing a purchase offer right on the spot. How much framing was required to convert the building into four units? Not much, and I'll tell you why.

This duplex had a layout similar to the single-family house I just described. It had the same front-hall setup, except that as the stairs reached the upper level, they connected to a U-shaped hall. This gave a natural traffic pattern for two different rental units on the upper level.

The lower level had some rooms off the main hall, so again, there was a natural setting for two units. By building a couple of partition walls and adding some plumbing, this two-unit building was turned into a quadplex. Extensive work was done for structural and cosmetic reasons, but the framing work required to create four separate living spaces was easy and inexpensive.

A basement apartment

I once created a basement apartment in a house I was living in. The framing work required in the basement was substantial. All of the walls were simple partitions, none of them supported any of the main house's weight.

A friend and I framed up the whole apartment on a Saturday. We built the walls on the floor and then stood them in place. The base plates were secured to the concrete floor with a powder-actuated nailing device and the top plates were nailed into joists and nailers. When we were done, the basement was a stand-alone apartment. The rent from the basement came close to covering all of my expenses for living in the house. It wasn't a bad deal.

So far we have looked at three different conversion jobs. The first two required little framing while the third job demanded a considerable amount of interior walls, but no structural changes. Let's look at a job where there was more framing involved.

The one that didn't fly

Up to this point I've told you only success stories. Now, I'm going to tell you about the one that didn't fly.

A few years back, my dentist was looking for a building to convert into a dental office that he could use. I wasn't his broker or builder, I was just a friend. The dentist found a residential property that had frontage on a busy road, and the house was zoned so that conversion wouldn't be a problem. There was even plenty of land to allow adequate parking.

On the surface the project looked good. The inside of the building needed a lot of work, but that wasn't important because most of the interior would be gutted and rebuilt. The dentist had some local remodeling contractors take a look at the building, and they provided him with price estimates for the job. After securing all of his information and mulling it over, he called me in to consult with him. Our consultation was on a professional level, but it was done without charge. One of the last people you want upset with you is your dentist.

I looked over the floor plans the dentist had prepared. They were drawn to scale and well done. I noticed some problems in the layout, but on paper, the project seemed okay. After reviewing the estimates from the remodeling contractors, I asked to do a site inspection of the property. We met at the house and my dentist showed me around. I took notes as we went.

One of the first things that struck me was the condition of the existing windows. They were old and extremely large, and they leaked air worse than a tire full of nails. I couldn't remember seeing windows listed on any of the contractor's estimate sheets. We moved through the house, room by room, as the dentist explained his plans to me in great detail. As our inspection progressed, I continued to notice problems with both the plans and the estimates. After we had toured the entire building, we sat down to go over my findings.

My dentist had done a good job drawing plans to show what he wanted in the building. But, he didn't take into consideration some framing obstacles, such as stairways, fireplace chimneys and other nearly immovable objects. Sure, all of the obstacles could have been moved or worked around in some way, but the expense would have been considerable.

Because the remodeling contractors left a lot of stones unturned when they inspected the building and costed the job, my dentist didn't get an accurate estimate of all the expenses he faced. For example, the house was to have central heating and cooling systems. But nobody discussed the fact that ductwork requires space, and the space was not shown on the plans. Also, if a cold-air return was run in a chase where it should go, one of the laboratory rooms would have to be a good bit smaller than planned.

As I went through the framing plan and showed my dentist the problems that I'd found, his high hopes began to drop. Although everything looked good on the floor plan he had drawn, no one had factored in duct chases or adding new stairs to get to rooms that had no means of access. Replacement windows had not been budgeted into the job, and the old windows were barely useable. The list went on and on. In short, it wasn't feasible to do the extensive framing work needed to convert this house into the kind of office my dentist wanted. My dentist didn't pursue the purchase.

Extensive framing

Extensive framing is not uncommon in conversion projects. Sometimes the inside of a structure must be completely gutted. When that happens, the entire building needs new framing.

Before you begin any framing work, have your game plan worked out, to scale, on paper. Traffic patterns are important in all areas of a building. Work triangles can make or break a kitchen design. Angled walls can give a contemporary look and provide a smoother traffic pattern to some buildings.

Make sure that the framing provides satisfactory use of the property. Since most of the other interior work depends on the framing, it is critical that you get the planning and framing work done properly.

11

Roofing

Roofing is an element of conversion jobs that often goes unnoticed and unchecked. Few people look up when inspecting a building. Unless there is evidence of water damage in a building, most buyers don't bother to inspect the roof. This lack of thoroughness can result in a costly lesson.

What comes to mind when the word roof is mentioned? If you're like a lot of people, you envision an A-pitch and asphalt shingles. This is certainly a common roof, but it is far from the only type. Do you think about the roof sheathing, or just the roof covering? Can you tell by looking at a roof how many years of useful life it has remaining? How expensive is it to repair or replace a built-up roof? Should a flat roof have roof drains installed? Can you install mechanical equipment on a flat roof to make the most of interior space? Are fiberglass shingles better than asphalt shingles? These are some questions that can pop up when the subject of roofs is mentioned.

If you can't answer these questions, this chapter can provide some help. If you still don't feel comfortable, call a professional roofer to assess the roof before you buy a building. Now, let's see what can be done do to make you a better roofing inspector.

Prepurchase inspections

Prepurchase inspections of roofs should be on your checklist of things that must be done. It's important to verify the type, condition, and expected life of the roofing materials (Table 11-1). Just because a roof isn't leaking today doesn't mean that it won't leak tomorrow.

I always depend on independent professionals to rate roofs. I'll take a cursory look from the ground or a window, and leave the climbing to others. Don't buy any building until you know the condition of the roof.

**Table 11-1. Potential life spans for
various types of roofing materials**

Material	Expected life span
Asphalt shingles	15 to 30 years
Fiberglass shingles	20 to 30 years
Wood shingles	20 years
Wood shakes	50 years
Slate	Indefinite
Clay tiles	Indefinite
Copper	In excess of 35 years
Aluminum	35 years
Built-up roofing	5 to 20 years

All estimated life spans depend on installation procedure,
maintenance, and climatic conditions.

Roofing changes

Roofing changes, other than replacing existing roof coverings, are not common in conversion projects. As long as a roof is in good shape, most contractors don't plan conversion work that requires the alteration of the roof.

However, there can be an exception to this rule with attic conversions. With the right roof, a lot of usable, rentable space can be made available by converting an attic. The roof change can be as simple as adding a couple of gable dormers. Or, it could be a major change requiring the removal the entire existing roof, including rafters or trusses, and building a new roof from scratch. Exactly what takes place has to be determined on a per-project basis.

While we are on the subject of roofing changes, let's talk about design decisions that can require major roofing work. Routine repairs and replacements are discussed a little later, but for now, let's expand on what might persuade you to raise the roof, so to speak.

Building up

You can gain a lot of additional square footage, at a reasonable cost, by building up. When building an addition to a house, many contractors think only of expanding horizontally. However, going up, instead of out, could save you a lot of money.

What do I mean by building up instead of out? It's simple, really—I'm suggesting that you remove all existing roofing and build a second story on top of the existing building. Or, perhaps all you want to do is convert the attic into living space, which might not require such extensive roofing and framing work.

Suppose you take a one-story building and add a full second story, as well as a modified attic for additional space. Think of the square footage you gain that can be leased on an annual basis. Going up can definitely be better than building out.

When you elect to build up rather than out, you eliminate the need for site work, footings, foundation, and some other expensive aspects of construction. The cost of construction, on a per-square-foot basis, is much lower. In some cases, ground-floor space rents for more then upper-story space, but this is something you can research on a local level.

While it might make sense to spend more money to purchase property with ground-level space, some properties have don't have enough land to allow you to build out. For these buildings, up is the only way to go. That means messing with the roof.

There is no question that attic conversions can offer the best use of affordable space. Generally, the appraised value of attic living space is higher than basement living space. The cost of the work might be about the same, but the return on your investment should be much greater if you spend the money converting the attic. Of course, roofing work is frequently a part of attic conversions, and so is a fair amount of framing. A major roofing change might be a good value, but it is expensive. Let's consider the various types of roof changes used for conversion work.

Cutting in gable dormers

Cutting in gable dormers is not a major job for experienced people, but it is not a job just anyone can tackle. Building a dormer into an existing roof requires both framing and roofing knowledge.

Framing and roofing are mixed together in this chapter, but there is a good reason for it. In big cities, roofers often do only roof covering. In rural areas, many carpenters also do some roofing jobs. In conversion work, a roofing job has two parts. The first part consists of the sheathing work, which is often done by framers, but plenty of roofers also install sheathing on remodeling jobs. The second part is the roof covering, which is a roofer's area of expertise.

When a gable dormer is added to a roof, the existing roof covering and sheathing must be cut away. The roof section is opened up to allow the framing of a dormer. This gets into structural work, and it should be done only by qualified individuals.

Once the dormer is framed, the flashing and roofing work follows. Flashing is an important part of roofing. Roofs leak when the flashing for dormers, skylights, pipes, and chimneys is not installed properly.

Adding a shed dormer

Adding a shed dormer is considerably more of an undertaking than sticking a few gable dormers on a roof. If you build a full-fledged dormer, you must tear off about one-half of the existing roof. The framing work can get complicated. Roofing is needed for the dormer, as well as some flashing. Roofing a new dormer is no more difficult than any other new-construction roofing. The flashing work requires a little old-work experience, but the job is very manageable for most professional contractors.

A shed dormer yields a lot more floor space than a gable dormer. Gable dormers are installed primarily to create a place to put a window. Shed dormers are used to add living area for bedrooms, bathrooms, or other habitable space.

Building a shed dormer can be an expensive option. But, if the rental market is strong, you can gain a lot of floor space to rent. If you're willing to get into major roof changes, a shed dormer might pay big dividends.

Changing a roof line

Changing a roof line is a big undertaking. It is not a job for those who lack confidence or money. Ripping off a roof and replacing it is certainly a major job, not to mention an expensive one. Taking a roof off is not always good business. However, it can be a cost-effective way to gain a lot of new space.

Since going up is less expensive than building out, changing a roof line could convert a property into a powerful profit center. Let's look at two different examples of rebuilding a roof. In the first example, changing the roof did not prove to be viable. In the second example, the roof replacement made sense, even though it was expensive.

You shouldn't do it

If you're thinking of removing an existing roof and building up, sometimes it shouldn't be done. Let's say you have found a good single-family residence that you want to convert into several rental units. With the existing layout of the house, you could create a duplex with only minor interior modifications.

However, you want three units. You plan to raise the roof to make room for an extra rental unit. Can one additional rental unit off-set the cost of a major roofing change? It might, but the odds are not favorable. The cash-flow from a single rental unit only amounts to so much. You must factor in how long it takes for the rental income to pay for the improvement.

What if you plan to sell the property after the conversion is completed? Adding the cost of a new roof line to the sales price of a building can price you right out of the market. Unless the rental income covers the additional expense, few investors are likely to want the property. This is clearly a situation where the cost of a major roofing job is not warranted.

A good move

There are times when raising a roof is a good move. As an example, let's say that you have stumbled onto a prime conversion property, one where a residential property can be converted to exclusive office space. The location is ideal, the structure is sound, and that the only thing holding you back is a lack of interior space.

The price is attractive, but the acquisition cost and the cost of construction make it difficult to project a positive cash-flow. You need more floor space to lease out. After assessing all the options, you decide that removing the roof and building up makes the most sense. It doubles the floor space. Also, the use of attic trusses creates storage space in the attic. The square footage gained from this approach adds four extra offices to the building.

The rental income from the four offices is more than you need to justify a major roofing project. Even with a higher-than-average vacancy rate, the increased size of the building makes it possible to perform major roofing changes without unusual risks. This is a situation where you would probably be a fool not to move ahead with the roofing project.

Roofing repairs

Roofing repairs are more common in conversion projects than major roofing changes. All sorts of repairs await your attention with older buildings. The work could be as simple as replacing one or two missing shingles, or as complicated as resurfacing a complete built-up roofing system. It is up to you and your property inspector to determine what type of work and expense is involved with your project.

Missing shingles

A few missing shingles are nothing to lose sleep over. It requires a trip onto the roof to replace the shingles, but the work is not extensive or expensive. You might have trouble finding replacement shingles that match the color of the existing shingles, but you can probably come close to making a match.

Flashing leaks

Flashing leaks are not uncommon in older buildings. Depending on the age of a building, the flashing could be made of any number of materials, including copper, aluminum, or lead. Replacing flashing that is leaking is not a very big deal for an experienced roofer. It is usually better to replace leaking flashing than to repair it. Sometimes a quick fix is appropriate, but it is normally better to invest in a good fix.

Rotted sheathing

You won't come across rotted roof sheathing very often, but when you do, the repair cost is notable. If an attic doesn't have proper ventilation, condensation can occur. When this happens, moisture invades roof sheathing from within the attic. If it goes unchecked, serious rotting can take place. Plywood turns black when it gets wet, a sign that big trouble could be brewing.

If the roof sheathing has to be replaced, expect to spend some major money. The roof covering and sheathing must come off. This work doesn't add to the income potential of a building. It is a full-out expense, and one that you don't want to encounter.

Other roofing problems

Other roofing problems can crop up. For example, a flat roof might not have roof drains. This can cause water to collect on the roof. A flat roof should have some arrangements for draining excess water. These arrangements might be as simple as weep holes or as extensive as roof drains. One way or the other, make sure there is a way to drain the water from a flat roof.

There are a number of other problems that can turn up with a roof. Shingles can become brittle. They can also blow off. Cedar shakes can be affected by too much moisture. Slate roofs can work themselves loose and create a safety hazard. They can also grow greenery if they stay too wet. Tin roofs can peel off or just leak. Every type of roof has potential problems. You should have all roofs checked by professionals before you commit to buying a building.

Replacing an existing roof

Replacing an existing roof can be a big job. Depending upon the type of roof, the expense could be moderate, or it could be major. If it's a typical shingle roof, you might be in luck. If the roof has only one layer of shingles, you should be able to install a new layer of shingles over the old ones. This saves a worthwhile amount of money. However, if the roof has layers of shingles, the old shingles should be stripped off before new ones are installed.

Replacing an existing roof can cost thousands of dollars. This is especially true of buildings with large or unusual roofs. If you are about to buy a property with a roof that needs replacement, you must be able to buy the building at a price that allows for the roofing expense, without eroding your profit.

New roofing materials

If you have to replace a roof, you need to chose the new roofing material for the job. To some extent, the decision is predicated on the type of roof you are covering. In most cases, you are going to be replacing asphalt shingles. You could replace this type of roof with the same material, or you might opt for fiberglass shingles.

Fiberglass shingles have become popular, but I recommend caution when using them in cold climates. Generally, I prefer asphalt shingles, but maybe I'm just old-fashioned. However, my feelings about the use of asphalt shingles in cold climates are based on reality rather than opinion.

I grew up in Virginia, but I've lived in Maine now for about eight years. Since moving to a colder climate, I've learned many variations on the building practices used in the South. One of these lessons involves fiberglass shingles. I am not an expert roofer or an expert on roofing. The information I'm about to give you is based solely on my personal experience.

Here in Maine, I have observed a number of roofs covered with fiberglass shingles, and many of them have had problems. Being a curious type who always wants to learn more, I talked with some local material suppliers. I asked if they get a lot of complaints from customers who use fiberglass shingles. The suppliers said the complaints were numerous.

It seems that fiberglass shingles don't hold up very well in Maine. The cold weather seems to cause them to crack and blow off. I have experienced this firsthand on some roofs. It is impossible for me to say that fiberglass shingles should not be used in cold climates, but my research to date indicates that, in Maine, there are considerably more problems with fiberglass shingles than with asphalt shingles.

I don't say this to turn you away from fiberglass shingles, but rather to give you some reason to question your local suppliers. Any new product might have some bugs which must be worked out before the product is at its optimum performance. From what I've seen and heard, I would say this is the case with fiberglass shingles.

Check with your local suppliers and contractors to see if they have experienced similar problems in your area. I suspect the cause of the problem is cold temperatures, but I cannot be sure. I can say, without a doubt, that the fiberglass-shingled roofs I've seen here in Maine seem to be prone to problems.

A big factor

As long as the roof on the building you are buying is in good condition, roofing should not be a big factor in your conversion project. The exception, of course, is if you plan major alterations to the existing roof to accommodate more upper-level space. But, in general, roofing is not a major concern in conversion projects.

12

Siding and exterior trim

The siding and exterior trim on a building can affect how fast the property is sold or rented. If the exterior of a property looks shaggy, the chances of selling it or finding good tenants falls off sharply. Maintenance is another factor, especially if you are planning to hold the property for several years. One good thing about siding and exterior trim is the fact that most problems associated with them are readily evident.

Many conversion projects do not require attention to the siding or exterior trim. A number of buildings can benefit from a fresh coat of paint or new siding, but it might not be necessary. The exterior appearance of some buildings is abominable. In these cases, you must dedicate a portion of your fix-up budget to the property's curb appeal.

How important is the siding and exterior trim? It can stand between you and a sale or a rental. First impressions are important. If prospective buyers or tenants are turned off as they approach the building, you might not get a chance to show the inside of the property. In many ways, the exterior of a building is more important than little details on the inside.

Crown molding is a nice touch in a dining room. So is a chair rail. Quarry tile makes a good impression in a foyer. Wallpaper can enhance a kitchen or bathroom. These interior amenities are nice, but they can't help sell a property if prospective buyers don't see them. You have to get people into your building if you hope to get it sold or rented. You have to work hard to create an attractive exterior appearance.

Assessing existing siding and trim

Assessing existing siding and trim doesn't require as much specialized skill as is needed for some types of inspections. You can tell immediately if the siding and trim looks good. Exploring further can reveal problems with rotting wood or loose sections of siding and trim.

A visual inspection can be done quickly since siding is not likely to have many hidden disasters. Check to see that the siding is attached firmly to the frame of the house. Also, look to see if the joints under the windows and at the cornerboards are sealed. It won't hurt to do a little probing here and there to see if the siding has gotten soft from moisture damage. When exterior wood trim is in bad shape, it usually turns black. Most types of siding last many years, as long as they are maintained.

Asbestos siding

Asbestos siding was installed on some houses in years past. This can mean trouble. If you are inspecting a house that has shake-type siding that isn't wood, you might be looking at an asbestos problem.

As long as asbestos siding stays intact and doesn't require physical disruption, you might not encounter any apparent trouble. However, if the siding begins to break, and it usually does, you might be faced with quite a dilemma.

Different jurisdictions deal with asbestos in various ways. I don't know the full extent of what you might be getting into by purchasing a building that is covered in asbestos, but I suggest that you check with local authorities to find out your liabilities. If you must hire a professional abatement team to remove the siding, the cost might be more than you can bear.

Peeling paint

When you find peeling paint on wood siding, you should suspect a moisture problem. Dampness can cause paint to crack and peel. The problem might be that the building is not protected with gutters and downspouts. It could be that foundation shrubs are too close to the house. Houses with crawl spaces might not have vapor barriers installed on the ground. There are many reasons why paint might be peeling, but none of them are good for the property owner.

Repairs and maintenance

Repairs and maintenance for siding are not normally major expenses. If you are looking at a building that has a piece or two of bad siding, you should be able to replace the damaged siding with minimal expense. The new siding might not match perfectly, but the difference in appearance should be acceptable. Some types of siding are more difficult to repair than others, but all types can be repaired while staying on budget.

Exterior trim usually deteriorates faster than siding, but the trim doesn't normally all go bad at the same time. Usually, the repairs are made by doing a little work here and a little work there. The cost of minor repairs for exterior trim are minimal. On the other hand, if all the soffits and trim boards have to be replaced at once, the cost can be high enough to present financial problems if you did not plan for them.

Painting

Painting the siding can make a dramatic difference in a building's outside appearance and appeal. Complete paint jobs are not cheap, but they won't break the bank. Old siding often has to be scraped before a fresh coat of paint can be applied. This is the hardest part of the job. If the siding is in good shape, you might be able to get by without doing a lot of scraping.

Painting and staining is one part of construction work that almost everyone feels qualified to undertake. While it is possible that nearly anyone can paint or stain exterior siding and trim, I feel the job deserves more respect. A lot of weekend painters tackle such jobs with less than acceptable results. Painting might be easier than plumbing, but it is still something of an art. If you are not an experienced painter, you might think twice before you commit to painting an entire building.

Sprayers

Painting with a sprayer is much faster than painting with a brush or roller, but it can have complications. Spraying uses more paint than brushing or rolling. The time saved when you spray paint more than offsets the wasted paint, but you need to account for the added cost of paint in your budget.

When spray painting, you might paint more than you planned, and that can create a much larger problem. When I was building houses in Virginia, I had a painter who was dependable and did good work. He used a sprayer for almost all of his jobs. However, on one occasion, this painter got both of us into a mess.

One of the houses was in a subdivision of nice homes. The building lots were small, so the houses were close together. The painter was working on a two-story colonial. It had a black roof and the siding was being painted gray. When I pulled up to the job site for a routine inspection, I couldn't believe what I was seeing. There was gray paint on the brand new black roof.

At first, this was all I noticed.

Then I saw a cloud of paint being carried through the air by a strong wind. Following the cloud with my eyes, I became somewhat horrified. The gray paint was drifting across the building lot and coming to rest on the neighbor's tan house and brown shingles. That did it, my blood pressure went off the scales, and I jumped out of my truck yelling for the painter to stop.

When the painter came down his ladder to find out what I was yelling about, I could hardly talk. My anger must have been very apparent, judging from the look on the painter's face. Of course, he had no idea what was wrong. As I calmed myself down, I had the painter step back, away from the house, and I directed his attention to the roof and the neighbor's house. As I recall, the painter's face paled and turned blank. I don't think he knew what to say. Here was an experienced, professional painter who had just damaged two houses with his paint sprayer, a sprayer that he used practically every day.

The painter took care of the trouble he had caused. After that incident, the painter never worked outside on windy days, at least not on my jobs. If this type of problem can come up with a professional painter, just imagine the trouble an amateur can get into with a paint sprayer. If you ever get involved in a painting job, either as a painter or a general contractor, I hope this story helps you avoid a similar mess.

Paint sprayers are wonderful machines. They save time, which saves money. In experienced hands, a paint sprayer is capable of doing fine work. I would not discourage you from using a sprayer, but make sure that it is used prudently.

Brushes

Painters have used brushes to ply their trade for years. While spray equipment has replaced a lot of brushes, painters continue to rely on brushes for some jobs. I'm not going to discuss the types and sizes of paint brushes that are available or anything like that. If you've been involved with construction and remodeling, you probably already know plenty about paint brushes. What you don't know can be explained by any competent paint store clerk. I prefer talking about the use of these tools.

Brushes can be used to paint entire exteriors. This method is slower than spraying, but less paint is used and the application of the paint is easier to control. Even with today's modern spray equipment, a lot of painting contractors still use brushes and rollers for all of their work.

I think brushes do a better job, but it might just be my perception. Brushes allow a painter to get into every nook and cranny. Also, since the painter works somewhat slowly and is close to the brush, it is less likely that spots are going to be missed.

Power washing

Power washing is an ideal way to make some types of siding look like new. If a building has vinyl, aluminum, or metal siding, a strong power washing can clean the siding and make the whole building look better. Vinyl siding, which is supposed to be maintenance-free, sometimes develops a build-up of mildew. A power washing can remove the ugly discoloration and restore the siding's appearance. Companies who do this work can usually be found in the telephone directory.

Replacing siding

Replacing the siding on an entire home is a considerable undertaking. It can be very expensive. Indeed, you can count on spending thousands of dollars to replace the siding on an average house.

The first step in replacing old siding is choosing new siding. A multitude of options are available. Let's take a few moments to discuss them.

Pine

Pine siding is very popular and reasonably inexpensive. This wood siding gives a good appearance and holds up well, as long as it is protected with paint or stain. If pine siding is not stained or painted promptly, it turns black as it is exposed to rain and moisture. If you're looking for an affordable wood siding, pine is probably going to be your best bet.

Some people claim that pine siding is not as good as cedar siding. Pine might not last as long as cedar, but the life span of pine is considerable. The key is to protect the wood by sealing it with paint or stain. Once the pine siding is installed and painted, the appearance mirrors that of cedar. Pine siding costs substantially less that siding made from cedar.

I have used pine siding on all of my personal homes, and I've had it installed on countless homes for my customers. I can't recall ever having a problem or complaint related to the pine siding. In my opinion, pine is a fine siding.

Cedar

The longevity of cedar is probably better than pine, but either type of siding can last for years when cared for properly. Cedar siding is more expensive than pine. I haven't installed a lot of cedar siding, and price is the primary reason. Most customers have not wanted to pay for the higher cost of cedar. After all, if the siding is painted, who's going to know the difference between pine and cedar?

Some houses I've built have been covered with cedar siding and then stained. This makes an attractive exterior appearance, but I can't say that the cedar looks better than pine. The two types of siding look different, as you might expect, but as far as one looking better than the other, I can't see it. Since appearance is a matter of personal preference, it's best left up to you to decide which siding looks better.

Cedar is a harder wood than pine. This serves the siding well in durability, but it makes installing the siding a bit more difficult. Cedar siding splits easily as it is being nailed into place.

Some people install cedar siding and never seal the wood. I think this is a mistake. Untreated cedar tends to turn gray as it weathers. Some people like this look, but I'm not one of them. Cedar is unquestionably a good siding, but you have to decide if it is worth the extra cost.

Hardboard

I installed a lot of hardboard siding on the homes I built in Virginia. This was especially true of the colonial-type homes I built. Once hardboard is painted, it looks very good, as long as it is installed properly. Hardboard siding normally costs about the same as pine siding.

Hardboard siding is quite floppy, and this can make for a sloppy installation. Siding contractors who don't pay close attention to what they are doing can end up with wavy siding. The wavy siding doesn't show up from a distance, but if you stand near a job like this, the undulating siding is quite noticeable.

Due to the nature of the material, hardboard siding shouldn't be stained. The material simply does not accept stain well. If the building is to be painted, hardboard siding is a reasonable option that is affordable.

Hardboard might not be the best siding choice for an old building that has walls out of plumb and studs that are not uniform thickness. These conditions exaggerate the wavy look of the siding.

Vinyl

Vinyl siding is very popular in some regions. It is a cost-effective siding that never needs painting or staining. An occasional power washing is the only maintenance normally associated with vinyl. When installed properly, vinyl siding can give a good account of itself.

Many people feel that vinyl siding cheapens the appearance and value of a property. To some extent, this is true. I've talked with a number of real estate appraisers over the years, and I've never found one who would give vinyl an equal value to wood siding. The cost between vinyl and pine siding can be quite competitive, at times, but pine has always done better for me on appraised values.

The fact that vinyl doesn't require routine painting or staining gives it a strong advantage when compared to other sidings. This is especially true when the siding is being installed on rental property. Any landlord knows that reduced maintenance translates into increased income.

Aluminum

Aluminum siding sort of bit the dust when vinyl siding became available. Over the years, many buildings were covered with aluminum siding, but very few new installations are done with aluminum. Aluminum and vinyl are similar in many ways, but vinyl has the upper hand. The color in vinyl siding is an integral part of the material, so it won't chip, crack, or peel.

The finish on aluminum siding can be damaged. Dents are also a problem with aluminum siding. If a child bounces a ball off the siding, there is probably going to be some damage. Normally, this is not the case with vinyl siding. I can see no occasion when aluminum siding would be used in today's market.

Other types

Plenty of other types of siding are available. There is a long list of material choices and design options. However, pine, cedar, hardboard, and vinyl are the materials used most often.

If you get into shiplap siding, metal siding, or plywood-type siding, you are probably making a mistake. Low-end siding does not appraise well, and it can affect both the rental and resale potential for a property.

Expensive siding and designs might be fine for a custom home, but there are few occasions when they are practical for rental property. I suggest you stick with the market trends.

Conformity

Conformity can become an issue when choosing a siding material. Putting vinyl siding on a building might make sense in terms of decreased maintenance, but it could kill the appraised value of your property. On the other hand, installing costly cedar siding might not increase your properties appraised value. Why is this? It is a matter of conformity.

When real estate appraisers put a value on a property, they use at least two or three different methods to arrive at a market value. One of these methods involves comparing the subject property to similar properties in the area that have recently sold. This is where a siding material that is nonconforming can hurt you.

Let's say that you have just purchased a single-family residence in a nice section of town. You are going to convert the house into a duplex. It is going to be used as one of your retirement rental properties. The house needs siding, and since you plan to hold the building for a number of years, you are considering vinyl. However, all of the other homes in the area have wood siding. If you install vinyl, your duplex is the only property in the area without wood siding. Would it be wise to use vinyl siding? Probably not.

Think about your situation. Your duplex is the only building covered with vinyl siding. The building would certainly stand out, but that's not always a good thing. Since all the surrounding comparable properties are sided with wood, you should probably use wood siding on your building. It might cost a little more and present more maintenance requirements, but it keeps the property in conformity with the rest of the area real estate. Installing vinyl under these conditions could have a detrimental affect on the appraised value of your property.

Some other time, you might be buying a home in an area where all the houses have vinyl siding. Going into an all-vinyl neighborhood with wood siding might be just as big of a mistake as going into an all-wood location with vinyl. Before you decide on a type of siding, inspect other buildings in the area. If the siding materials vary from house to house, you should be safe installing the siding of your choice. However, if a particular siding seems to be prominent, you should probably choose that same siding for your building.

Installing new siding

Installing new siding on an old building can be quite an experience. All sorts of surprises can pop up.

I remember once when siding installers were pulling off old siding, several bats came flying out of the exterior wall. I've never seen people move so quickly. On a different occasion, I saw a swarm of honey bees come out of a wall when the siding was removed. I've also heard stories about snakes, squirrels, rats, and even a raccoon.

Then there are the stories of how siding installers have found cached loot when opening up old walls. You can never be sure what you might find when you open up an old wall.

Sometimes new siding can be installed directly over existing siding. This practice is seen frequently when vinyl siding is used. If the existing siding is not rotting and is in pretty good shape, it should be safe to go over the top of it with a second layer of siding. When the old siding is ragged and rotting, it should be removed.

Installing new siding over existing siding has the obvious benefit of reducing the labor cost. Tearing off old siding can take as long as installing new siding, so you might reduce your costs by as much as 50 percent.

A common problem with adding a second layer of siding is getting flat, even lines. The new siding must be installed to surfaces that are level and plumb or there can be some displeasing visual effects.

Should you side your property in layers? My gut reaction has always been to remove existing siding before installing new material. I know there are contractors who are going to disagree with me, but this is my opinion.

Staging or pump jacks

Some type of staging or pump jacks are required on most siding jobs. Pump jacks allow installers to move around more quickly, but staging or scaffolding can offer a safer base from which to work. Even with a one-story house, some type of elevated platform is going to be needed when working with the gable ends. Most of my siding installers have used pump jacks, but a few have used staging. The choice is up to the installer.

Debris

As with many elements of a conversion project, the removal of existing siding creates a sizable pile of debris. This debris, and all the other trash that accumulates over the course of a conversion job, must be dealt with in some manner. Portable trash containers are normally the best way to deal with site debris. Burning is not allowed in a lot of areas, and many dumps and landfills are reluctant to take construction debris. My experience has proven that trash containers are the best solution to on-the-job debris.

Nails

The nails used to attach siding can become very important. For example, if common nails are used to install wood siding, rust stains are likely develop in short order. Stainless steel nails should be used to prevent rust and stain. When working with products, always read and follow instructions when they are provided by the manufacturers.

Keeping it straight

When installing siding, especially on older buildings, keeping it straight can be the biggest obstacle to overcome. Siding should be started at the bottom of a wall and installed upwards. Chalk lines can provide reference points to help maintain an even installation. Straight siding is nearly impossible on some jobs, but you should strive to keep the overall appearance as nice as possible.

Seal the gaps

After the new siding is installed, you should seal the gaps found around butt joints. A clear silicone caulking works well for this purpose. If the gaps are not sealed properly, rain can get behind the siding and do a lot of damage. Inspect the seams a week or two after the job. Check to make sure that the caulking didn't shrink and provide opportunities for water problems.

Installing new exterior trim

In most cases, installing new exterior trim is not a very big deal. Almost any type of wood can be used as trim. Also, vinyl and aluminum trim is available to help assure a maintenance-free exterior for buildings covered with vinyl siding. Replacing trim boards and soffits is not complicated work. If you can cut angles and aren't afraid to work above the ground, this phase of a job is simple.

The chances are good that you might not ever have to repair or replace any siding with your conversion work. You probably are going to cut through some of it to add windows and doors, but most properties don't require major siding work. A couple of coats of paint can normally get an old building up and running.

13

Windows, doors, and skylights

Windows, doors, and skylights can turn a dull property into a bright, cheerful place to live, work, and play. Your conversion plans might not call for skylights, but there is a good chance that windows and doors are a part of your project. Even if you are not required to install new windows or doors, you might find that adding them can do a lot for your property, especially in certain rooms.

When you actually begin shopping for windows, doors and skylights, you might be surprised at the number of choices available. The doors alone can fill an entire catalog, and windows are more numerous than doors. The maze of products you must wade through is extensive. Prices vary tremendously, and so do features and benefits.

Planning natural room light

Kitchens and bathrooms almost always benefit from more natural light. So can breakfast areas. Other rooms sometimes beg for light. Surveys have indicated that home buyers are favorably impressed by rooms that have an abundance of natural light. It can improve the odds to sell or rent your building. Even if you are converting a property into professional space, windows can win you tenants and buyers.

Since natural light is a great asset, you should consider ways to allow more light into your building. To some extent, the existing construction of your property can affect your options, but most buildings can be adapted to accept a wide variety of windows, doors, skylights, and roof windows.

Kitchens

Kitchens are one of the most important rooms in a home. Surveys have shown that property buyers are influenced by kitchens more than any other room. From a financial standpoint, remodeling a kitchen is one of the safest home improvements you can make. Kitchens are certainly an ideal location to spend your improvement money. It stands to reason, then, that kitchens deserve a little extra attention.

When you buy an older building, the chances are good that the kitchen is going to have a window over the sink. The chances are also good that the only light source in the entire kitchen is going to be that one window. The result is a dark and gloomy kitchen. People won't enjoy being in that kitchen. People won't spend time in a room if it does not make them feel comfortable.

When you are trying to rent or sell your conversion project, you can't afford to have potential buyers who are uncomfortable in the rooms you have created. Your goal is to make people feel at home as soon as they walk in the room. You want to design rooms that make people want to stay. How can you do this? The process has many steps, but one of them is covered in this chapter.

A kitchen should be bright, cheerful, and inviting. It must also be functional. First impressions are important, and to get a great first impression, you must appeal to people's desires. A functional kitchen can sell a house or rent an apartment, but a kitchen with a fantastic visual aura can sell the house or rent the apartment even faster.

Flooding a small kitchen with natural light can make it appear larger and more appealing. How can it be done? Because of the kitchen cabinets, wall space might be at a premium. If so, you can't add a window without sacrificing cabinet storage. Storage is a big factor in a functional kitchen, so you shouldn't do away with the wall cabinets.

If there is attic space or just a roof over the kitchen, you can turn to skylights. Installing skylights in the ceiling can do wonders for a kitchen. If skylights won't work, you might consider a garden window. These big windows are shaped in a way that allows them to fit nicely in most kitchens, without consuming unnecessary wall space.

Wall space can limit light in a kitchen. Not only are cabinets an obstacle, counters limit you as well. A tall window cannot be installed in an average kitchen. Wide windows won't fit between wall cabinets. With these two factors combined, you don't have a lot of options. A garden window and skylights are usually the most appropriate choices.

Of course, not all kitchens are so limited. Country kitchens, for example, are spacious and offer plenty of opportunity for natural light. You have to assess your project on its own merit, but you should strive to let the light shine in.

Another way to get extra light into a kitchen might be the use of a nine-light glazed door (a door with nine panes of glass in the top half), a terrace door, or a sliding-glass door. If your kitchen space is large enough to accommodate a door in an exterior wall, you could produce a lot of light.

Let's say that your breakfast area is a little cramped. You would like more space, and you desperately need more light. You can solve both problems with one improvement. Installing a bay window gives you both extra floor space and plenty of light. Another option might be to install a terrace door or sliding-glass door and add a deck. The deck provides a cozy place to enjoy morning meals in good weather. A glass-top table and an umbrella can give residents the feel of being in Europe, at a sidewalk cafe. Windows, doors, and skylights provide an abundance of opportunities for creative conversion contractors.

Bathrooms

Bathrooms are said to be the second most important rooms in a home. Houses and apartments need bathrooms for obvious reasons, and the more bathrooms, the better. Bathroom remodeling has historically proved to be profitable.

Modern bathrooms are often spacious and bright. This is not the case in many older homes. Most bathrooms in older homes are small, dark, and uninviting. This problem is something that you, as a conversion contractor, can change. Some contractors only add new fixtures to existing bathrooms, but they don't consider other changes. This is like shooting yourself in the foot.

It is tempting to avoid enlarging the size of existing bathrooms. When you run the numbers on what it costs to enlarge and improve a bathroom, it is easy to take the path of least resistance. I know this from personal experience. My first conversion project had two bathrooms, and I didn't bother to expand or improve them beyond new fixtures and wall coverings. This was a mistake. I made the same mistake on my second conversion, but then I learned my lesson. Every since, I've been careful not to take bathrooms for granted. I expand and enlarge if possible. Consequently, my rental rates and resales have gone smoother.

It is not always feasible to enlarge bathrooms. When it is, you should give the option serious consideration. However, when you don't have room to expand, you have to turn to other means of making existing bathrooms more desirable.

When the bathroom is located on an exterior wall, you might be able to add a window. Skylights might also be possible. Bathrooms situated in interior sections of buildings don't allow many choices for creative improvements. Keep this in mind when selecting projects to convert. I'm not saying that interior bathrooms are enough of a deterrent to make you walk away from a deal, but your options are limited.

Family rooms

Family rooms are meant to be fun rooms. Unfortunately, designers of older homes often neglected to include windows and doors in family rooms. Adding a large sliding door or two and some spacious windows can wake up a family room. Letting extra light into the room can make it appear much larger. Installing glass doors in one wall of the room is going to reduce the energy efficiency of the building, but it makes a major improvement in how the room is perceived.

Bedrooms

Conversion projects often involve the addition of bedrooms. Bedrooms are required by code to have a suitable means of egress. This rule is usually met by using windows. These windows don't have to be anything fancy, but they must be large enough to meet local code requirements.

Attic conversions

Attic conversions require the installation of windows. This can be a problem. Since tall walls are at a premium in an attic, gable dormers are usually required if you must have windows. Gable dormers get expensive, but there is a way around them.

A dormer is actually required only when you need more floor space, as might be the case if you are adding an attic bathroom. If your attic has adequate floor space, you can minimize expense by using roof windows. Roof windows are a viable substitute for gable dormers.

Most attics can handle a few rooms without the need for a shed dormer, but it is not uncommon for shed dormers to be needed when a centrally located bathroom is required.

Any room

Almost any room can benefit from more natural light. Windows, doors, skylights, and roof windows are available in an abundance of sizes and configurations. With all the available options, you are sure to find products that can fit your needs.

Windows

Windows are often needed during conversion projects. Sometimes it is necessary, or at least desirable, to replace all existing windows. Local code requirements might insist that new windows be added as the use of space is changed. When a building is being converted from residential to commercial use, window costs can be a big part of the total expense. There are a wide variety of window styles from which to choose.

Double-hung

Double-hung windows are, by far, the most common type of window. If you choose this type, you are almost always be safe in your decision. The resale value of double-hung windows is good, and so is the market appeal. You'll find many variations in price and quality when shopping for windows.

The type of conversion you are doing can dictate the class of window needed. For example, if you are creating a triplex in an area of low-to-moderate-priced homes, you are wasting your money using top-of-the-line windows. However, if you are converting a building into medical offices, where image is everything, you can justify using more exotic windows.

Sometimes it's worth spending more money for energy-efficient windows. If prospective buyers can appreciate and pay for more efficient windows, you should be safe having them installed. Buildings that you plan to keep for a good while are also prospects for better windows.

Single-hung

Single-hung windows are not used very often. They look much like double-hung windows, but there is one big difference. Only one of the sashes moves in a single-hung window, while both sashes move in a double-hung window. In some low-end projects, you might find an occasion when single-hung windows make sense. But, generally, you are better off staying with double-hung windows.

Casement

Casement windows cost more than double-hung windows, but they offer some special advantages. They are extremely tight in the energy-efficiency department. Since casement windows crank out, you can get full air flow through the window. Single-and double-hung windows can't compete with this feature.

Only on limited occasions can you justify using casement windows in rental property. Due to their expense, these windows are not normally cost-effective in small rental jobs. However, if you are doing an up-scale conversion, casement windows can work out just fine.

Awning

Awning windows are not used very often. They are a type of specialty window. An awning window raises up from the bottom, a big advantage because it allows the window to remain open even in heavy rains. This window also works well in bathrooms or other areas where privacy is desired. The windows can be mounted high in a wall to allow light and ventilation while blocking exterior views.

Bay and bow

Bay and bow windows are expensive. Rarely can the cost be justified in a rental property. Since bay windows can add floor space to a room, such as a small eat-in kitchen, you might be able to make a case for installing one where a breakfast nook is needed. Bow windows are less costly to install than bay windows, and they still provide a lot of light. You are going to have to assess your personal circumstances, but I doubt you can find many situations that call for a bay or bow window in a conversion project.

Fixed glass

Fixed glass is one of my favorite money-saving ways to get extra light into a building. I have used fixed glass in every house I've built for myself, and I've used it on a lot of other jobs. The cost of stationary glass panels is a fraction of what you pay for operable windows. Although fixed glass won't provide ventilation, you get plenty of light.

Fancy windows

Some very fancy windows are available on the market. Unfortunately, their cost usually knocks them out of consideration for most conversion projects. A commercial conversion is about the only project that can absorb the high cost of fancy windows.

Adding windows

Adding windows is a job that anyone with basic carpentry experience can usually handle. Cutting in the rough opening for a new window can be a little tricky, but as long as you take your time and work carefully, you shouldn't have much trouble. Once the wall is opened up, framing the window opening is pretty simple.

Some windows are held in place with a nailing flange. The flange is set against the exterior wall sheathing and screwed in place. Siding is installed over the flange. Not all windows have nailing flanges. Some windows are made so that they are nailed into place through their sides. Follow the manufacturer's recommendations when installing any window.

Doors

Doors are likely to be needed when doing a conversion project. You might need to add exterior doors, and you are going to almost certainly have to install some additional interior doors. Just as with windows, a wide selection of doors is available.

Exterior doors

Wood

Wood doors have been used for years. They are a satisfactory door, but they do have some disadvantages. Wood doors don't have great insulating qualities. They are also subject to swelling and sticking. A wood door can swell to a point where it can't open. One good thing about a wood door is that it can either be painted or stained, so cosmetic choices are abundant.

Fiberglass

Fiberglass doors are relatively new. Unlike wood doors, fiberglass units don't swell and stick. The insulating qualities of a fiberglass door are better than those found in wood doors. It is possible, at least with some brands, to stain a fiberglass door. These doors are made to look like a wood door, but they give longer, better service.

Metal-insulated

Metal-insulated doors are not only inexpensive, they have good insulating qualities and they offer good security. Metal doors are available in different styles and designs. Six-panel embossed versions are very popular. One drawback to metal doors is that they cannot be stained. Aside from this one drawback, metal doors are an excellent, affordable way to go.

Sliding-glass

Sliding-glass and gliding-glass doors can transform a dark family room into a fun place to spend your time. While these doors do allow more heat loss than a standard door, their visual appeal and ventilation qualities make them very desirable in some circumstances. Security, however, is not a strong feature of a glass door, and this factor might have some bearing on when and where to install an all-glass door. In general, glass doors are not used very often in conversion projects. But if you have a dark, dismal room that needs help, a glass door might do the job.

There is one other disadvantage to some glass doors. Inexpensive doors are often plagued with condensation. In winter, the condensation can turn to frost. You can avoid, or at least minimize, the sweating problem by purchasing high-quality doors, but the cost of these doors can be intimidating. A good clad door can cost three or four times what its low-end competitor is going to cost. While it is quite feasible to spend $300 for a door, $1200 can be too much to deal with when balancing a conversion budget. However, if you decide to install a cheap sliding-glass door, be prepared for problems with condensation.

Terrace

Terrace doors are very popular. They are often used in place of sliding doors. A terrace door has one stationary panel and one panel that swings. Since the door swings, rather than slides, it is easier to open. This can be a major factor if you are converting a property that might house elderly residents. You can install deadbolt locks on terrace doors. That gives terrace doors a security edge over sliding-glass doors.

Interior doors

Wood

Wood doors are very popular for interior use, but they are not cheap. A six-panel wood door can cost twice as much as a composite-type door, and even more than twice that of a flat luan door. Wood doors can be stained or painted. If you are doing a project where clear trim is being used and stained, wood doors are the most logical choice available.

Flat panel

Flat panel doors are inexpensive, but they don't have much going for them in the appearance department. If you are doing a low-budget job, flat luan doors can keep your costs down, but they don't give your building much of a personality.

Six-panel composite

Six-panel composite doors are a great compromise between cheap panel doors and expensive wood doors. If your door is to be painted, composite doors work fine. Once painted, composite doors look very much like their wood cousins. The only disadvantage to composite doors is that they do not take stain.

French

French doors are pretty and elegant, but they are also extremely expensive. They are far too expensive to be used in most conversion projects. Unless you are creating space that depends on flair for its success, these doors are going to be out of your league.

Prehung doors

In my opinion, prehung doors are the only type to install. Some carpenters buy all the necessary components and build their own door units on site, but this seems like a terrible waste of time to me. Prehung units don't cost much more than slab doors and the components needed to make them operational, but they can be installed in a fraction of the time needed to fabricate a complete door unit.

When you buy a prehung door, it usually comes complete with a split jamb and prefabricated trim. The door can have either solid trim or lower-cost fingerjoint trim. Either trim is fine if it is to be painted, but fingerjoint trim looks out of place when it is stained. The lower cost of fingerjoint trim might be tempting, but don't buy it if you plan to stain.

Skylights

Skylights come in different shapes and sizes. Some are operable, allowing them to be opened, and others are fixed. Operable and fixed skylights look much the same. They both allow the same amount of light to enter a home, but operable skylights also provide ventilation.

Operable skylights

Operable skylights are great for many uses, although for certain applications they are not worth the added expense. Many operable skylights have screens, and that can be a big advantage during bug season.

Rooms that develop a lot of moisture, like kitchens and baths, can benefit from the installation of operable skylights. Excess moisture can be very destructive in a building. Skylights not only let in extra light, they provide a means for venting the moisture. When you are planning to install skylights in either a kitchen or bathroom, take a hard look at skylights that open and have screens.

It's not impossible to open an operable skylight mounted on a high ceiling. You can use a long pole (sold by the manufacturer) or you can buy an electronic opening device. Either way, you should not have any problem getting the skylight open.

When you convert attic space into living space, you might discover that the rooms tend to be too hot in the summer months. If you don't have air conditioning, you can relieve some of the discomfort by installing operable skylights. These skylights can do a super job expelling upstairs heat.

Fixed skylights

Fixed skylights are less expensive than operable skylights. There are times when it is best to invest in operable skylight, but many times justifying the extra expense is difficult. Sometimes it just makes sense to stick with fixed units.

I have just finished building a new home for myself. The living room has two fixed skylights, while my office has a single operable skylight with a screen. What made me choose one type over the other?

The operable skylight in my office serves as one of my windows. I wanted the skylight to open so that I could achieve good cross ventilation during the warm months of the year. This skylight brightens my work area and allows a nice breeze through the office.

The fixed skylights in the living room were installed to provide light, not ventilation. For my needs in the living room, I didn't need to pay extra for skylights that could open.

Many rooms in a home can benefit from extra light. Only some rooms, like kitchens and baths, have particular needs for extra ventilation. For much of your living space, fixed skylights work just fine. Many types of fixed skylights are available, and their costs cover quite a spectrum.

Plastic bubbles

Plastic bubbles are the least expensive type of fixed skylight available. These units might be curb-mounted or self-flashing, but in both cases, the cost is low when compared to other types of skylights. The bubbles are available either clear or tinted. I've always used the tinted models, but some people might prefer the clear units. I tend to like the tinted models because they are not as bright and are less likely to fade carpets.

One drawback to the plastic bubble is heat loss. Since the bubble is not insulated, a lot of heating and cooling expense can be attributed to their lack of energy efficiency. Condensation is another possible problem with uninsulated skylights. I have seen skylights sweat with condensation to a point where carpeting in the room became soaked.

Not all plastic skylights are shaped like bubbles. Some are rectangular, and dimensions of 2 feet by 4 feet are common. Other shapes are also available. Some skylights have flanges that are installed under shingles. Other types are designed to be attached to a raised curb that is built on the roof. Care must be taken to ensure that water does not leak around the edges of skylights. For best results, follow the manufacturer's installation suggestions.

More expensive

Skylights made with glass are more expensive that those made with plastic. Today, glass skylights are much more common that plastic ones. They are also heavier and a little more difficult to install, but this is offset by their improved energy efficiency.

Glass units come in varying degrees of quality and cost. Some have only a single layer of glass, while others have multiple layers. High-priced skylights are filled with argon gas to keep the glass from fogging up. It is not difficult to spend several hundred dollars on a good skylight. Some skylights have blinds installed between the layers of glass. Peruse the brochures of various manufacturers, and you'll be amazed at the many options available.

Installing a skylight

Cutting a skylight into an existing roof is not normally a big problem. The skylight can be purchased in a size that allows it to fit between existing rafters. In vaulted ceilings, the job is not complicated at all.

If there is attic space between the roof and living space, the task takes on a few twists. A light box must be built for this type of installation.

Building a light box doesn't require an extensive knowledge of carpentry. The concept is really quite simple. After locating a place for a skylight, a plumb bob is used to find an appropriate spot on the ceiling below. This is done in the attic. A hole is cut in the roof for the skylight. The ceiling is also cut out. Now you have a hole in the roof and a corresponding hole in the ceiling below.

Once both holes are cut, lumber is used to frame the light box. This is normally a simple job because the framing can be attached to the rafters on either side of the holes. The inside of the light box should be framed so that the skylight can give maximum light. After the framing is done, drywall is hung and finished. The completed project sheds new light on the room where it is installed.

Skylights and the bottom line

As nice as skylights are, they can put a job over budget. For example, installing two good skylights in a room could cost over $1000. How much of this money would be returned on an appraisal? It's hard to say, but it is unlikely that it would all come back to you. You would probably be losing money by installing expensive skylights.

There is, however, another way of looking at this expense. If skylights make the living area more desirable, the property might sell faster or fill with tenants quicker. If that happens, you have made a wise investment. It doesn't take long for an empty rental space to cost you hundreds of dollars. It also doesn't take long for extended interest on a construction loan to add up. If skylights can help make your deal fly faster, they are a good buy.

Watch the budget

When you are working on your budget, plan the prices of windows, doors, and skylights carefully. These components of your project are expensive. Forgetting a couple of windows could cost you anywhere from $500 on up. A few mistakes like this can rob you of your profit. Windows, doors, and skylights are not the only aspects of a conversion job where a lot of money can be lost. Plumbing is one phase of conversion work that is almost always needed, and it is rarely cheap. A lot of potential problems are associated with plumbing systems, so let's find out what they are in the next chapter.

14

Plumbing

Plumbing is one phase of conversion work that strikes fear into many general contractors. It is also where a lot of money can be lost due to poor planning. Most building codes require plumbers to have a special license, so unless you have that license, you are going to need to hire a plumbing contractor. Some areas have an exception to the licensing rule. The exception allows a resident of the property to do the plumbing without a license. However, the work must still be checked and approved by the local building inspector. Not all areas follow the same plumbing codes, so check with your local plumbing inspector before plotting the course of your plumbing.

Site assessment

The site assessment of a plumbing system can be difficult. Normally, much of the piping is concealed and inaccessible, so the inspection process isn't easy. You can flush toilets, drain sinks, and run water from faucets, but you can't see inside walls, floors, and ceilings. It might be possible to inspect some of the plumbing from the basement, cellar, or crawl space. Sometimes all you can see is a small section of pipe, but what you see should give you an idea of what kind of pipe to expect in the entire system. Also, look under any cabinets that have plumbing (such as kitchen and bathroom cabinets) to find out the type of materials used for water pipes, drains, and vents. This information can prove to be very helpful.

Before you buy any conversion project, the plumbing system should be inspected by a competent professional (see Chapter 3). A thorough, accurate inspection report can help you understand and plan all the plumbing work that must be done. However, the job might not always go the way you plan. Plumbing work is often filled with surprises. Don't assume all the pipe in the building is plastic just because you see a plastic drain pipe under the kitchen sink. That plastic drain pipe might have been installed as a replacement for an old cast-iron pipe. When you open the wall, expecting to see plastic pipe throughout, you could be confronted with cast-iron or galvanized steel pipe. A surprise like this could get expensive.

You can usually expect some plumbing changes whenever you convert a building from one use to another. Depending on the project, the work involved can range from pleasantly easy to painfully difficult. For example, if you plan to convert a single-family house into a duplex, you might only have to add a kitchen sink if the house already has at least two bathrooms and one kitchen. The plumbing costs would be minimal. But, suppose you converted this same property into a hair salon? You would have to purchase several new sinks. Hot water, and plenty of it, would be needed. A public restroom might be required. You might have to consider plumbing codes for persons with disabilities. The plumbing needs for a building can quickly change depending upon how it is going to be used.

There is a lot to consider when you assess the plumbing requirements of your conversion project. The plumbing system must be solid and in good working order. Local codes probably require that you bring the system up to current code standards if you embark on extensive rehab work. Also, you might have to relocate, add, delete, or reconsider plumbing to accommodate the new use of the building. With this in mind, I'll discuss the various phases and situations most likely to affect the plumbing in your building.

Primary service

The primary service of your plumbing system is the first concern. This issue should be addressed before you buy a building. Is the sewer large enough for the new use of the building? Is sewage disposal a problem? Is the water service going to be adequate? These questions must be answered.

You might be able to come up with answers to some of these questions if you have a general background in plumbing and are willing to do some research. You can also talk to your local plumbing inspector. The utility company should be able to shed some light on issues pertaining to the water mains and sewers. If you have limited experience and feel that the entire subject is over your head, consult a licensed plumber. Before you get too involved with a building, you should have answers to all the key questions.

Existing drains and vents

You can probably continue to use the existing drains and vents in the building. They might have to be altered or relocated, but most of the materials should be salvageable. One exception to this is the galvanized steel pipe used for drains. This pipe is notorious for its ability to clog up and rust out. If your building has galvanized steel drain pipe, I would have it replaced. You might get by if you leave the pipe in place, but there is going to come a time when replacement is mandatory. Better to head off the problem early and avoid having to tear out the walls and ceilings of a recently renovated building.

Many older buildings have cast-iron pipe for drainage. This pipe is normally satisfactory for continued service. Cast-iron pipe has a long life, and few problems are associated with it. Modern plumbing systems use Schedule-40 plastic pipe. If your building has this type of pipe, you should not need to have it replaced. Occasionally, lead pipe turns up in old houses. If you discover any lead bends, traps, or pipes, they should be replaced. The soft lead deteriorates over time, and problems are sure to follow. Aside from these tips, the remainder of what you should look for are leaks and slow-running drains.

Leaks in drainage and vent systems are hard to find once the piping is concealed. However, if there is a significant leak, it usually shows up somewhere. It's a good idea to do a visual inspection of each drain. Fill the fixture with water, then allow the water to empty into the drain. If the drain has a leak, you should be able to spot it. Another telltale sign of a drainage leak can be the discoloration of a ceiling. Leaks under and around bathtubs are common. So are leaks around the bases of toilets. When these fixtures are installed above a ceiling, the ceiling is usually the first place to show the evidence of a leak.

It's easy to test for slow drains. When you flush the toilets or run water in the fixtures, the water should promptly flow down the drain. Hair clogs are common in lavatories and bathtubs. These minor clogs can give the appearance of a much bigger problem. If you have a problem with either of these fixtures, check the outlet and trap before you condemn the drain pipe.

Water pipes

Water pipes in your building might have to be enlarged. If new plumbing fixtures are added, you might need to increase the pipe size of risers and main arteries. Most codes do not allow more than two plumbing fixtures to be served by ½-inch pipe. Some old houses have only ½-inch pipe throughout. Newer buildings have ¾-inch feed pipes with ½-inch supply pipes. In any event, adding new fixtures might mean running new piping. Check with a licensed plumber or your local plumbing inspector to be safe on this issue.

A majority of houses have copper water pipe. This pipe gives many years of good service and rarely needs repair or replacement. Some old houses might have galvanized steel pipe, not just for the drain and vent service mentioned earlier, but also for the water service. All galvanized steel pipe should be replaced, whether it's used for drain, vent, or water service. This pipe can be a consistent source of problems.

Some modern homes use CPVC plastic pipe for conveying water. This pipe is brittle and is prone to cracking when under stress, but once installed, it gives reasonably good service. As long as the pipe is not subjected to abuse, it can last a long time. One of the newest materials used for water piping is polybutylene. This gray plastic pipe is very flexible and extremely durable. Installed properly, polybutylene is one of the best materials for carrying water.

Plumbing fixtures

Plumbing fixtures can be tested and assessed by most anyone. If the fixtures look good and perform properly, they should not need to be replaced. However, many older homes are equipped with outdated fixtures. If the fixtures date the property, it is normally a wise decision to replace them. Why spend a lot of money creating a new rental unit only to blemish it with antique plumbing fixtures?

Some fixtures can be in good working order, but look awful. As a general rule, unsightly fixtures should be replaced, even if they work perfectly. However, if the eyesore is a bathtub, it might make sense to have it refinished rather than replaced. Refinishing a tub should be a lot cheaper than the cost to buy and install a new one. Some companies can come to your building and refinish the plumbing fixtures on site. They can refinish nearly all fixtures. Also, they can repair most fiberglass fixtures. This can be a cost-effective way to avoid the expense and hassle of replacing bathing units.

It isn't terribly expensive to replace plumbing fixtures, and the new fixtures can give a fresh look to any bathroom or kitchen. If your budget can stand it, replacing old fixtures with new ones is a nice touch.

Adding new fixtures

Adding new fixtures to a plumbing system is common in conversion projects. When a building is changed from one use to another, its requirements for plumbing facilities often changes as well. In an earlier example, I mentioned that a substantial number of new fixtures might be needed to convert a residence to a beauty shop. Converting a house into multifamily residential rental units can also put demands on you for new fixtures. If you are converting a building into a dental office, the new fixture costs are likely to be exorbitant. When you need to add new plumbing fixtures, be prepared to pay some steep prices.

The cost of a toilet and lavatory is not very much. But the cost of having these fixtures installed by a licensed plumber is a whole other issue. Plumbers don't work cheap. Depending on how accessible and usable existing plumbing is, the cost of adding a new bathroom can be measured in thousands of dollars. A real estate appraiser I spoke with gives an average value of $3500 for a full bathroom. If you have to install three of these in your new four-unit building, you might have to part with more than $10,000. The cost could be higher, depending upon the plumber's rates and working conditions.

Another problem with adding new plumbing fixtures is the disruption it can cause. The need to get pipes hidden in walls and ceilings can mean tearing out the existing walls and ceilings. Then these areas have to be restored. The cost of plumbing can involve somewhat more than just the plumbing. You might have to factor in costs for drywall work and painting.

If your building conversion creates a greater demand for hot water, you are likely to need more water heaters. Water heaters are not too expensive, but when installation costs are included, you can be looking at hundreds of dollars for each one. Those costs quickly add up when you're counting pennies.

Permits

Permits are required for most plumbing work if it exceeds routine repairs (like fixing a leaking faucet) and minor replacement work. Local plumbing codes vary, but most of them require a permit for the replacement or installation of a water heater. A permit is also required to install new fixtures or relocate existing fixtures. Typically, a fixture can be replaced by a similar fixture, in the original location, without a permit. Due to the code requirements and regulations, there is not a lot of plumbing that an unlicensed individual is approved to perform. Most codes allow unlicensed people to perform maintenance and repairs, but that's about all.

Inspections

After the permits are issued, the plumbing work must be inspected by a local plumbing inspector or approved representative. The inspection can include new sewers and water services, underground plumbing, plumbing fixtures and all plumbing that is concealed. Pipes that are to be concealed must be tested and inspected before they are covered. Local requirements vary on how the tests must be conducted, but most plumbers use air pressure to test new installations. Inspections are the responsibility of the permit holder, usually the master plumber, so it is unlikely that you are going to be involved directly.

Find a specialist

When you get involved with plumbing and conversion projects, you should find a specialist in the field of plumbing remodeling. This might not be possible if you work in mostly rural communities, but you should be able to find a specialist if you live in a large metropolitan area. Plumbers who concentrate on new construction are not the best choice when it comes to conversion work. Neither are plumbers who devote most of their time to service and repair work. You need a plumber who knows remodeling inside and out. It might cost you a few extra dollars to hire a specialist, but the time and frustration saved can more than offset the cost. Let me give you a few examples that show why a plumber who regularly does remodeling work is a good bargain, even at a higher price.

In addition to my building credentials, I'm also a master plumber. Over the last couple of decades, I've seen a lot of plumbing and a lot of plumbers. Some of what I've seen has been enough to make me shake my head and wonder how some plumbers make it through the day.

A lot of old houses have cast-iron drains. When installing a new fixture, it is normal to cut the cast-iron drain in order to insert a new fitting. With the proper tool, a ratchet cutter, a plumber can cut a 4-inch cast-iron pipe in just a few minutes. Without this tool, all sorts of things can happen. I've seen plumbers cut cast-iron pipe with a hacksaw. It can be done, but you can enjoy a leisurely lunch while the cut is made. Other plumbers use reciprocating saws with metal-cutting blades. This type beats a hacksaw, but it can still take 30 minutes or more. Some old-timers can cut cast iron with a hammer and chisel. I've done it this way, but it is as much an art as a skill, and modern plumbers are likely to have trouble learning the proper technique. If untrained hands take a hammer to cast-iron pipe, the result can be disastrous.

When a cast-iron pipe is hit improperly with a hammer, the pipe often cracks. The crack can run for a long distance. I remember one occasion when a plumber was using a hammer to get into a building drain and cracked the pipe so badly that the yard outside had to be excavated in order to make the repairs. The crack ran right down the pipe and out through the foundation. Choosing the wrong plumber could make the work go slower and perhaps add some unexpected work to the job.

Plumbers who are not experienced in remodeling often open up interior walls in order to run the pipes. This might be necessary for some installations, but sometimes a plumber can drill through the top and bottom plate of an interior wall and snake the piping right through it. It not only saves time, you won't need to pay to have the wall repaired.

My list of plumbing horror stories could go on and on. Let me simply say that you owe it to yourself to find good subcontractors in each of the trades that are needed for your project. Finding the right people for the job is half the battle of winning in the conversion game.

15

Heating and air-conditioning

The heating and air-conditioning systems in conversion projects almost always require some attention. They can also require a lot of your money. Rarely are existing systems adequate to handle a conversion project. Both heating and air-conditioning systems are important to the comfortable use of habitable space. In some locations, they are crucial. For example, here in Maine, a failed heating system is a serious problem when the outside temperature is 20 degrees below zero. In hot spots, such as Arizona, a failed air conditioner can also cause serious problems. Even if these systems don't fail completely, they might not perform at a level that's satisfactory to the tenants and occupants. As the landlord or seller, you don't want to burden the existing heating and air-conditioning systems to the extent that you anger the occupants and buyers.

How much do you know?

Unless you are a skilled heating and air-conditioning technician, you should plan to hire competent subcontractors to work with these systems. For one thing, a special trade license is usually required in this area of work. For another, amateur attempts at either heating or air-conditioning can result in a very costly lesson.

As you know, it's important to have buildings checked out before you commit to buying them. However, in the conversion business, it is not enough to simply confirm that existing systems are in good working order. Since you are changing the use of a property, you probably are altering the needs of the heating and air-conditioning systems. Savvy conversion contractors cover this issue with the experts before they buy a property. Some people either don't remember or don't bother to investigate the heating and air-conditioning systems thoroughly. They generally lose money. Since your goal is to make money, have at least one professional review the systems in a building before you buy. Ask for a report that covers both the current condition of the equipment as well as what must be done to upgrade the systems to meet the demands of the building's new use.

Cost factors

Two cost factors must be considered when altering, replacing, or installing heating and air-conditioning systems. The first is the cost of the purchase and installation. Some systems cost much less than others to buy and install. This is certainly a factor for anyone wishing to make a few extra dollars on a conversion deal. However, it is not wise to look only at the cost of purchase and installation.

The second factor to consider is the cost of operating the various systems. If you plan to keep the property for yourself, the long-range effect of high operating costs can make you wish you had spent a little more at the time of conversion. Even if you are going to sell or rent the property, prospective buyers and tenants (who pay their own utility expenses) might frown upon systems that cost a lot to operate. Before you take the cheapest way out on installation costs, weigh all of the options and potential scenarios.

As a real estate broker, I've sold and leased all types of properties. I'm almost always questioned about the type of heating and cooling systems that are used. I've shown properties to people on the verge of buying, only to lose the deal to concerns about the cost of electric baseboard heat. The same has proven to be true with prospective rental tenants. Electric heat can be expensive, and concerns of high monthly utility bills can send good, qualified prospects running in search of another property. This is only one example, but I'll explore others as I delve into the various types of systems to be considered.

Types of heating systems

Numerous types of heating systems exist. The type found in your building is likely to be determined by your geographical region and the age of the property. Different types of heating systems vary in their fuel usage, performance, and cost. To bring the picture into better focus, let's examine each of the major heating systems.

Forced hot air

Forced hot-air furnaces were popular for many years. They are still manufactured and sold. Overall, a forced hot-air system provides good service in any climate. However, this system does have a drawback in that the furnace moves dust around almost constantly. Allergy sufferers frequently have trouble living in homes with forced hot-air systems.

Hot-air furnaces can be purchased to run on various fuels, including oil, gas, or electricity. The efficiency of hot-air furnaces is acceptable, and aside from noise and dust, not much is bad about them. However, some factors make these systems less than ideal for a conversion contractor.

Hot-air furnaces use heat ducts to convey warm air to the living space and also to return cold air to the furnace. If your conversion creates additional space that must be heated (as in an attic conversion), the heat duct is probably going to need to be enlarged. In most instances, the furnace must also be enlarged, which gets expensive. Also, you must get both the supply and return ducts into the new space. Unlike plumbing and electrical components, which can sometimes be snaked through existing walls, heat ducts require a good deal of space. You must build chaseways or open walls and ceilings to allow the installation of new ducts.

Some people look at buildings equipped with hot-air furnaces and get excited about using the existing ducts to distribute cool air from new air-conditioning equipment that is planned for the project. This idea normally won't work very well. Common ductwork can be shared by both heating and cooling systems, but the ducts should be sized based on cooling needs, rather than on heating needs. Ductwork for air-conditioning is typically larger than that required for a heating system. Tying a new air conditioner into existing heat ducts usually results in poor performance.

Forced hot-air furnaces operate at reasonable energy costs. But, unlike heat pumps, they don't combine the advantage of having both heating and air-conditioning in one package. A lot of forced-air furnaces are in operation, but I don't feel they are the best system to install when converting a building. If you must buy a larger furnace, it might be better to change the type of system serving the property.

Heat pumps

Heat pumps are extremely popular in many parts of the country. A heat pump provides both heating and cooling from a single source. This is a big advantage. Heat pumps use ductwork and forced air, similar to the hot-air furnace system. Dust and airborne irritants can still be a problem with heat pumps.

There are many misconceptions about heat pumps. Many people think that heat pumps are not effective in cold climates. To some extent, this is true, but the case against using a heat pump in frigid regions is not as clear cut as some people would lead you to believe. As author of *Troubleshooting and Repairing Heat Pumps* (McGraw-Hill, 1995), I feel qualified to talk about heat pumps. The book was the result of extensive research along with my personal knowledge of the subject.

Heat pumps perform at their best when installed in geographic regions that have moderate temperatures. An average balance point for a heat pump tends to be just a little below the freezing temperature. If the outside temperature dips below a heat pump's balance point, supplementary heat comes on to offset the change in temperature. Usually, the heat is created with electric elements, and the operating cost can get expensive when the electric heat is kicking in. However, in many areas, such as Virginia, heat pumps are extremely efficient. All of the new homes I built in Virginia were equipped with heat pumps.

In cold locations, such as Maine, heat pumps are not popular in residential applications. There are different types of heat pumps, and some work just fine in cold regions. Air-to-air heat pumps are best suited to moderate temperatures. Water-based heat pumps can be cost-effective in areas where extreme cold sets in for long periods. The installation cost of a water-based heat pump is prohibitive at times, but the operating cost is attractive.

Regardless of the geographic region of your building, you should be able to match a heat pump to the building's heating and cooling needs. In areas with extreme temperatures, the biggest drawback is the acquisition and installation cost. Once that is behind you, the low operating cost can keep you happy for a long time to come.

Heat pumps normally require two major pieces of equipment, an inside unit and an outside unit. Space limitations are rarely a problem. Compared to other heating systems, the ductwork used with an air-type system is more difficult to install. That's due to the bulk of the ducts and the lack of places to conceal them. You can overcome this disadvantage by opening walls and ceilings or building chases. Heat-pump ducts are sized for their cooling requirements, so the performance from both the heating and air-conditioning is normally satisfactory.

If you are doing a conversion that involves a minimal space, such as a garage or attic, a single-unit heat pump might be the answer to your heating and cooling needs. Motels often use this type of unit.

Part of the unit sits in the living space while the other part extends outside. Basically, the heat pump sits in an outside wall where it works very well. This unit can help you avoid problems associated with extending ductwork, and you can continue to use existing systems for the unaltered space. A one-piece heat pump can be expensive, but the operating costs are affordable.

Forced hot-water

Forced hot-water heat is unquestionably the most popular system in areas where winter temperatures are brutally cold. When it comes to beating extreme winter temperatures, it's hard to find a better heating system. But, this type of system doesn't do one much good in the summer months, since it does not include air-conditioning. If you also want air-conditioning, a separate system is required.

Buildings that have hot-water heat can sometimes be easier to convert. With this kind of system, it is not uncommon for the boilers to be oversized to the point where an extra zone of heat can be added without having to upgrade the size of the boiler. This, however, is not always the case, so don't assume that you can heat additional space without the expense of a larger boiler.

The copper tubing that carries water from the boiler to the heating units is small, usually ¾ inch in diameter. Small tubing like this can be snaked through existing space, a procedure that is much easier than trying to hide bulky duct work. The baseboard heating units normally used with forced hot-water heat are attached directly to exiting walls. Since registers or returns don't have to be cut in, you eliminate some risk of damaging existing walls and ceilings. Hot-water systems have another advantage. The boiler can be set up to heat domestic water (the water used for cooking, showers, and the like), at a lower cost than it would be with an electric water heater.

People in Florida and other deep-South states have little need for hot-water heat. A heat pump probably can serve their needs much better. But, if your building is in a northern state, hot-water heat is hard to beat.

Electric heat

Electric baseboard heat is the most economical heating system to install. It is also easy to install in conversion projects, because the electrical wires can be easily snaked to the heating units. Electric heat might be easy and inexpensive to install, but it is expensive to operate. This is not such a big deal in areas where the winters are mild and short, but it can be a serious expense in colder climates.

I installed electric heat in my first home. The cost was too good to pass up, but I later regretted it. The operating cost for heat in that house was horrendous. When I first moved to Maine, I rented a house. Guess what? It had electric heat. Houses in Maine with electric are not in demand, and I found out why. Even using wood stoves as my primary source of heat, the electric bills during the heating season hit $300 a month. The kitchen stove was fueled with gas, so that was not even a part of the electric bill. As you might imagine, I moved when the lease expired.

Although electric heat is expensive to operate, it can make a lot of sense in geographic regions that have mild winters. Electric heat is easy and inexpensive to install, and if it isn't used very often, the operating costs are not a big factor. Regions that have mild winters generally get pretty hot in the summer, so air-conditioning is likely to be also needed. If that's the case, it might make more sense to simply have a heat pump installed.

Air-conditioning

When you decide to add air-conditioning to a conversion project, you have three basic options. You can install a heat pump that provides both heating and air-conditioning. This is usually a good choice. Another option is to keep the existing heating system and install an independent air-conditioning system. This can be a sensible decision. Your third option is to install individual air conditioners on a room-by-room basis. This eliminates the need for ductwork, but it is not as attractive and it might not be as efficient. Let's discuss the options in more detail.

Heat pumps

You've already heard about heat pumps. In many geographic areas they are an ideal combination system. But in some areas, it costs so much to get a unit that can perform well in the winter that you might not be able to justify the expense. If your building has an existing heating system that is sufficient, it might be radical to tear out the heating system and put in a heat pump. However, the long-range savings in operation costs might prove otherwise. You need to do some research and see how the numbers work out for your building.

Straight air-conditioning units

Straight air-conditioning units are expensive to buy and install. Your building might require such an expense, but the costs are significant. I would try to avoid this situation.

Individual units

Individual units have merit in many ways. For one thing, occupants can control their own comfort. If a central unit is used, some people can be chilly while others are warm. Independent units are easy to install. Unlike central units, which require extensive ductwork and considerable time to install, independent units can be put in place quickly and inexpensively. Independent units have another advantage. If a central system goes out of order, your entire building is uncomfortable. When an independent unit shuts down, only a portion of your property is affected.

So many variations and possibilities are linked to conversion projects that you must assess your needs on a personal basis, even on a building-by-building basis. My best advice to you is to set aside time to look into all of your options carefully. Don't jump into anything. Once you have narrowed the field, talk to the experts. When you have all the facts, you can make a safe and informed decision.

16

Electrical improvements

The electrical systems in older buildings can sometimes leave a lot to be desired. They can also represent a major expense in your overall budget. A trade license is usually required for electrical work, so you normally need to hire a subcontractor. Making old buildings safe and bringing them up to current code requirements can be very expensive. Adding rental units can require the installation of new electrical services, which can also bust your budget. Electrical work can puncture your profit balloon in plenty of ways.

Starting point

Before you can budget for electrical improvements, you must have a starting point that tells you exactly what you have in the building and what work needs to be done. The starting point should be established before you purchase a building. The information you use to establish the starting point should come from your inspector. You want your inspector to inform you of all the existing electrical conditions.

Also, it's a good idea to contact your local building inspector to find out if any past or present electrical violations are related to the building. The inspectors are usually cooperative and conscientious.

If you know how you plan to convert the building (and you should), the inspector can also give you a good idea of what to expect as you begin the conversion process. For example, if you are making three apartments out of a single-family home, the inspector should be able to tell you that you need two additional electrical services. If the wiring is extremely old and must be entirely replaced, your inspector should file a report to that effect. To realize profits in the conversion business, you must collect all the facts before making any financial commitments. Otherwise, you could lose your shirt on your first deal.

Electrical services

Electrical services are needed for all of your residential rental units. Each apartment should have its own electrical service. The same is true for commercial tenants. The cost of installing individual electrical services can get steep. You'll encounter the cost of a panel box, the circuit breakers, a weather head, assorted other items, plus the labor costs of a licensed electrician. It is not difficult to spend in the neighborhood of $1000 for each service that is installed.

When it comes to new electrical services, there is more to consider than cost. You, or your electrician, are going to have to find suitable locations for each service panel. The panel locations can have a bearing on the cost of wiring your new units, so choose them carefully. You want the panel boxes as close as possible to your wiring paths.

Old houses might have fused electrical systems. It is not unusual to find 60-amp services installed in older homes. These electrical services are not adequate for modern electrical demands. A 100-amp service should be considered a minimum size for each residential rental unit. A 200-amp service is best for houses, but a 100-amp service can usually handle the requirements of an apartment. If you get into commercial conversions, you might have to switch to 200-amp services. In either case, if the building is protected by fuses, you should upgrade your building and install circuit breakers.

In my opinion, the upgrading and addition of electrical services should only be done by experienced, licensed electricians. An electrical permit is usually required for this work, and these permits are normally issued only to master electricians. The electrical power in a panel box can kill you on the spot. This is no place to learn by experience. Your experience could terminate your life.

I wired my new home, but I didn't get very involved in the installation of the electrical service. I mounted the panel and assisted a master electrician, but I kept my fingers well away from the power cables. Doing my own wiring was pretty simple, but I had no desire to fry myself at the panel box. All of the wires and devices that I worked with were cold. The main breaker at the panel box was turned off whenever I was working with the electrical system.

Old wiring

Buildings that have old wiring can present conversion contractors with some real challenges. Depending upon the age of your building and the condition of its wiring, you might need to replace all of the wiring. Most jurisdictions require that all electrical, plumbing, and heating systems be brought up to current code requirements if extensive work is done to the systems. This requirement can have a major effect on your budget. To protect yourself, you have to understand the local rules and regulations and plan accordingly.

On occasion, the existing wiring might be on the verge of being in violation of current codes. This situation probably puts the ball in your court. You must make a judgment call and decide whether or not to upgrade the wiring. Some builders would take the path of least resistance and cost, and choose not to do anything. I would upgrade any wiring that is questionable. Money is money, but people's lives could be at stake in this situation. Given a borderline situation, the call is yours, but I would heartily recommend that you upgrade the wiring to make it safer.

Conversion projects usually involve an increase in the use of mechanical systems, such as electrical wiring. While a house might have functioned flawlessly as a residential property, the wiring could be inadequate when you convert the building for another use. Electrical systems can start fires, and fires can kill people and destroy property. New electrical wiring might not be the best cash-on-cash return you invest in a building, but it certainly is good for the comfort of your peace of mind.

Wiring codes have changed over the years. As new products have become available, the need for better wiring has increased. I can think back to my grandparent's home and remember a lot of little extension cords that were used daily. I can also remember when fuses frequently blew as my grandparents began to accumulate modern appliances. In fact, I can remember electrical situations in my grandparents' house that today would scare me to death. I was too young to know about the dangers, but now that I understand what's going on, I realize it was fortunate that we didn't have a devastating fire.

The memories I hold from my grandparents' house go way back, probably 30 years. It is understandable how the conditions in that house came to be. What I can't understand is how similar situations can still be present in today's homes. Less than five years ago, I was active as a broker in the multifamily market. I spent considerable time listing and showing apartment buildings. During this time, I saw many of the same problems that existed in my grandparents' home some 20 or 30 years earlier.

Granted, these properties were not top-notch units, but they were not slums either. Yet they had minimal electrical services. Fuse boxes with 60-amp service were common. So were six-outlet power strips plugged into thin extension cords. More times than not, the buildings were not even equipped with three-prong plugs. Ground-fault interrupters (GFIs) were nonexistent, and very few of the buildings had operational smoke detectors.

The buildings should have been periodically inspected by local authorities, but they made no apparent effort to bring the apartments up to code standards that would provide the residents with a safe level of living conditions. The point of all this is to caution you that a lot of buildings have electrical systems that still require extensive work in order to meet current codes.

Bringing buildings into compliance

Bringing buildings into compliance with current electrical codes can be very expensive. Depending upon how bad the existing wiring is, it might be necessary to strip all walls and ceilings and replace the old wiring. Normally, it isn't necessary to go to such extremes, but sometimes it's the only option. However, many smaller jobs often have to be done. This work is easier and less expensive than rewiring an entire building, but the costs can still affect your profit.

Water heaters

Electric water heaters in older buildings were typically wired with 12-gauge wire. It was considered adequate at the time, but current codes require a 10-gauge wire. You might not need to make this change until it's time to replace the water heater, but you should check with your electrician or electrical inspector to determine your status and liability on this issue.

Current electrical regulations require that a disconnect box be installed near an electric water heater. This rule also was not in effect several years ago. A lot of electric water heaters currently in use don't have a disconnect box installed. Like wire sizing, you might not have to make the upgrade change until the water heater is replaced, but you should check to make sure.

Smoke detectors

Under current code regulations, smoke detectors are required in various locations in a living space. One is required near bedrooms, another is needed in a kitchen. Other locations, such as halls, can be required to have smoke detectors. Requirements can mandate that the smoke detectors be hard-wired and connected so that if one detector goes off, they all sound an alarm. You might be able to get by with battery-powered detectors, but you should check out the requirements with local authorities or a licensed electrician.

Carbon monoxide detectors

Carbon monoxide is a colorless, odorless gas that can be lethal. A detector can provide an early warning to the build-up of carbon monoxide in a house. These detectors are relatively new on the market, but they are gaining use in many areas.

Ground fault

Ground-fault interrupter (GFI) circuits are required in all wet areas. Such areas include kitchens, bathrooms, laundry rooms where a sink is installed, garages, and outside outlets. You have two options when faced with ground-fault rules.

You can install a GFI outlet in each of the wet locations so that it is the first outlet that power is fed to on the circuit. This provides ground fault protection to the entire circuit. The difficult part of installing a GFI outlet is in determining which outlet is the first outlet to be fed on the circuit. If you can tell which outlet is the first, you can simply replace it with a GFI outlet. Another option is to install a GFI circuit breaker for the circuit. GFI breakers are expensive, but they are sometimes less of a hassle to install than a GFI outlet.

Enough outlets

Many buildings do not have enough outlets to meet current codes. Normally, you do not need to add outlets to meet the current code until major work is done to the electrical system. Chances are good, however, that you are going to have to upgrade and correct this deficiency in order to make your converted space suitable for sale or lease. This is especially true if the conversion is going to be used as an office.

According to the codes, a lamp with a 6-foot cord should be able to be plugged into an outlet from any point along a wall. This essentially means that outlets should not be spaced more than 12 feet apart. Kitchen outlets must be spaced at 4-foot intervals. These examples cover most outlet situations, although there are some variations and exceptions. Check with your building inspector for local code requirements.

If you are converting a building into professional office space, you should install more outlets than required by the electrical code. It is also helpful to supply some split-circuits on the outlets. With the massive amount of electrical equipment used in offices today, it is easy to overload a single circuit. Split circuits are required in kitchens, and they are a good idea in any location where a lot of electrical devices operate simultaneously.

Overhead lights

Older homes often had overhead lights, but these lights are not installed as often in modern homes, I suppose to lower construction costs. I think rooms with overhead lights are more useful than those that depend on light from lamps, and a number of my customers share my feelings. It's my opinion that the majority of the public prefers overhead lighting to lamps. You might want to consider this when setting a budget for your electrical work.

Older buildings generally have ceiling lights. If the wiring is safe and adequate, it is a simple matter to upgrade the old fixtures. Rooms that are not equipped with existing overhead lights can present a problem. Depending upon the direction of the ceiling joists, it might be impossible to snake wires through the ceiling to a suitable switch location. The ceiling could, of course, be opened to allow easy access for wiring, but this gets into higher costs. If the joists are running in the direction of a switch location, it is very feasible that wiring could be snaked through the ceiling and walls with minimal damage.

Lighting in office buildings and professional service buildings must be plentiful. The odds are that ceilings are going to have to be opened to allow adequate fixture installations. This isn't all bad, however, since such a conversion project is probably going to require substantial wiring work. As long as you plan your electrical work in advance and budget properly, you can do just about anything.

While you are wiring

While you are doing the electrical wiring in a building, give some thought to other kinds of wire that might need to be installed in the walls. For example, since telephones are going to be needed in certain rooms, it makes sense to prewire the phone jacks. You might also want to think about installing wires for cable television, security systems, door chimes, and thermostats. Running future-use wires when walls are open is a lot easier than working with them after everything is sealed up.

Electrical fixtures

Electrical fixtures frequently carry a high mark-up. It is not unusual for a fixture that costs $20 wholesale to be sold for $40 resale, or more. If you have access to wholesale fixtures, you should be able to save yourself a few hundred dollars. I have sources where I can buy light fixtures for less than $10. These are not the type of fixtures that you would install in a high-end, custom home, but they're not junk, either. Fixtures don't have to cost a fortune to look good and work well. Shopping is the key to affordable light fixtures. You might do okay buying fixtures through your electrician, but less-expensive fixtures are probably available.

I purchase a lot of my fixtures through a couple of mail-order outfits. My savings on a myriad of items is phenomenal. Light bulbs, light fixtures, accessories, plumbing fixtures, hardware, and a long list of other items are available at prices about 30 percent less than my local wholesalers. The service from these catalog distributors is great. I call one day, and in no more than two days, my order is delivered to my door. This type of outfit is well worth looking into. Effective price shopping can lower the overall cost of your conversion job by a considerable amount.

Electricians

When you do conversion projects, try to hire electricians who have experience working on old buildings and remodeling. This same thinking applied to your search for a plumber in Chapter 14. Electricians who specialize in old buildings and remodeling know how to work wires through walls and ceilings, a valuable skill on conversion projects.

Electrical work requires a trade license, so electricians that you consider for your project must be properly licensed and insured. Once you have found a seasoned master electrician that you can work with comfortably, you should be able to work through the wiring phase with a minimal of difficulty.

17

Insulation

Insulation has a lot to do with the operating cost of rental property. A well-insulated building costs less to heat and cool than one that is poorly insulated. Money saved on operational expenses goes directly into the pocket of a landlord. Whether you are doing conversions to sell or rent, an efficiently insulated building is more attractive than one that lacks adequate insulation.

Experienced remodelers usually have a good idea of what to expect in the way of insulation when working on older buildings. Some old buildings have no insulation in the outside walls. If the buildings have any insulation at all, it might be found in the attic. Some old homes have newspaper and cardboard serving as insulation in the exterior walls. The old newspapers make for interesting reading, but their insulating qualities are not very good. The quality and quantity of insulation varies. Fiberglass is, by far, the most common type of insulation discovered in walls and attics. But other types are often found.

Two schools of thought

There are two schools of thought when it comes to conversion projects and insulation. You can either take steps to insulate the building to modern standards, or you can leave well enough alone. Deciding which path to take depends on your individual circumstances. If you are going to replace exterior siding or open up exterior walls from the inside, you are going to be ahead of the game by bringing the insulation up to current standards. When the siding and interior of exterior walls do not require any major work, you might be better off to leave the wall insulation alone.

If a real estate agent is involved when you buy a building, the chances are good that you are going to receive a written disclosure statement. One category on the statement is going to be about the insulation. Many sellers simply state that they do not know what quantity or type of insulation is installed in exterior walls. If you receive this type of disclosure, you're free to make the same statement, assuming that you don't know what's in the walls. A disclosure statement like this is your ticket out of having to upgrade the wall insulation, but it doesn't mean you shouldn't invest in additional insulation.

Buyers and tenants who pay their own utility expenses commonly want to know the R-values for the insulation in a building. It might be acceptable to say you don't know the R-values, but you stand a better chance of selling or renting the property if you can provide a statement showing that the insulation meets current industry standards.

What is the R-value? It is a measurement used to determine the resistance of insulation. The higher the R-value is, the more resistance an insulation provides. An R-19 insulation has much less resistance than one with a rating of R-30. As long as you remember that the higher the R-number, the greater the insulating value, you should be all set (Table 17-1).

Table 17-1. R-values for insulation

Material	R-value per inch of insulation
Fiberglass batts	3
Fiberglass blankets	3.1
Fiberglass loose-fill	3.1 to 3.3 (when poured); 2.8 to 3.8 (when blown)
Rock-Wool batts	3
Rock-Wool blankets	3
Rock-Wool loose-fill	3 to 3.3 (when poured); 2.8 to 3.8 (when blown)
Cellulose loose-fill	3.7 to 4 (when poured); 3.1 to 4 (when blown)
Vermiculite loose-fill	2 to 2.6
Perlite loose-fill	2 to 2.7
Polystyrene rigid	4 to 5.4
Polyurethane rigid	6.7 to 8
Polyisocyanurate rigid	8

Of the many phases of work involved in a conversion project, the insulation is one of the least expensive, and it is one that can pay for itself over time. Increasing the insulation results in savings from heating and cooling costs. A lot of people are happy to pay a little more up front in order to save a lot more in the long run.

If you decide to upgrade the insulation in a building, you have several options available. The right choice depends heavily on the type of building you have and the conditions under which the new insulation must be installed. Some contractors blow insulation into exterior walls and attics. A lot of contractors use fiberglass batts to insulate habitable space. When adding extra insulation to attics, be sure to avoid blocking ventilation. There have been cases where added insulation blocked ventilation at the eaves, resulting in severe mildew and other problems throughout the house.

Insulation options

Insulation options available to a conversion contractor are numerous enough to create some confusion. Should you use rock wool or cellulose? Is fiberglass better than perlite? What's the best insulation for my budget? How difficult is it to install loose-fill insulation? These are just some of the questions that might come up when you plan the insulation phase of your conversion project. A look at the various types of insulation on an individual basis can help to clear the murky water.

Batt insulation

Batt insulation consists of glass fibers or mineral wool. Glass-fiber batts are the most common. These rolls of batt insulation are available in various thicknesses and R-values. Batt or blanket insulation (as it is sometimes called) is usually available in widths of either 16 inches or 24 inches. The 16-inch wide batts are used between wall studs, and the 24-inch wide batts are used between ceiling joists. This insulation is available in 3-, 6-, or 9-inch thicknesses. The thickness affects the R-value. For example, a 3-inch batt has an R-value of 11. A 6-inch batt has an R-value of 19.

Batt insulation is available either faced or unfaced. The facing can be either a foil or paper backing on the insulation. The facing provides a vapor barrier. Insulation installed in walls is usually faced, while insulation in attics is usually unfaced. Batt insulation is commonly stapled to wood studs as it is installed in exterior walls. When this insulation is used in a crawl space, it is normally stuffed between floor joists and held in place with little metal supports. It is also laid in the floors of attics. Of all the types of insulation available, fiberglass (or glass fiber) is probably the most common. It is used in all types of projects.

Fiberglass insulation can irritate some people. It is famous for its ability to make people itch. Proper clothing is the best defense against itching. Long-sleeve shirts and long pants should be considered mandatory equipment. Gloves can also be worn to reduce skin irritations. Closing the ends of shirt sleeves and pants legs with rubber bands or tape can help prevent fiberglass particles from finding a way to exposed skin. Wearing safety goggles is a good idea, too.

In addition to causing some skin irritations, fiberglass can affect the respiratory system. The tiny glass fibers that become airborne during the installation process can invade the nose and mouth, causing coughing and further irritation. This problem can be reduced by wearing a mask when working with the insulation.

Fiberglass is relatively inexpensive and easy to install. Glass fiber is good because it does not tend to settle and create voids. If settling occurs, there is a loss in insulating qualities. Water can reduce the resistance of fiberglass insulation. Fiberglass is durable and remains effective for years. Another advantage to this popular insulation is its low risk as a fire hazard.

Foam

Foam insulation doesn't have much of a place in remodeling conversions. This liquid foam can be injected into existing walls with a special machine, but there is little need for it unless a building has a brick exterior. Urethane foam insulation was popular for awhile, but then it was discovered to offer health hazards, and many locations restricted or banned its use. When this form of insulation is used, it is extremely efficient, but it is flammable. If burned, urethane gives off cyanide gas. This deadly gas is one of the primary reasons that some areas are restricting the use of urethane.

Loose-fill insulation

Loose-fill insulation is sold in bags. It is meant to be spread over an area or blown into a space. The loose-fill material might consist of cellulose, glass fiber, mineral wool, perlite, or vermiculite. All of these are available in loose form. This insulation is frequently blown into existing walls and attics, and it can be a good option for a conversion contractor.

Blowing insulation into an attic is very simple, assuming that you have a machine designed for the job. These machines can be rented from tool rental centers, but many suppliers can loan you a blower if you buy enough insulation. If you have plenty of space to move around in an attic, you don't need a blowing machine. You can simply walk around and distribute the insulation from the bags.

Blowing insulation into walls is a bit more difficult. Fire-stops can get in the way and cause only half the wall to get insulated. To overcome this, assuming that fire-stops are in place, you have to make two access holes in each stud bay to introduce the insulation into the wall. When you blow insulation into exterior walls from the outside, the access holes must be plugged, a job I don't enjoy. In a conversion project, I prefer to make the access holes on the inside walls because it's easier to patch them. Also, inside patches can be made to look invisible, which is not always the case with patches in exterior siding.

Cellulose

Cellulose is a common form of loose-fill insulation. It can be made of recycled paper. The insulation is inexpensive and easy to install. However, if it gets wet, cellulose loses much of its insulating value. Untreated, cellulose presents a high fire risk, but a treatment can be applied to retard the fire hazard. I recommend installing only fire-retardant cellulose.

Since cellulose insulation is made from paper, it doesn't irritate the skin or respiratory system as do some types of loose-fill insulation. This is one reason why I've used cellulose every time that I have had to personally installed loose-fill insulation. As far as I know, there are no environmental risks involved with cellulose, and added benefit that keeps people happy.

Mineral wool

Mineral wool can irritate the skin and respiratory system much like fiberglass insulation. A mask, gloves, and full body protection should be worn when installing mineral wool. The insulating qualities of mineral wool are good, but if I am required to install loose-fill insulation myself, I choose cellulose.

Vermiculite and perlite

Both vermiculite and perlite are used in loose-fill insulation. Neither of these insulators are flammable, and both of them are considered to be free of any harmful fumes and gases. It might be well worth your time to investigate these two materials when it's time to insulate your conversion project.

Rigid insulation

Rigid insulation can be installed on a roof to increase the insulating value. This is a big plus in buildings where attic space is limited or nonexistent. Basement walls are another place where board insulation can be used to reduce utility costs. If you are replacing the siding on a building, and have stripped the old siding off, you can add rigid insulation to the exterior sheathing before the new siding is added. The insulation can add to the R-value of the exterior wall.

Rigid insulation boards are generally available in widths of 16, 24, and 48 inches. These boards can range in thickness from ½ inch to a full 7 inches. The wide range of available thicknesses allows you to tailor this insulation to meet any of your needs. Once you decide to use rigid boards, you must select a material. This insulation can be made from polystyrene, urethane, or glass-fiber. The polystyrene and urethane do a better job than the glass-fiber. However, polystyrene is very flammable. Urethane was discussed earlier.

Vapor barriers

Vapor barriers play an important role in the insulation of a building. For example, rigid insulation boards that are installed without a vapor barrier can lose up to half of their R-value to moisture. When insulation is installed in walls and crawl spaces, a vapor barrier should also be installed. If you are using a fiberglass insulation, it can be purchased with a vapor barrier already installed. Another way to create a vapor barrier is to wrap the interior of outside walls with plastic.

If you use faced insulation, the facing should be installed on the heated side of the wall. The goal is to keep house moisture from entering the wall cavity. If this goal is not met, the sole plates, siding, and studs can rot. Many modern contracting firms install unfaced fiberglass batts in exterior walls and then cover the interior of the walls with plastic, to act as a vapor barrier.

Ventilation

Ventilation is needed for insulation to perform at its best. Foundation vents, soffit vents, and attic vents can all serve to provide adequate ventilation. An attic that is not ventilated properly can sweat with moisture. When warm air from the building collides with cold air outside, condensation occurs. This condensation can ruin insulation and structural members, such as rafters and roof sheathing. Gone undetected, the damage can amount to tens of thousands of dollars, and it doesn't take long to happen. The condensation in an attic can reach such an extreme that water can leak through ceilings and run down interior walls. This situation should not be taken lightly. Make sure your buildings are well ventilated.

18

Wall and ceiling coverings

Wall and ceiling coverings can do a lot to spruce up an old building. Structural work and mechanical systems are quite important to a building, but when it's time to sell or rent the property, often the cosmetic improvements have the most impact. A buyer might be happy to know that your building has all new copper electrical wiring, but the bathroom wallpaper and kitchen tile are more likely to be the features that push the buyer into a decision. Buying strictly on looks is not good business, but it is frequently the way properties are sold and leased.

Investors look past pretty little fix-ups to find flaws in a building. This hard-nosed group is experienced in the business of buying structurally sound buildings. Rarely are they swayed by artful stenciling along a ceiling. However, veteran investors make up only a portion of the buyers in the market for conversion projects.

Rookie investors are known to act on impulse. If they like the look of a building, they buy it. This group is easily influenced by cosmetic touches. Installing wallpaper and a chair rail in a dining room can help make a sale to these buyers. A tile splash guard behind the kitchen range can prove impressive. There are all sorts of ways to stir the emotions of prospective purchasers and tenants.

It has been my experience, as both a seller and a broker, that inexperienced investors purchase properties that they like, not necessarily properties that are good buys. Successful investors learn, the hard way, to overcome this major weakness. But you can sell a lot of buildings to rookie investors as they are working their way through the learning curve. Is this wrong? If you are honest and present your properties in a reputable manner, there is nothing wrong, in my opinion, with selling to a person's passion. In fact, I call it knowing your market and making sound marketing decisions.

Taking a look

A look at existing walls and ceilings can tell you what must be done to improve them when the conversion is completed. A coat of paint might be all that's needed. However, there is a good chance that some of the walls and ceilings are going to be damaged during the conversion work. They might have to be opened up for plumbers, electricians, heating crews, or other trades. If this is the case, you must come up with a plan for restoring the affected areas. The walls and ceilings you start with can influence your decision. Let me give you a few examples.

Drywall

If the building you are converting has walls and ceilings covered with drywall, you are not likely to have many problems. Drywall is easy to cut and patch. New drywall can be blended into existing drywall very well. A coat of sealer, followed by a coat of paint, is all that is needed to camouflage any disruption of the walls or ceilings. However, not all buildings have existing drywall in the walls and ceilings. That makes some of them much more difficult. Keep a record of the paint used in case you need to make touchups later (Fig. 18-1).

Paint Record Form			
Type of paint	**Supplier**	**Color**	**Paint number**

18-1 *Paint record form*

Plaster

Plaster was a common covering for walls and ceilings at one time. Plenty of buildings still have walls and ceilings covered with plaster. If you buy one of these buildings, it's going to be substantially more difficult to repair cuts, cracks, and holes in plaster than it would be if you were working with existing drywall.

Plaster can throw you some curves, and I mean this literally. When plaster is applied to lath, it is seldom smooth. The plaster has rises and depressions that create an uneven surface. When making a repair, it's not easy to match drywall to a surface like this. It can be done, but some skill is needed to make a good match of the patch.

The wood strips and wire used in conjunction with plaster can make life difficult for any of the trades that must work with it. With drywall, a plumber can take a hammer and knock out a channel for a pipe in moments. To make the same opening in a plaster wall requires a saw and a lot more time. Plaster also creates considerably more dust. Not only that, your hand and arm are probably going to get a few nicks, cuts, and scratches. In short, plaster makes the job harder for plumbers, electricians, and others to do their installation work. It is also more difficult to patch. If your project has plaster, be sure to factor the extra work into your overall production schedule and budget.

Logs

You might not think of logs when you think of wall coverings, but there are log buildings in the real estate market, and some models incorporate logs for their interior walls. A building like this is a nightmare to convert. Personally, I would avoid log buildings altogether. If you don't take my advice and decide to buy a log building, do your homework first.

I have worked with several log buildings during my career. I've never bought one as a conversion project, but I have done plumbing work on a number of them. I can tell you from first-hand experience, they present very difficult work for all of the mechanical trades. This is particularly true when you have a log building that has interior walls made from logs. The mechanical costs for a log building are likely to be considerably higher than they would be for a conventional building.

Masonry walls

Masonry walls are rare in modern residential construction, but many buildings have brick and block exterior walls. These walls present a real challenge not only to the mechanical trades, but also to those who must repair and cover them. You can deal with most of the problems presented by exterior masonry walls, but expect higher production costs.

Paneling

Wood paneling has seen bursts of popularity from time to time. It has been used in family rooms, bedrooms, bathrooms, and probably every other type of room. If your building has paneled walls, budget in enough money to replace it if you think it might be disturbed. Repairing or matching old paneling is next to impossible.

Tile

At one time ceramic tile was used heavily in bathrooms. Tile covered the showers and the floors, and it routinely ran about half way up the walls. Tile is a good wall covering, but old tile is hard to match. When remodeling a bathroom (or any room with tiles), some tiles are sure to be damaged. That means you must budget to replace all of them. If you try to get by with a little patch here and there, the appearance of your conversion project is likely to suffer.

Ceilings

Ceilings in modern buildings usually consist of painted drywall. The ceilings are frequently covered with a texture to hide flaws in the finish work (Fig. 18-2). There is nothing wrong with this type of ceiling. It is cost-effective, and most people like it, including those in real estate market. Since the cost of construction is a key factor in the conversion business, a simple drywall ceiling is usually the best choice.

Probable Causes for Ceiling Defects

Cracked ceilings:
- Settlement in the building or foundation
- Vibrations in the building or foundation

Nail-pops:
- Nails pulling loose

Drywall tape coming loose:
- High humidity
- Improper installation

18-2 *Probable causes for ceiling defects*

Drop-in tiles

Drop-in tiles (Tables 18-1 and 18-2) and the framework that holds them can become a part of a conversion project. This type of ceiling is readily accepted in commercial circles, but it is generally looked at unfavorably in residential properties. A dropped ceiling is sometimes needed to conceal wiring, pipes, and heating and air-conditioning components. The use of a dropped ceiling can reduce your conversion costs. I'll explain.

Table 18-1. Ceiling tile comparison

Type of material	Cost	Features
Mineral-fiber	Very expensive	Noncombustible
Fiberglass	Mid-range price	May be fire resistant
Wood-fiber	Inexpensive	May be fire resistant

Table 18-2. Ceiling tile applications

Material	Use
Wood-fiber	Can be applied over plaster or drywall with adhesive
Mineral-fiber	Drop-in panels that work with a grid system
Fiberglass	Drop-in panels that work with a grid system

Let's assume that you have bought an old house that has plaster walls and ceilings. The ceilings are almost 10 feet high. You want to add bathrooms on the second story, and you also need new electrical work up above. Then, too, there is the task of extending new heating and cooling ducts to the upper level. How are you going to do this?

One option is to cut out the ceiling and work all of your equipment, in some way or another, through the ceiling joists. This, of course, would be time-consuming and expensive. There would also be the trouble and expense of repairing the ceiling. A better option is to run all of your mechanical components below the existing ceiling and hide them with a dropped ceiling. The building has plenty of ceiling height to allow such an installation, so you might be wise to consider this option.

You could install a dropped ceiling consisting of removable tiles and a grid work of framing. This allows the new installation work to remain easily accessible. It can be reached simply by removing the tiles. However, if you dislike the look of drop-in tiles, you could frame a new ceiling system and cover it with drywall. Either way, you create an easy installation path for your mechanical equipment.

Drywall

Drywall is, without a doubt, the most common wall and ceiling covering in use today. It is inexpensive, relatively easy to install, and provides a good-looking finished product. If you have a building with an old plaster ceiling, you might consider leveling the ceiling with wood strips and then covering them with drywall. This technique hides any channels or holes in the existing plaster ceiling and gives a nice finished look to the building.

As convenient as drywall is, it requires a skillful set of hands to finish it properly. Almost anyone with a strong back can hang drywall, but taping and sanding drywall requires talent. I learned this the hard way, and although this story is embarrassing, I'll share it in hopes of saving you from a similar mistake.

I built my first home about 12 years ago. At the time, I was very active as a plumber and remodeling contractor. I was getting into home building, but had yet to perfect all the skills necessary to build a house with my own two hands. My wife and I decided, however, that we could do much of the work in our dream home, and we did. Some parts of it turned out better than others.

When we got to the drywall stage, we had no problem hanging the boards. It was the finish work that did us in. We installed the cornerbead, taped the joints, and set about sanding out the mud. After several attempts, it became apparent that neither of us had the skills to achieve an acceptable finish on the walls or ceiling.

Not having a lot of money, we decided to get creative. The ceilings were coated with drywall mud and stomped with a potato masher. The textured ceiling hid our taping mistakes and looked fine. It was the textured walls that were a bit weird. Yes, we actually textured the walls to hide our inability to finish the drywall in a professional manner. Since that time, I've become much more proficient in the finishing of drywall, but I would never again attempt to tape an entire house. It is my opinion that the finishing of drywall should be left to the experts.

Walls

Walls in older buildings are likely to be covered with plaster. This offers the same challenges we discussed for ceilings. If only minor repairs are needed, it is worthwhile to retain the plaster walls. However, if major destruction is going to take place, as is often the case with conversion projects, you should plan on replacing the plaster with drywall. I'll warn you now, the stud walls behind the plaster are not likely to be even. You are probably going to have to use furring strips to get the walls acceptably even for the drywall. This process is time-consuming and adds to your overall cost.

Kitchens

The walls in kitchens can be drywalled and painted, or they can be drywalled and covered with a more pleasing wall covering, such as tile or wallpaper. Kitchens are good rooms in which to invest a little extra money. If you're going to get fancy somewhere in the property, the kitchen is one of the best places to do it.

Bathrooms

Modern bathrooms don't have as much tile work as they once did. It's not that tile has become unpopular, the cost is simply prohibitive. Like kitchens, bathrooms are excellent places to spend some extra cash. It is my opinion, which is shared by many real estate appraisers and surveys, that kitchens and bathrooms are the rooms that sell houses and rent apartments. They are less important in commercial buildings, but in residential properties, bathrooms and kitchens deserve much of your attention.

Painted drywall is fine in a bathroom, but wallpaper adds a touch of elegance. Depending upon the type of property you are creating, it might not make sense to go too far overboard with fancy wall coverings in any room. However, bathrooms are one place you are not likely to lose the money you invest.

Bedrooms

Bedrooms can be dolled up with special wall coverings, but the effort is usually wasted. The best course of action in a bedroom is to stick with drywall and paint.

Family rooms

Family rooms look fine with painted walls. They also look nice with wainscoting, but this quickly gets expensive. Paneling has historically been used in family rooms, but many styles of paneling darken a room. This effect is not desirable. In general, I would stick with light-colored painted walls.

Living rooms

Formal living rooms are no longer common. They are not expected in most rental properties. With this in mind, painted walls can suffice in almost all living rooms found in apartments.

Laundry rooms

If you are creating laundry rooms in your building, painted walls are going to be fine. A laundry room is rarely on the list of most-important places to occupy and enjoy. They must be functional, but they don't have to be exceptionally pretty.

Other rooms

Other rooms in your building should have a fresh coat of paint. If any money remains from the wall and ceiling budget, I would invest it in the kitchen and bathroom.

Accents

Special accents can enhance the appearance of the walls. These little extras don't cost a lot, but they can make a big difference in how the finished job turns out. For example, adding a stenciled border around the top the kitchen wall can set a tone for the room. Depending upon the design of the stencil, it can give a kitchen a country or contemporary look.

Ceramic tile can also accent a kitchen. Installing tile behind a range, as a splash guard, is just one way to use tile in a kitchen. If you have a budget that allows a bit more expense, you could tile the walls between the top of the kitchen counter and the bottom of the kitchen cabinets. This type of work sets a kitchen off and gives it considerable appeal.

Wallpaper is another accent that can be used to give your kitchen a special look. Of course, wallpaper, tile, and stenciling can be used in other rooms, like bathrooms. Perhaps one of the best ways to dress up a room is with the use of interior trim, a subject I discuss in the next chapter.

19

Interior trim

Interior trim is often taken for granted. The casing around windows and the baseboard around walls is not usually a feature that many people find exciting. Some trim looks better than others, but overall, it goes unnoticed. This is not true in all cases. As a conversion contractor, you can use interior trim to make your project command attention, and you can do it without spending a lot of extra money.

Installing interior trim is not heavy work. It is a job that any handy person can manage, as long as that person has patience. The most difficult part of installing trim is making cuts that are going to match up when joined together. This process can be a struggle for some people, especially in a conversion project, where the walls might not be plumb. Carpenters who install trim as a specialty make the job look very easy. For the rest of us, it's not all that easy, but it is a phase of work that doesn't require any special license or long years of training. Experience, of course, makes everyone better, so if you decide to install your own trim, don't expect the results to be as good as the work of a professional.

Existing trim

Conversion jobs frequently require the removal of some walls and the addition of others. Depending upon the type of building, its age, and your conversion plans, you might want to salvage and reuse some of the existing trim. Old houses often have ornate trim, which can add to the charm of some types of conversions. But if the interior trim isn't anything special, you must decide if you want to take the time and effort to salvage the trim, even if it's in good shape. Attempting to use existing trim for baseboards can be a bother.

Removing trim without damaging it is time-consuming work. Before starting, check to find out if you can match the trim you salvage with new trim. You might be able to, but it's best to verify this before you cast your budget numbers in stone. If you can't match the old with the new, it might mean buying all new trim, an expensive proposition.

When the existing trim is of an antique nature, you can seek out special suppliers for help. Some sources sell replica trim, although it is usually expensive. Ordinarily, it is not cost-effective to purchase specialty trim, but on occasion the expense is justifiable. For example, if you are adding three new interior doors to your project, and all the other doors have old-fashioned trim, it would probably pay to buy replica trim for the new doors. However, you do have to be careful about how much money you are pumping into a conversion project. The budget can get out of hand quickly.

When most of the windows and interior walls are to be kept intact, you should be able to leave existing trim in place. It probably is going to need some attention with a paint brush, but that's a minor cost. If you can get by without replacing interior trim, you can save a considerable amount of money.

Picking a new style

A new style of trim might be appropriate for your building. This is especially true if you are converting from a residential use to a commercial use. Several types of trim are available, but only three are used in most residential applications. I'll discuss each of them.

Clamshell

Clamshell trim is about the least expensive wood trim you can buy. It is a plain trim that does little to make the interior of a building more interesting or attractive. The strongest feature of this trim is its price. As I have said before, you must tailor your buying decisions to the property you are converting. In some properties, it would be a waste of money to use anything more expensive than clamshell trim. On the other hand, it would be a mistake to install this trim in a professional office or an upscale apartment.

Colonial

Colonial trim is something of a universal trim. It's not cheap, but neither is it at the top of the pricing structure for wood trim. I use this trim in most of my projects. It has also been the choice for all of my personal homes throughout the years. Colonial trim is well accepted. It does well on real estate appraisals, and the cost is bearable.

Plain trim

Plain trim boards can be used as interior trim. The square-cut edges and plain facing of a stock trim board create a rustic look. I've seen this trim in expensive homes of various designs, but it fits best in houses that have a country look. Common practice when using this trim allows the boards to simply butt together, eliminating the need to cut angles and saving installation time. In the right houses, the look is certainly acceptable.

Fingerjoint trim

Fingerjoint trim is less expensive than solid trim. It is made from short lengths of wood that have been joined end-to-end to make a longer section of trim. The special joint that joins the boards end-to-end is called a *fingerjoint*. Fingerjoints are glaringly apparent on the trim, and they look unsightly. However, if you plan to paint the trim, fingerjoint trim is the best choice. It costs less, and once it's painted, you can't see the joints.

Fingerjoint trim should not be stained. The end result gives a poor appearance. I can recall a new house in Virginia that had colonial trim on the windows, baseboards, and door casings. All the trim was stained. The windows and baseboards had solid trim and they looked fine. The doors didn't fare as well.

Apparently the doors were ordered as prehung, pretrimmed units. Unfortunately, someone dropped the ball when specifying the colonial door trim. The doors came with fingerjoint trim for the door casing rather than solid trim. The fingerjoint trim was stained and it looked awful. Every joint in the casing stood out and captured your attention. You want trim to be a focal point in your building, but not in this way. It's okay to mix fingerjoint trim and solid trim, but don't do it if the trim is to be stained.

Solid trim

Solid trim is more expensive than fingerjoint trim, but it can be stained without having unsightly joints show. Some contractors refer to solid trim as clear trim. Whatever you call it, this trim does not have any joints in it. The entire length of trim is all one piece.

There is no point in paying for solid trim if it is going to be painted. When painted, solid trim doesn't look any better than fingerjoint trim. The only time that I would pay extra for solid trim would be when it was going to be stained.

Trim kits

Trim kits can cut down on production time. These kits contain precut pieces of trim. They are typically used to trim out windows. Since all of the wood is precut, the amount of labor required to trim a window is reduced drastically, which should translate into increased profits through lower labor costs. Trim kits cost more than wood bought in standard lengths, but the money saved in labor costs should more than offset the expense of the kits. Also, you get the job done faster. Remember to specify if the trim is to be solid or fingerjoint.

Prehung doors

Prehung doors can be ordered with the trim casing already surrounding them. In the case of interior doors, where the jambs are split, installing the trim permanently is a very quick job. I know carpenters who buy prehung doors without the trim attached, but I can't imagine why. As with window trim kits, you must specify whether you want fingerjoint or solid trim.

Shoe molding

Shoe molding, also called quarter-round, is often installed in rooms where vinyl flooring is used. This molding holds the edges of vinyl flooring in place and does not allow them to curl up. Most contractors I know use shoe molding. It is an optional trim, but one I believe is worthwhile.

Other trim

I've discussed baseboard trim, casing, and shoe molding. What other trim items are there to discuss? We could talk about chair rails, crown molding, handrails, and accent items. Some of this trim is not appropriate for rental apartments.

For example, crown molding, molding that goes around the top of a wall where the wall meets a ceiling, is a bit fancy for most apartments. It is also expensive, so you should avoid it in common rental conversions. Chair rail falls into this same category. While decorative molding is expected in high-priced homes, it is not usually associated with apartments. However, if you are doing a conversion to create professional space, both of these trim items could be on your material list.

Stairways need handrails. You can go cheap and simple, or you can spend thousands of dollars in a handcrafted railing. You should keep this part of your trim package simple. A few metal brackets and a rounded handrail can do nicely in most rental situations.

Trim accents could include any number of items. Wood covers for electrical outlets can be considered trim accents. The same goes for switch covers. Bathroom accessories, such as towel bars, towel rings, tissue-paper holders and so forth can be lumped into the accents category. You could even install trim to create a herringbone design on one of the living room walls. Your use of trim to create a unique environment is limited only by your imagination. Bear in mind, however, that you are working within a budget for profit, so don't get carried away with the personal touches.

20

Floor coverings

Floor coverings are an important element in your conversion project. The flooring is an aspect of your job that people are going to see right away. If it's nice, they'll notice it. If it's not, they'll notice it even faster. Finished flooring can be extremely expensive, but you can achieve a beautiful floor without high costs.

Existing flooring

When a building is going to be converted, the existing flooring normally has to be replaced. Some of it might be salvageable, but most vinyl and carpet floors are not worth trying to save. If it's feasible, try to work around wood and tile floors so they can be saved. But if you are making major modifications to a building, you can't expect to retain all of the original flooring.

If you have existing flooring, such as tile, that you want to avoid damaging, I'll let you in on a little trick I learned along the way. Place a carpet pad over the flooring and tape the pad in place, then cover it with plastic. I've found this method to be very helpful during remodeling and construction. The soft pad absorbs blows that might break tile or cut vinyl, while the plastic protects the floor from paint, water, and other liquids.

Vinyl flooring

Vinyl flooring is typically used in rooms that are likely to have spills. Kitchens, bathrooms, and laundry rooms are all good candidates for vinyl flooring. Foyers and entry areas are also sections of a home or apartment where vinyl flooring is common. Since vinyl is easy to clean and impervious to water, it is a smart choice for such areas.

When you shop for vinyl flooring, you are going to discover that it is available in different styles and in a wide range of prices. Sheet vinyl is the most common type of vinyl flooring. Since the flooring is all one piece, there are no seams to come loose or leak. However, large rooms, usually over 12 feet, are going to require seams with most types of sheet vinyl. Some manufacturers produce wider rolls of vinyl. Wider vinyl costs more, but it might be worth it to avoid seams.

Individual vinyl tiles are available, but they are not often used. They take longer to install than sheet vinyl, and because each tile is installed independently, there is a risk of problems. The tiles can come loose, one by one. Also, cracks between the tiles can catch dirt, making the tiles difficult to clean.

Individual tiles are sometimes used in foyers to simulate quarry tile or slate. I suppose this is fine, but I've yet to see a vinyl floor that looks enough like real slate, stone, or hard tile to be worth the risk of having so many seams. In my opinion, sheet vinyl is a better choice.

Installing sheet vinyl

Installing sheet vinyl is a job that is usually best left to flooring professionals. The flooring can be installed by amateurs, but the work is a lot more difficult than it might seem. If you are working in an empty room, the job might not be too tough. But, if you have to cut around cabinets and fixtures, the job quickly gets fussy and difficult.

The prep work required before installing sheet vinyl is crucial to success. If the surface that's to be covered with new flooring is rough, the finished job is not going to look good. It is possible to install new vinyl over old vinyl, but the existing floor must be in prime condition.

When preparing an old floor for new vinyl, I always install new underlayment. It provides a clean, porous base for the adhesive that secures the vinyl in place. New underlayment isn't always required, but it is always a good idea. On a few occasions, I've installed the underlayment over the existing floor, buy I usually have the old floor removed before adding the underlayment.

Warning! If you have a building where the flooring is made up of individual tiles, you might be faced with an asbestos problem. A variety of old flooring materials were manufactured with asbestos in them. You could run into a serious abatement expense if this type of flooring is to be removed. If you have any doubts about the composition of existing flooring, consult with a flooring expert before removing the flooring.

Even when new underlayment is installed, it might be necessary to fill cracks that form between the sheets. A floor ready for vinyl installation should be very smooth. It is also important to make sure that no nail or screw heads are protruding from the underlayment. Any that stick up are going to show in the new vinyl.

If you are going to install your own vinyl, follow the manufacturer's recommendations carefully. You must make sure that the vinyl is warm and pliable before installing it. The manufacturer's instructions can tell you the proper working temperature, how to roll the vinyl prior to installation, what type of adhesive to use, and so forth.

Picking your vinyl

Selecting your vinyl floor might be harder than you think. A multitude of choices are available. Not only are there countless colors and patterns, there are many different grades of material. Contractor prices can range from as little as $7 per square yard to as high as $30 per square yard or more. No-wax finishes are common, but some of these finishes are better than others. You can invest a substantial portion of your time choosing the best floor from the many options.

When choosing vinyl, you need to consider the amount of traffic it is going to endure. A laundry room floor does not receive the constant use that a kitchen floor does. You might find that it makes sense to use lower grades of vinyl in some areas and higher grades in others.

My philosophy has been to use mid-range, FHA-approved materials in most of my speculative work. Then I have plenty of materials to choose from and can keep my budget in line. In all the years I've been using this type of vinyl, I've never had a serious problem. Before I would spend $25 a yard for vinyl, I would install tile.

At times I've used cheaper vinyl. I even used vinyl squares in a kitchen once, although I'd never do it again. There was a time in my career when I concentrated on cheap properties in rundown neighborhoods. I was speculating that the neighborhood would come around and revitalize. It never did, at least not while I owned houses there.

These houses were old and the location would not support expensive finishes. I used cheap vinyl and got away with it. It was common to replace the flooring each time a tenant moved out. Sometimes it pays to go for bargain-basement remnants.

Carpet

Wall-to-wall carpeting is an industry standard for flooring. There is no question that carpeting is popular. Almost every new home or office building has carpeting in it. There are good reasons for this. Carpet makes a floor warm to the touch. The combination of carpet and pad creates a soft walking surface. Cost is another good reason for using carpet—it is much less expensive than some other types of flooring, such as hardwood.

Only rarely is the existing carpeting worth saving in a major conversion project. If the existing carpeting should be in good shape, it might pay to protect it, have it professionally cleaned, and leave it as your finished flooring. Unfortunately, the conversion process usually changes the interior of a building to the extent that existing carpeting doesn't fit the new space. You might, however, be able to cut out sections of the carpeting for use in any new, smaller rooms.

Buying carpet

You are going to find a wide range of prices when you shop for carpeting. There are also several types of carpeting. Some don't crush as much as others. Some resist stains better (Fig. 20-1). Is one type of carpet better than another? I think so, but you have to weigh the differences and choose a type of carpeting that fits your needs. In many ways, choosing a carpet mirrors the principals that are used to buy vinyl flooring.

- *Polyester:*
  ~Bright colors
  ~Resists mildew and moisture
  ~Stays clean
- *Olefin:*
  ~Very durable
  ~Resists mildew and moisture
  ~Very stain-resistant
- *Wool:*
  ~Durable
  ~Abrasion-resistant
  ~Reasonably easy to clean
  ~Should be protected against moths
  ~Resists abrasion

- *Acrylic:*
  ~Resists mildew
  ~Resists insects
  ~Remains clean
  ~Resists abrasion
- *Nylon:*
  ~Extremely durable
  ~Resists abrasion
  ~Resists mildew
  ~Resists moths
  ~Remains clean
  ~Tends to create static electricity

20-1 *Carpet features*

Just as with vinyl, I normally use a mid-range, FHA-approved carpeting for projects I'm doing on speculation. This has always served me well. The pad is an important part of a carpet installation. If money is tight, spend more money to get a great pad and less money on the carpet (Table 20-1). A moderately-priced carpet on a quality pad looks better and lasts longer than an expensive carpet on cheap padding.

Many years ago, a carpet salesman showed me a trick. He took three samples of carpet pad and laid them on the floor. The pads represented the low, middle and high price ranges. Then the salesman took a carpet sample off a rack, laid the sample on the low-priced pad and told me to stand on it. I was wearing boots with heavy, aggressive soles. After standing on the carpet for a moment, the salesman told me to step off and to notice how long it took for my footprints to disappear.

Table 20-1.
Cost comparison
of carpet fibers

Polyester	Moderate cost
Olefin	Prices vary
Wool	Expensive
Acrylic	Moderate cost
Nylon	Prices vary
Polyester	Moderate cost

Next, he put the same carpet sample on the mid-priced pad and I repeated the process. The footprints seemed to go away quicker. When the same test was conducted on the high-priced pad, it was obvious that the prints vanished faster. This simple demonstration proved a point to me that I've never forgotten. The pad is the most important part of a carpet job.

The installation of wall-to-wall carpeting should, in my opinion, be left to the pros. The work is physically demanding and requires skill. If you tackle the job yourself, follow the manufacturer's recommendations for installation.

In bathrooms

Should carpet be installed in bathrooms? Overall, I would say no, but there are special circumstances where it would be appropriate. If I were converting a building where residents would be elderly or physically disadvantaged, I might put carpet in a bathroom. Providing such a nonslip surface seems logical to me under the right conditions. Normally, however, carpeting is a poor choice for a bathroom, especially a full bath, where baths and showers are taken. Spilled water and ambient moisture can become trapped in the carpet and pad, leading to mold and mildew, not to mention rotted flooring.

At the request of customers, I've installed carpeting in bathrooms and kitchens, but I feel that these rooms are better suited to a more water-resistant type of flooring. My preference is a textured tile, but for most of my projects, vinyl is what gets installed in the bathrooms and kitchens.

Wood floors

Wood floors were abundant in the houses of yesteryear. If your building has wood floors, you should try to save them. You might do well to look under any carpeting or vinyl that is in your building. It was not uncommon for contractors to cover up perfectly good wood floors with the trendy materials of their time. You might discover a gold mine of hardwood flooring that you didn't know existed.

Old floors that have discolored can be brought back to a vibrant life. It requires some sanding and refinishing, but wood floors can endure a lot and still come out looking good (Fig. 20-2). With the high cost of installing wood floors, you would be foolish to destroy such a floor during your conversion.

Installing wood floors is not normally going to pay for itself in rental conversions. The expense is just too great to recoup. If the rental unit has a small, separate dining room, you might consider putting wood floors in it. In general, I would not install any wood flooring in an average conversion project.

- *Polyurethane:*
  - ~Expensive
  - ~Resists water
  - ~Durable
  - ~Scratches are difficult to hide
- *Varnishes:*
  - ~Less expensive than polyurethane
  - ~Less durable than polyurethane
  - ~Resists water
  - ~Scratches are difficult to hide
- *Penetrating sealers:*
  - ~Provide a low-gloss sheen
  - ~Durable
  - ~Scratches touch up easily

20-2 *Finishes for wood floors*

Tile

Tile can be used on walls and on floors. It makes an excellent flooring in high-traffic areas, such as foyers and entryways (Fig. 20-3). Tile is also attractive in a kitchen or bathroom. There are, however, a few drawbacks to tile. One is its cost. Tile is expensive when compared to carpet or vinyl flooring. Another problem is that tile can become very slippery when it's wet. There is still another complaint to be made against tile. If something is dropped on it, there is a good chance damage is going to occur, either to the tile or to the object that was dropped. For example, a drinking glass is not likely to survive a

- *Ceramic tile:*
  ~Sizes range for 1-inch squares to 12-inch squares
  ~Most tiles have a thickness of ⁵⁄₁₆ inch
- *Ceramic mosaic tile:*
  ~Sizes range from 1-inch squares to 2-inch squares
  ~Also available in rectangular shapes, generally 1 × 2 inches
  ~Average thickness is ¼ inch
- *Quarry tile:*
  ~Sizes range from 6-inch squares to 8-inch squares
  ~Rectangular tile is available in 4-x-8-inch size
  ~Typical thickness is ½ inch

20-3 *Tile sizes*

fall to a tile floor. Conversely, a tile floor can become cracked if a heavy object, like a pan full of water, is dropped on it.

I use a lot of tile in my jobs, but I use it sparingly. Quarry tile is frequently installed in the foyers and entryways. I sometimes put tile in bathrooms, but I rarely install it in kitchens. As for other rooms, I like to install tile in sun rooms and occasionally in breakfast areas (Table 20-2). Cost, of course, prohibits me from always doing what I like. To make money in the conversion business, you must know your limitations.

**Table 20-2. Difficulty
rating for installing tile**

Ceramic tile	Fairly Easy
Ceramic mosaic tile	Easy
Quarry tile	Fairly Difficult

Other types of flooring

Other types of flooring have their place under certain circumstances. For example, I've used old bricks to create floors in rustic family rooms. Some people use stone in their foyers as a flooring. I've seen a variety of wood floors used that were not exactly conventional. I think you are going to find, however, that it is best to stick with market standards and to control your costs when converting a building. Getting too cute or creative can hurt you a lot more than it can help.

21

Cabinets
and countertops

Cabinets and countertops can account for a huge portion of your remodeling budget if you are converting a house into a multifamily building. If you're adding three complete kitchens, you could easily spend between $10,000 and $15,000 on cabinets and countertops. When you factor in vanities and tops for three new bathrooms, you can tack on another $1000 or so. With this kind of money at stake, you have to shop prudently and make smart buying decisions.

Can you imagine a kitchen without cabinets? Where would you store your dishes and flatware? Where would you keep your pots and pans? Where would you put the food? Obviously, cabinets are an important element in a kitchen. Without them, the kitchen loses all of its appeal. Also, cabinets play a large role in how well a rental unit rents or a building sells. Cabinets and countertops are going to be an important part of your conversion project.

A new look

You can save money by giving old cabinets a new look. This new look can be achieved by refinishing the existing cabinets. Just changing the cabinet doors can make a big difference. If you then add new drawer fronts and pulls, the cabinets take on a new personality. Finish the job with a new veneer and the cabinets can look as good as new at a fraction of the cost.

This scenario can certainly work for the remodeler who is concerned with simply upgrading an existing kitchen. But what about you, the conversion contractor? Chances are good that in addition to remodeling an old kitchen, you are going to need to add one or more new kitchens. You need to buy new cabinets and countertops. This chore is not as simple as it might seem. Price and quality vary greatly in countertops and cabinets.

Kitchen countertops

Kitchen countertops are used for everything from desk space, to storage, to food preparation, to unofficial closet space. The countertops in a kitchen get plenty of use, so they must be durable. It is also important that they be attractive and functional.

When you design a kitchen, you determine how much countertop is needed. However, it is best to wait until the base cabinets are installed before ordering preformed countertops. A small mistake in a measurement can have you storing a countertop for years to come.

When it comes to countertops, you have some decisions to make. Are the countertops going to be made up on site, or do you plan to order preformed countertops? Which way is cheaper? Is one better than the other? Many questions must be answered.

Preformed countertops

Preformed countertops are common in residential properties, as well as commercial buildings. They are cost-effective, relatively easy to install and do a good job. Preformed countertops are made of a base material, usually pressed board, and covered with plastic laminate. There is nothing wrong with using a preformed countertop in your kitchen. But at times it is more sensible to have custom countertops built on the job.

Custom countertops

You might assume that a custom countertop is going to cost you more than a preformed countertop, but oftentimes that is not the case. I'll give you an example. I just finished building a new house for myself. The kitchen has a double-bowl corner sink. Because of the sink location, I didn't want to use a preformed countertop that would place seams under the sink drains. As it worked out, that is exactly where the joints between the sections of countertop would have fallen. I decided to look for another option.

If I was willing to accept the preformed countertop, it was going to cost me in the neighborhood of $320. Since I didn't want to do this, my next step was to investigate the cost of a preformed top with a different seam configuration. I was quoted a price of around $600. Not wanting to pay double the price to avoid two seams, I talked to my carpenters. They built the countertop right in my kitchen. I got a stronger, better countertop for around $400. That's a little more than a stock unit would have cost, and a lot less than the price for a custom preformed unit.

Tile countertops

Tile countertops can be quite attractive in a kitchen, but they are also expensive. I've used tile countertops in two of my personal homes and many of the custom homes I've built. Tile countertops have also proved to be popular in kitchen remodeling projects I've done, but I've never installed tile countertops in a conversion project. I don't think the return on the investment is good enough to warrant it.

More expensive countertops

You can get countertops that cost more than tile countertops. In fact, if you have an unlimited budget, any number of countertop options are available. These countertops might be splendid, but in a conversion project, expensive countertops don't look as good on the profit-and-loss statement. I advise you to stick with standard laminated tops and avoid getting too fancy.

Kitchen cabinets

If you've been a contractor for a while, you've probably seen advertisements that claim you can buy enough cabinets to outfit an entire kitchen for some price that seems ridiculously low. These sale prices are usually for unfinished cabinets. The quality of construction for the cabinets may or may not be good (Table 21-1), but in most cases, the purchasers must finish the units. It takes a lot of time and patience to do a good finishing job. I'd prefer not to have to take on that task.

Price wars rage in the construction and remodeling fields. Many businesses run ads claiming they offer products that are better or cheaper (or both) than the competition. You need to sift through the hype and determine which claims are real and which are nothing more than exaggerated sales pitches.

The kitchen cabinets just installed in my house are of a better-than-average quality for production cabinets. They cost around $3000, not counting the countertop. If I believed every sales flier I read, I could have bought great cabinets for about half the cost. Could I really? I don't think so. The brand of cabinets that I normally use has been around for a long time, and I've installed a lot of them with no real problems. When I find a winner, I stick with it. It's finding that winner that can be difficult.

Table 21-1. Kitchen cabinet features

Type of cabinet	Features
Steel	Noisy
	May rust
	Poor resale value
Hardwood	Sturdy
	Durable
	Easy to maintain
	Excellent resale value
Hardboard	Sturdy
	Durable
	Easy to maintain
	Good resale value
Particleboard	Sturdy
	Normally durable
	Easy to maintain
	Fair resale value

Base cabinets

If you are not familiar with kitchen designs, you can be amazed at the number of variations available in base cabinets. I was looking through a catalog for one manufacturer just recently, and there were pages upon pages of cabinet variations. Some of the decision you have to make involve sizes, styles, colors, and features.

Standard base cabinets are about 32½ inches high. Once a countertop is installed on the base cabinets, the finished height is usually around 36 inches. Base cabinets come in different widths. Sink bases are usually 5 feet wide. Other base cabinets might be as narrow as 12 inches or as wide as 3 feet. There are, of course, other sizes available, and custom cabinets can be made to your specifications. Custom cabinets, however, tend to be more expensive, and they can take months to get. At one time, I used custom cabinets in many of the homes I built, but the long lead time discouraged me. Also, I found that some production cabinets are just as good as custom cabinets.

Cabinet materials can consist of solid wood, plywood, or particleboard. Many production cabinets use a mixture of these materials. Choosing the cabinet material is only part of the buying decision. You need to look at the construction features of the cabinets. For example, dovetail joints should last longer than butt joints. You must also consider whether or not the cabinet is going to have doors, drawers, appliance openings, or special accessories. Also, take a look at how well the drawers glide. Insist on a cabinet with quality glides and rollers.

Wall cabinets

Choosing wall cabinets is not much different than shopping for base cabinets. You have to consider sizes and styles that are going to best suit your requirements. Do you want cabinets with glass or raised-panel doors? Should the doors have porcelain pulls or finger grooves? Wall cabinets offer plenty of choices.

The heights and widths of wall cabinets vary. Most wall cabinets are about 30 inches tall. Cabinets designed to fit over refrigerators frequently have a height of 15 inches, and wall cabinets installed over ranges are normally about 18 inches tall. Standard widths start around 12 inches and go up to 3 feet. Various manufacturers offer cabinets in other sizes. When considering cabinets, keep in mind that cabinets are sold in a variety of widths, in 3-inch increments.

Look for quality in the shelves and latches of wall cabinets. The shelf supports should be adjustable to allow for random spacing of the shelves. Magnetic catches are usually favored over plastic latches. Inspect hinges, structural supports, and all other structural aspects of wall cabinets before you buy them.

Delays

Delivery delays are common with some cabinets. Custom-made cabinets can take months to arrive on a job. Some production cabinets can take six weeks, or longer, to be delivered. Stock countertops generally take a week or two to arrive. Make sure that you order the cabinets early enough to arrive at the job site on time. Once you get to the cabinet stage, your job is going to grind to a halt if the cabinets and countertops are not available when you need them.

I recommend that you use standard, stock cabinets whenever possible. There are two good reasons for this advice. First, stock cabinets cost less than custom cabinets. More importantly, at times, stock cabinets are available when you need them. I've had new houses sit unfinished for weeks, just waiting on custom cabinets. Customers get frustrated, subcontractors are thrown off schedule, and cash flow dwindles. It is best to deal with products that you know and trust and that are going to be available when you need them.

Bathrooms

You choose bathroom cabinets and countertops in much the same way you choose kitchen cabinets and countertops. The same quality concerns apply to the cabinets, but there are some variations on the countertops. For example, a cultured marble vanity top is a good choice for a bathroom, but you wouldn't use one in a kitchen.

Some contractors use laminated countertops for vanities. When this is done, the bowl is cut into the top. There is nothing seriously wrong with this approach, but I don't like this type of setup. I feel the combination cheapens the look of a bathroom. Additionally, self-rimming and drop-in lavatories can leak where the bowl is set into the countertop. Also, the combined cost of a lavatory bowl and laminated top is not much less, if any, than the cost of a cultured marble top. Since the lavatory bowl in a marble top is molded right into the countertop, there is no place for water to seep around the bowl.

Low prices

Low prices (Table 21-2) on cabinets usually mean trouble. Either the cabinets come to you unfinished, or they come without doors, or they are a cash-and-carry deal where you have to haul the cabinets to your job site. However, some good deals are available from time to time. If a supplier is liquidating display models or closing out inventory on a discontinued model, you can get some legitimate savings. You should shop prices and try to reduce your acquisition cost, but don't walk into a trap set by gimmick advertising and sales efforts. Before you buy cabinets, be darn sure of what you are getting for your money.

Table 21-2. Kitchen cabinet price ranges

Type of cabinet	Price range
Steel	Typically inexpensive, but high-priced units exist
Hardwood	Typically moderately priced, but can be expensive
Hardboard	Typically moderately priced
Particleboard	Typically low in price, but can reach into moderate range

22

Laundry facilities

Laundry facilities are not usually given the attention they deserve. This is true in both new construction and conversions. Many of the remodeling jobs I've done over the years have involved laundry rooms. Designers and contractors don't seem to understand what the public wants out of a laundry room. I wouldn't go so far as to say that a laundry area ranks in importance with a kitchen or bathroom, but it is a space that can make your property more appealing. That's a plus when you are looking for either buyers or renters.

People wash, dry, iron, and mend clothes. Clothes are big business, and laundry facilities can improve the cash flow in your rental business. Coin-operated, on-site laundry facilities can really add to the income from your building. Many landlords don't recognize the full benefit of installing coin-operated laundries. I can tell you from experience, however, that a good laundry setup can help you boost the income performance of your building.

Two types

There are two types of laundry facilities to consider if you are converting buildings into residential rental properties. You could be a thoughtful contractor and supply private hook-ups in each apartment. Tenants are going to love the arrangement. Or you could be more profit-orientated and install a centrally located coin-operated laundry. You and prospective purchasers of the building are going to appreciate the financial return on this choice. Since most of us enjoy making extra money, let's talk about the money-making route first.

Coin-operated laundry

How much income can a coin-operated laundry produce? The answer depends on several factors, including the number of tenants using the laundry, how often the tenants use the laundry, and the local competition. Some of this you are going to have to guess. However, you can determine the average number of tenants who are available to use the laundry. You can also check the area to see what local laundromats are available and what they charge. Once you have your estimates, you can start pushing some numbers around. I'll give you an example.

Estimating income

Let's say that you have recently purchased a building that you are going to convert into six rental units. There are going to be two one-bedroom apartments, two two-bedroom apartments, and two three-bedroom apartments. How many tenants does this translate into? Let's run the numbers two ways, conservatively and aggressively.

Taking the conservative approach, let's say there is one occupant in each one-bedroom unit, two occupants in each two-bedroom unit, and three occupants in the three-bedroom unit, for a total of 12 occupants. Looking at it aggressively, let's assume there are two occupants in each one-bedroom unit, three occupants in each two-bedroom unit and four occupants in each three-bedroom unit, for a total of 18 occupants.

Next, let's figure out how many loads of laundry the tenants are going to generate. If you assume an average of two loads of laundry for each tenant every week, the conservative number is 24 loads per week (2 loads × 12 occupants), the aggressive number is 36 loads per week (2 loads × 18 occupants).

A commercial laundry is located a little more than a mile away from your building. Parking facilities are poor, and there are not enough machines to support large groups. The customers often have to wait in line to use a machine. All of this is to your advantage. The laundry charges 75 cents to wash a load, and $1.75 to dry it. With this information, you can now project some cash flow-figures.

Using the conservative figure of 24 loads per week, and figuring each load is washed and dried, the income from a coin-operated laundry in your building would be $60 per week ($2.50 × 24). If you use the more aggressive numbers, the weekly income is $90 ($2.50 × 36).

When the high and low numbers are averaged, they come out to $75. Now, if you take $75 a week, multiply it by 52 weeks and divide it by 12 months, you arrive at an estimated income of $325 per month. Plug this number into your spreadsheet and see how much the value of your building goes up when using the income-approach to property valuation.

The example I've just worked through is just that, an example. I'm not trying to say that you can make an extra $300 a month by putting a coin-operated laundry in your building. The point I'm making is that an income-producing laundry room can provide extra cash flow, and the increased cash can raise the value of many apartment buildings.

Private hook-up

Another approach to take when considering laundry facilities is to put yourself in the place of a tenant. If you were looking for an apartment and found two apartments that were both very nice, you would have to find something to help you decide which unit to rent. That something could be a private laundry hook-up. Given the choice between using a community coin-operated laundry and a private facility in your own apartment, most renters would opt for the latter.

Providing private hook-ups does not help your cash flow in the same way that a coin-operated facility can, but it can reduce your vacancy rate and allow you to charge a higher rental rate. Both of these factors give you increased income and better building values. So, which approach should you take?

Six-units

Buildings with six or more units present a landlord with enough tenants to make a coin-operated laundry viable. These commercial-grade residential rentals are normally appraised with an income-approach method. This being the case, increased income brings the value of a building up. This isn't the way it works with residential-type buildings (buildings with four units or less). Residential properties are appraised with a comparable-sales approach. In reality, appraisers often use three methods of appraising buildings. The individual methods I'm discussing just happen to be the ones that normally have the most impact on the final computed value of a building.

Since commercial-grade buildings benefit more from increased income than residential-type buildings do, the bigger buildings are the ones where coin-operated laundries make the most sense. Residential properties don't offer as many tenants to use laundry facilities. Also, any additional gross income from a coin-operated laundry does not affect the value of these buildings as much. With all of this in mind, I would use coin-operated machines in big buildings and individual hook-ups in small buildings.

Finding a location

If you are going to install laundry facilities in your conversion project, where should you put them? Some designers seem to favor putting washers and dryers in basements. This is certainly a common practice. However, I can't count the number of customers who have paid me to relocate laundry equipment from the basement to another location in the residence. This, along with my personal feelings, prompts me to think that basements are not great places to put laundry facilities.

Basement laundries have some advantages. Noise from the equipment is not as likely to disturb tenants. Dust and lint are kept below the main living areas. Also, if a washing-machine hose breaks, only the basement gets flooded, a considerable advantage. But, basement laundries have some disadvantages, too.

When laundries are in basements, residents have to lug their laundry down to the facility, and then back up again. This can be a real chore, especially for older tenants. Basement laundries tend to be damp and musty with little ventilation. Plumbing drains can present problems if they are not installed low enough to accept the discharge from washing machines. That means you might have to install basins and lift pumps. If you do, you have an added expense and the potential for maintenance problems. Now that you've read some of the pros and cons, it is up to you to decide where to place your equipment.

Near living space

When I build a house or remodel a building, I try to locate the laundry facilities near other living space. For example, I might build a laundry room along a hall or off a breakfast area. I keep two thoughts in mind when I select a location: noise and convenience. I attempt to find, or create, a location where the noise from laundry machines is not going to be offensive. Whenever possible, I position laundry rooms near bedrooms, since that is where dirty laundry originates and clean laundry returns. It cuts down the amount of travel during laundry duties.

Some people are opposed to putting laundry facilities on second and third floors. Usually, the main concern is flooding, and this is a valid point. However, by placing pans under washing machines, checking hoses regularly and keeping valves closed when machine are not used, accidental flooding is unlikely. In my opinion, the convenience of having laundry facilities on the same level as sleeping areas more than offsets the fear of flooding.

In the case of multifamily buildings, where not every apartment has its own hook-ups, I usually plan laundry facilities along a hall on each level of the building. A conveniently located laundry room can be a real asset to your property. Where you position your facilities is strictly up to you. To a large extent, the decision is based on the building you are converting.

How big?

How big should you make a laundry area? It depends on the circumstances. In a custom home, I would make a laundry room large enough to accommodate a washer, dryer, laundry tub, ironing board, and small folding/sewing table. However, most apartments don't have that much space. You can squeeze a single washer and dryer into an area that measures at least 30 inches by 60 inches, but this is a tight space. If you choose stackable appliances, you can get by with less area.

If you are installing a community laundry, the room must be large enough to accommodate all of the equipment, plus the people who are going to use the facility. In large rental buildings, a room like that requires substantial space. Each building has different circumstances that influence the size of the laundry facilities.

23

Storage facilities

Storage facilities are usually very important to tenants. When converting a building into multifamily use, you must make arrangements for the storage of the tenants' possessions. This step in the conversion process is one that many inexperienced contractors overlook. Oftentimes, they don't realize their error until someone brings up the issue of storage after the project is completed. Then, of course, it's too late. It is much easier, and usually less expensive, to plan and create storage areas during the conversion stage.

Allow adequate time to design your storage space. Don't just stick a little storage space here and a little storage space there. Come up with a plan that is both cost-effective to produce and attractive to tenants. A super storage facility can help you attract new tenants.

Chicken wire

If you've ever lived in a large apartment building, you've probably seen tenant storage areas made from chicken wire. This might be fine if you expect only chickens are going to try to gain access to someone else's belongings. In fact, chicken wire offers little security and no privacy.

I've lived in buildings that used chicken wire for storage cubicles, and I didn't like it. Storing old tax records in such a place made me uncomfortable, so there was no way I'd put items with financial value in the locker. In my opinion, wire enclosures are not suitable storage space.

Individual closed-in spaces

Individual, closed-in storage spaces are much more desirable than those that are open to the full view of anyone in the area. If you're going to gang up all of the storage in one place, at least provide some privacy for your tenants. Drywall, studs, and plywood cost more than chicken wire, but they give tenants a much safer feeling.

Whenever the layout of a building makes it possible, I like to create individual storage areas. This is several steps better than a communal storage area. Most storage cubicles are smaller than a walk-in closet, so you should be able to fit some private facilities into each apartment. Not only is this safer for the tenant, it is also more convenient.

Where can you find space?

Where can you find space for storage facilities? It depends on the property. Many of the larger multifamily buildings in my region are old. They often have covered porches off the back of each level. Typically, these porches run the entire length of the building and individual space is created with party walls. Porches like this are an ideal place to create storage. The porch already has a floor and a roof. A little framing and siding, along with a door, is all it takes to make a storage cubicle on the porch. The porches I'm describing are large enough to provide storage facilities, yet there is still room for an area that allows the tenants to enjoy the outdoors. Keep in mind that load requirements might be more stringent for storage, so check first to make sure the porch structure can withstand the added weight.

Since walls are often added or moved during conversion projects, it might be possible to build storage space within an apartment, in the form of closets. Sometimes, however, there isn't enough floor space available to create a major storage area.

Basements are not ideal storage locations. They can be damp, sometimes even downright wet. Moisture can damage items in storage. If you don't have other options, the basement is going to have to suffice as a storage location. Some basements are better than others for this purpose. But what can you do if the building doesn't have a basement?

Add on

If you have searched your building (and your brain) without finding any existing space to use for storage, you might consider an addition. It doesn't have to be complicated or expensive work. Building a small addition on the side of your structure is not a major expense. However, you must first do some research.

If your building sits close to the property line set-backs, you might not be able to add to the building. Most communities have zoning regulations that dictate how close to a property line a building can sit. Most buildings have enough room around them to allow small additions, but some might not. If you build your storage units and then find out that you have encroached into a set-back zone, you've got problems. You might be able to get variance and keep your addition, but it's not unreasonable to assume that you would have to remove the addition. Check your zoning situation before doing any exterior additions.

Freestanding storage

Freestanding storage buildings are another way to overcome storage problems in small buildings, assuming that there is enough land to accommodate the new buildings. Freestanding storage units can be quite cost-effective. They can even be less expensive than building add-on space. Be sure to check with your zoning office before you get started. Set-back requirements for freestanding buildings are usually the same as those for additions to a building.

Outside storage facilities should have an attractive appearance. Sticking a metal shed in the backyard isn't going to do much for the general appearance of your property. The shed is going to be cheap but not attractive. A better option is a wood-frame building. You can either build it yourself, or buy a prefabricated unit. The prefabricated models can sometimes be bought for less than what it costs to build one from scratch. Since prefabricated units are built on skids, they can be moved around, which could become an advantage to you at some time in the future.

I recently had a need for an 8-foot-by-10-foot storage unit. Originally, I planned to build the structure myself, then I injured my shoulder and couldn't do the work. The storage need couldn't wait, so I got my carpenters to work up prices on what their labor would be to build the unit. I did a material take-off and priced out the list. When I combined the material prices with the labor prices, I came up with a total of about $1500. This seemed like a lot, so I went to work doing some research.

After some investigation, I found a man who would sell me a prefabricated building for $1100, including delivery and set up. All I had to do was write the check. The building was delivered on time and it is beautiful. It has a gambrel roof, wood siding, wood framing, a floor, asphalt shingles, attic vents, and double doors. Not a bad buy for $1100. This purchase convinced me to buy prefabricated units for all my future storage needs. This type of building comes in various sizes and prices, and it is well worth considering for your outside storage needs.

Extra income

Storage space might be able to earn you some extra income. Some buildings already have excellent storage facilities on the property. The storage facilities would need to be converted, but the financial rewards might make it worthwhile. Can you think of situations when an existing property has a storage opportunity just waiting for you? I'll give you a few ideas.

If you're dealing in residential conversions, the buildings you buy are likely to be either houses or multifamily properties. Houses frequently have a garage. Sometimes the garage is attached, but not always. Either way works fine for what I'm about to share with you.

Garage storage rental

I had an investor a few years back who bought a four-unit building. The rental units were maxed out, and there didn't seem to be anything the new owner could do to stimulate a better cash flow. I found a way to help him.

The building had an attached, two-car garage. Since the building had four rental units and the garage had only two bays, the previous owner had not allowed access to the garage for tenant use. After looking at the garage, I showed my investor buddy how he and his wife could turn a few extra bucks. I gave him two options.

In my first plan, the investor could set a rental price for the garage bays and offer them to his tenants on a seniority basis. Since the building was in Maine, where the winters are cold, snowy, and long, a garage is a nice asset. I'm sure the tenants would have been happy to pay extra if they were able to park their cars out of the weather. This idea was a good one, but it is not the one the owner chose. Personally, I think it is the route I would have taken.

My other idea for the garage was to divide it up into individual storage units, with doors cut from the outside walls. The spaces could be rented out, either to the tenants or anyone else who needed storage. Have you checked the prices at private rental places lately? Believe me, they're high. This option appealed to the new property owners, and they made the conversion.

The garage, as I recall, contained about 576 square feet, with dimensions of 24 feet by 24 feet. We sat down and worked through various plans for the conversion. The hard part was making as many units as possible while retaining suitable access to each. The plan chosen by the owners created six rental units. Each space had between 80 and 90 square feet (some space was lost to framing). All the units were accessible from outside of the building.

The last I heard, the investor had all six storage units rented, and was collecting $75 a month from each one. That translates to $450 a month for the six units. In this particular building, apartments were renting for $395 a month. So, this creative investor took a garage that was deadweight and got it to produce an income that exceeded one of his apartments. Since storage space is less labor-intensive than habitable space, this type of deal is very attractive to a landlord.

Barn storage rental

Before closing this chapter, I'd like to give you one more example of how a storage conversion can make sense. In rural locations, such as where I live, houses often have detached barns nearby. These barns can sometimes be converted into apartments, but not always. Don't let such a barn go to waste. Use the barn as a storage facility. Partition off the top level, if it has one, for individual storage of small items. Use the expansive lower level as storage for cars, motor homes, boats, and other big-ticket items. People often pay premium prices for this type of storage. I'm not trying to put you into the private storage business, but if you have existing facilities, you might as well capture all the profits you can.

24

Decks, porches, and balconies

Decks, porches, and balconies can all add to the appeal of your conversion project. These amenities are appreciated by tenants and owners alike. From an appraised value point of view, there is a good return on your investment when you build outside leisure space. But you have to keep the size of your decks, porches, and balconies within reason in order to maximize your equity gain. Contractors often make the mistake of overbuilding when adding these types of structures. I am going to talk about this more as we go along in this chapter.

You must first check to make sure that your building has a large enough lot and also that it is not encumbered by zoning restrictions, deed restrictions, or covenants that prevent you from adding outside living space. If no restrictions can keep you from building, there is a good chance that adding one of these outside structures can increase your rental income and the market value of your property.

Decks

Decks are fun places to be in warm weather. They make cooking out more enjoyable, and if you're someone who likes to lay out in the sun, a deck is ideal. Decks also provide a nice location for outside parties. If you have kids, it's a lot easier to clean up after a birthday party on a deck than it is in the house or apartment. People who grow plants love to set them out on decks. The list of reasons why decks are popular could go on and on.

Decks are not inexpensive to build, but they do hold their value well on appraisals. If you are a carpenter and build the deck yourself, the return for your time in equity is quite good. Even if you subcontract the work out to a carpenter, there is probably still going to be some room for you to pick up an equity gain. Equity in a building you own translates into better borrowing power while you own the property and more money in your pocket when you sell.

Deck locations

Deck locations are usually chosen in areas where the deck can connect to the building it serves. Normally a door opens out onto the deck. This setup, of course, is the most convenient. But, sometimes isolated decks are appropriate. For example, let's say that you have an enclosed courtyard in the back of your building. You might build a free-standing deck to house an outdoor spa. I realize this is not feasible for most rental buildings, but if you have upscale tenants, a spa in the backyard could increase your rental income and the quality of your tenants. This is a goal every good landlord seeks to fulfill.

Most decks attach to buildings. They are generally set off to a side or the back. If you're dealing with first-floor living space, constructing a deck is not much of a job. You put a band board on the building (don't forget to flash it in), dig some holes for a pier foundation, and then build the deck. Of course, the job takes a little time and could get complicated if there are multiple level and fancy designs, but a bread-and-butter deck is not much trouble to build.

Whenever I build a deck, I use pressure-treated (PT) lumber. Untreated lumber can be used for much of the job, but I prefer the enduring qualities of pressure-treated wood. There is a downside to PT lumber. It doesn't take paint very well, and it can't be stained. If you don't mind a greenish tint in the wood, PT material is fine. If you have your heart set on a pristine white deck, untreated wood is going to suit your needs better.

How big?

How big should a deck be? This is determined, to some extent, by the number of people who are going to use it. Since I can't speculate on how you are going to use the deck, let's concentrate on the money angle of deck size.

I've talked with appraisers on many occasions in an effort to refine my procedure for spending less and making more. By this, I mean that I like a strong equity return on my investment. To get it, you have to know what limitations exist and what the optimum improvements and sizes are. This is why I rely on consultations with appraisers. It would be a good idea for you to find an appraiser to talk to from time to time. Let me give you an example of one of my last meetings on the issue of decks.

I went to one of my favorite appraisers and asked for help planning for equity gains on a new project I was about to start. Part of our discussion revolved around decks. The deck size I had in mind was 10 feet by 12 feet. It proved to be a good size. The smallest deck that made sense, financially, was 8 feet by 10 feet. The largest size that worked was 12 feet by 14 feet. Smaller decks didn't have enough value to even break even on the cost of construction. Larger decks began to loose their higher price-per-square foot rating, bringing their overall value down. The big decks still didn't lose money—they appraised out for more than they cost to build—but the mid-range decks appraised with a higher equity average. In other words, if I built a 10-by-12-foot deck, I would recover all of my construction cost and pocket a nice equity profit. This is what I needed to know.

Since decks are typically appraised on a square-footage basis, I decided to build a 12-by-14-foot deck. It gave me the biggest bang for my buck. If I did not have a conversation with my appraiser, I might have gotten in trouble. Fortunately, I have enough experience in both building and real estate to have a good idea of what to expect on an appraisal. This is not the case for everyone. If I had built a dinky little deck, I would have lost money. Building a mammoth deck would not have allowed me to make much money over my cost. The mid-range size was the best equity producer.

You can follow this same line of thought in all of your conversion work. If you want to know what the equity spread is when adding a bathroom, an appraiser can tell you. They can also tell you how a floor covered with quarry tile will stack up against one with sheet vinyl. It costs a little money to consult with a good appraiser, but the cost is next to nothing when you consider how much money it can save or make for you.

In some geographical locations, decks are not as good an investment as they are in other locations. Maine is one such location. When the weather becomes agreeable for sitting out on a deck in Maine, the biting bugs are out in full force. If you've haven't sat outside with black flies and mosquitoes the size of small moose biting you, then you probably haven't lived in Maine. Areas where bugs are a bother are good places to consider screened porches.

Porches

It costs a good deal more to build porches than it does to build decks. Since a porch is covered with a roof, it stands to reason that it is going to be more expensive to build. In general, I would say it is not a good idea to build porches on rental property, but this theory doesn't always hold true. To discuss this completely, we have to designate what we mean by a porch.

For the sake of this discussion, I'm calling anything with a floor and a roof a porch. This definition could include a small covered stoop, but for the most part, I'm talking about areas with enough square footage to allow people to lounge about and enjoy being outdoors. Porches that are enclosed with screen are also covered here, no pun intended.

Stoop covers

Adding stoop covers over existing stoops is not going to do much for your appraisal. It gives occupants a dry place to stand and search for keys in the rain, but the cost-effectiveness of this type of work is not very good. Stoop covers can make better architectural statements for a building, but again, it is rarely worth the cost.

Open-air porches

Open-air porches are nice. Lots of older buildings, especially those in the South, have long front porches or wraparound porches. I do love wraparound porches on farmhouses. I grew up in a house with a big front porch, and it was a great place to play when it was raining or when it was too hot to be out in the sun. My grandfather and I spent hours each day playing on the front porch and waiting for the mail to come. Porches just bring out fond memories for me. However, I didn't tell you about my childhood just to get my feelings on paper, although it was enjoyable. I'm actually making a point with my story. People often have good memories of playing on porches. Given an opportunity, they would like their children to experience the same fun. Building a porch on your rental units can provide the chance for tenants and their children to spend quality time out on the porch, so it's not a bad marketing strategy.

I can't see building a simple porch on a rental property. If I were going to invest in the cost of a porch, I would take the job a little further and have it screened. I don't think you get your money out of building an open-air porch, unless your building has some unique circumstances.

Screened porches

Screened porches are a long step up from decks in terms of cost. Fortunately, they hold their own very well on an appraisal report. This can't be said for an open-air porch. Screened porches add usable, warm-weather living space to a home or apartment. People can enjoy a quiet breakfast in the sanctuary of their screened porch. Children can play out on the porch. Cool breezes can be captured while the family remains under the shade of a roof. Screened porches certainly do offer some nice advantages.

The key to getting your money back from a screen porch is the same as I discussed for decks. You have to build them in a moderate size. Too small is no good, and too big is not good enough. Take the middle of the road and your equity gain should be there. This is, however, subject to your local market conditions. The wise thing to do is to consult with an appraiser before you budget your money.

Screened porches are most frequently built off the end or side of a building, which is fine for a single-family home, but it might not make sense in a multifamily environment. If you have four apartments, you are not likely to want to build four screened porches. A better idea is to build a screened gazebo that all of the tenants can use. In this way, you make four tenants happy with one structure. If you have enough land, you can use the gazebo as a focal point for a quaint garden that tenants can use for cooking out, relaxing, and enjoying the outdoors. This type of arrangement can pull better tenants for your building.

I can give you a word of advice from some hard-earned experience. If you decide to build a screened porch where young children are active, cover the lower 4 feet with plywood, install a drink rail, and then screen in the upper half of the structure. A low screen is almost guaranteed to get damaged by children at play.

Sun porches

Sun porches are very nice. In fact, they are too nice for most rental buildings. A Florida room, sun room, or sun porch (or whatever you want to call it) is great on a custom home, but don't spend your money on one with rental property.

Balconies

Balconies are essentially elevated decks. If you have a multistory building, balconies can give tenants a place of retreat outside of their apartments. This is nice, but you could be increasing your liability by providing an elevated space for tenants. I can't advise you on this issue, since I'm not an attorney. Balconies do have value in rental properties, but I'm not sure that their value is worth the risk of potential lawsuits.

If you choose to provide balconies for your upper-level tenants, I suggest that you make the structures very secure. Angled braces can support the balconies, and you are going to need a sturdy railing to enclose the space. Check your local code requirements for the spacing between pickets, and make sure you install enough of a barrier to meet code regulations. I would build the balconies with pressure-treated lumber.

Ground-level decks can be good investments in conversion projects. Screened porches might be safe investments, but due to their cost, I suggest that you do a good bit of research into market values and demand before jumping into building one.

I would not install balconies. If a building I purchased had balconies that were structurally sound, I would convert them into storage space for the tenants. I don't like the idea of people sitting on the rails or leaning over them. Also, an added danger is that people can drop things over the rails.

25

Security measures

In many places, security measures continue to be a topic of conversation. It's unfortunate, but many people no longer feel safe in their homes. Crime is a fact of modern life, and people are afraid. If your building is in an area with a high crime rate, security might be a mandatory part of your conversion plans.

I moved to Maine about eight years ago. My wife and I made the move for many reasons, but at the top of the list was a desire for better living conditions to raise a family. Our neighborhood in Virginia was safe enough at the time, but crazy crimes were getting closer to home. All the other good neighborhoods were affected, too. My family is still in Virginia, so I get periodic updates on what's going on. Now, there are ride-by shootings, drug deals going bad, weapons in schools, and a lot of other activity that we hope to shelter our children from. I was able to move away before my neighborhood became a fringe area of a combat zone. Unfortunately, for many people, it isn't possible to just pack up and move. They must dig in and persevere, perhaps as a tenant in your rental building. If this is the case, the more security you can offer, the more likely you are to get and keep tenants.

What can you do?

What can you do to instill confidence in your tenants? Many approaches can help put their fears at rest. Some of the options are expensive, and others are not. Little things, like adding some exterior lighting and trimming back shrubbery, can make a big difference in how the safety of your building is perceived. Let's look at some security measures that might work for you.

Alarm systems

Alarm systems are one of the first deterrents to crime that most residents think of. They believe that a few pieces of wire, a couple of contacts, and a siren is going to protect them. I don't think so, but it doesn't matter what I believe, it only matters what tenants think. I don't doubt that alarm systems can be a deterrent, and that they can help to avoid some criminal activity. In other areas of security, such as fire safety, they are very good.

Professionally-installed alarm systems can reduce the risk of crime. Weak-kneed criminals bail out when the lights start flashing and the siren is shrieking. Hard-core bad guys are going to know how to defeat such a system, so you're still in trouble, maybe more trouble than you would be without the alarm. The system might give you a false sense of security, making you more vulnerable to full-time criminals.

Hard-wired alarm systems can be installed at any time, but they are easiest to install during the conversion project. Most electricians can wire an alarm system, or you can hire a company that specializes in security. Costs vary from company to company, building to building, and region to region.

If crime is a big concern in your community, a security system can be good for you and your tenants. The physical safety of your tenants could be at stake, and your building is in the line of fire, so you both benefit from a security system. A few phone calls can get security companies sales reps out to talk with you. If you think a security system might be valuable, I suggest you make the calls.

Lighting

The addition of lighting to both the outside of your building and the common areas inside can provide one of the least expensive, yet most effective, deterrents to some types of crime. Adding spotlights on the sides of your building is not expensive. Mounting exterior security lights on poles around your property is not a bank-breaking expense, and adding extra lighting in the halls and common areas is no big deal. Motion-sensing lights might be a good idea. Extra lights can make your tenants more comfortable, and therefore, longer-term tenants.

Landscaping

Landscaping can sometimes add to security risks. Villains have a place to hide if your building is surrounded by tall trees or large, bushy shrubs. You and your tenants don't want these hiding places. Trim back shrubbery and open up the grounds surrounding your property to make it difficult for anyone to find a hiding spot. Very little cost is involved in this tactic, yet it works.

Window bars

I've seen buildings with bars on the windows, and I know the bars add protection for occupants, but I can't see buying into this type of neighborhood. If I'm inspecting properties and see a lot of overkill security features, I look to buy in another area. Putting bars on the windows of your building might be necessary, but it sure gives the impression to tenants that there are better places to live.

Locks

Locks are inexpensive and simple to install, yet a lot of landlords don't provide quality locks on the doors. If you want to appeal to the security-minded tenant, have some deadbolt locks installed. Also, have security sash locks installed on the windows. They won't prevent someone from breaking a window and climbing through, but the perpetrator is not going to be able to raise to window to gain access.

Doors

I think all rental units should be equipped with solid entry doors. My preference is a six-panel, steel-insulated door. Cut a peep hole into the door or provide an intercom system for the tenant, but avoid doors with excessive glass in them. If sidelights are installed in conjunction with a solid door, make sure the door is fitted with a key-only type of deadbolt lock.

If your building has a common hall that serves multiple apartments or offices, a special security door could be in order. Ideally, you want a small foyer with two security doors. This setup gives occupants a chance to get into a secure area before unlocking the door to the main building. It can be expensive, but if your location warrants it, do it.

Fences

Fences are usually ineffective except as deterrents to animals and kids. As far as keeping criminals out, you would need a major security fence installed. The fence might create more of a risk than an advantage. Once criminals cut through or climb over fences, they are afforded some protection from the view of a passerby. Fences are not cheap, and many of them are not attractive. Unless I was having a real problem with kids cutting across my property or stray animals bothering my tenants, I would not install a fence.

Phone jacks

Installing phone jacks in several rooms can bolster the confidence of tenants. Cordless phones make it easy to move from room to room with a phone, but installing extra connection ports for standard phones could help calm the security fears of some tenants.

Security personnel

Hiring security personnel is out of the question for small multifamily ventures. Unless you have a very large complex, you cannot afford to have routine security patrols or a guard at the main door.

Valuables and such

If you want to create security caches for valuables and such, you might build in security safes during construction. This step would normally be considered going overboard, but there are times when it makes sense. For example, if you are converting a building to be used as medical offices, it might be wise to build a secure storage area for medications, needles, and other items used by medical professionals. Built-in fireproof filing cabinets could be a good idea when converting a building into commercial space.

Emergency lighting

Emergency lighting might not be required in your halls and other common areas, but it is a good safety feature. Battery-powered lights can be installed without much trouble, so you might want to look into this option, depending upon your personal circumstances.

Attitude

Security is often nothing more than a sense of attitude. If you convert your building and provide features that make people feel safe, then their attitude is going to tell them the building is secure. In reality, security is a difficult goal to achieve. As in physics, for every action there is an equal but opposite reaction. For every security device you install, someone is out there devising a way to get around it. Sure, security equipment and measures help to reduce risks, but they don't eliminate them.

Here we are

Well, here we are, at the end of our time together. I've enjoyed sharing my experience with you, and I trust you have learned a thing or two about conversion projects. You are going to learn a lot more once you become immersed in the field work. I've been in the trades for over twenty years, and I'm still learning.

I wish you the best of luck in all of your conversion endeavors. If you stub your toe, don't get too discouraged. Focus on the future, learn from your mistakes, don't make the same mistakes twice, and you can grow to be a successful person.

Appendix A

Contractor forms

Punch List
Bathroom Remodeling Project

Item/Phase	O.K.	Repair	Replace	Finish work
Demolition				
Rough plumbing				
Rough electrical				
Rough heating/ac				
Subfloor				
Insulation				
Drywall				
Ceramic tile				
Linen closet				
Baseboard trim				
Window trim				
Door trim				
Paint/Wallpaper				
Underlayment				
Finish floor covering				
Linen closet shelves				
Linen closet door				
Closet door hardware				
Main door hardware				
Wall cabinets				
Base cabinets				
Countertops				

A-1 *Punch list*

Item/Phase	O.K.	Repair	Replace	Finish work
Plumbing fixtures				
Trim plumbing material				
Final plumbing				
Shower enclosure				
Light fixtures				
Trim electrical material				
Final electrical				
Trim heating/ac material				
Final heating/ac				
Bathroom accessories				
Clean up				

Notes

_____

_____

_____

_____

_____

A-1 *Continued*

Punch List

Phase	Okay	Needs Work

A-2 *Detailed punch list*

Certificate of Subcontractor Completion Acceptance

Contractor: _____

Subcontractor: _____

Job name: _____

Job location: _____

Job description: _____

_____

_____

Date of completion: _____

Date of final inspection by contractor: _____

Date of code compliance inspection & approval: _____

Defects found in material or workmanship: _____

_____

_____

Acknowledgment

Contractor acknowledges the completion of all contracted work and accepts all workmanship and materials as being satisfactory. Upon signing this certificate, the Contractor releases the Subcontractor from any responsibility for additional work, except warranty work. Warranty work will be performed for a period of one year from the date of completion. Warranty work will include the repair of any material or workmanship defects occurring between now and the end of the warranty period. All existing workmanship and materials are acceptable to the Contractor and payment will be made, in full, according to the payment schedule in the contract, between the two parties.

_____   _____

Contractor   Date   Subcontractor   Date

A-3 *Subcontractor completion acceptance*

Change Order

This change order is an integral part of the contract dated _____, between the Customer, _____ , and the Contractor, _____, for the work to be performed. The job location is _____.
The following changes are the only changes to be made. These changes shall now become a part of the original contract and may not be altered again without written authorization from all parties.

Changes to be as follow:

_____

_____

_____

_____

_____

These changes will increase/decrease the original contract amount. Payment for theses changes will be made as follows: _____. The amount of change in the contract price will be _____ _____ ($). The new total contract price shall be _____ ($).

The undersigned parties hereby agree that these are the only changes to be made to the original contract. No verbal agreements will be valid. No further alterations will be allowed without additional written authorization, signed by all parties. This change order constitutes the entire agreement between the parties to alter the original contract.

_____   _____
Customer   Contractor

_____   _____
Date   Date

_____
Customer

_____
Date

A-4 *Change order*

Code Violation Notification

Contractor: _____

Contractor's address: _____

City/state/zip: _____

Phone number: _____

Job location: _____

Date: _____

Type of work: _____

Subcontractor: _____

Address: _____

Official notification of code violations

On (date) _____ , I was notified by the local code enforcement
officer of code violations in the work performed by your company. The
violations must be corrected within two business days, as per our contract
dated _____. Please contact the codes officer for a detailed
explanation of the violations and required corrections. If the violations
are not corrected within the allotted time, you may be penalized, as per
our contract, for your actions in delaying the completion of this project.
Thank you for your prompt attention to this matter.

_____

General Contractor   Date

A-5 *Code violation notification*

Appendix B

Landlord forms

Tenant Rental Application

Name _____

Social security # _____ Home phone _____

Current address _____

How long at present address _____

Landlord's name _____

Landlord's phone _____

Reason for leaving _____

Previous Addresses for the Last Three Years

Address _____ From _____ to _____

Landlord's name _____ Phone _____

Reason for moving _____

Address _____ From _____ to _____

Landlord's name _____ Phone _____

Reason for moving _____

Address _____ From _____ to _____

Landlord's name _____ Phone _____

Reason for moving _____

Driver's license # _____ State _____

Vehicle license # _____ State _____

Car make _____ Model _____ Year _____

Credit References

Name _____ Account # _____

Address _____ Account # _____

B-1 *Rental application*

Name _____ Account # _____

Address _____ Account # _____

Name _____ Account # _____

Address _____ Account # _____

Name, address, and phone number of nearest relative, not living with
you _____

Name, address, and phone number of two personal references, not
related to you: _____

_____

Names of all people planning to reside in your rental unit:

_____

_____

Other Pertinent Information

_____

_____

_____

_____

_____

_____

B-1 *Continued*

Rental Lease

This lease is between _____, landlord
and _____, tenant, for a
dwelling located at _____
_____, unit number _____.
Tenant agrees to lease this dwelling for a term of _____,
beginning _____, and ending _____, for
$_____, per _____, payable in advance on the first
day of every calendar _____. Rent shall be paid to _____
_____.

Payments shall be mailed to _____, at
_____.

The first _____ rent for this dwelling is $_____. The
entire sum of this lease is $ _____. The
damage deposit on this dwelling is $ _____ and is
refundable if tenant complies with this lease and leaves the dwelling
clean and undamaged. If tenant intends to move at the end of this lease,
tenant agrees to give landlord notice, in writing, at least thirty days before
the lease expires. A deposit of $ _____ will be required
for two keys. This deposit will be refunded to the tenant when both keys
are returned to the landlord. Landlord will refund all deposits due within
ten days after tenant has vacated the property and returned the keys.
Only the following persons are to live in the above mentioned dwelling:

_____

_____.

Without landlord's prior written permission, no other persons may live in
the dwelling, and no pets shall be admitted to the dwelling, even
temporarily. The dwelling may not be sublet or used for business
purposes. Use of the following is included in the rent, at tenant's own risk:

_____

_____.

Tenant agrees to the terms set forth in the attached rental policy. This
attached rental policy shall be considered a part or this lease and the
tenant's signature on this lease indicates his acceptance of all terms and
conditions of the rental policy.

B-2 *Short lease*

Violation of any part of this agreement, or nonpayment of rent, when due, shall be cause for eviction under appropriate sections of the applicable code and law. The landlord reserves the right to seek any legal means to collect monies owed to him. The prevailing party shall recover reasonable attorney's fees incurred to settle disputes. Tenant hereby acknowledges that he has read this agreement, understands the entire agreement, agrees to the entire agreement, and has been given a copy of the agreement.

_____   _____

Landlord   Date   Tenant   Date

B-2 *Continued*

Rental Lease

This agreement is between _____,
Owners and _____,
Tenants, for a dwelling located at _____
_____, unit number _____.

Tenants agree to lease this dwelling for a term of _____,
beginning _____, and ending _____,
for $_____, per _____, payable in advance on the
first day of every calendar _____. Rent shall be paid to
_____.

Payments shall be mailed to _____, at
_____.

The first _____ rent for this dwelling is $_____. The
entire sum of this lease is $ _____. The
security deposit on this dwelling is $ _____. It is
refundable if Tenants comply with this lease and leave the dwelling clean
and undamaged. If Tenants intend to move at the end of this lease, they
agree to give Owners notice, in writing, at least thirty days before the
lease expires. A deposit of $ _____ will be required for
two keys. It will be refunded to the Tenants when both keys are returned
to the Owners. Owners will refund all deposits due within ten days after
Tenants have moved out completely and returned the keys. Only the
following persons are to live in the above mentioned dwelling:

_____

_____

Without Owner's prior written permission, no other persons may live in
the dwelling, and no pets shall be admitted to the dwelling, even
temporarily. The dwelling may not be sublet or used for business
purposes. Use of the following is included in the rent, at Tenant's own
risk:

_____

_____

Tenants agree to the following: 1) To keep yards and garbage areas
clean. 2) To keep from making loud noises and disturbances. 3) To play
music and broadcast programs at all times so as not to disturb other
people's peace and quiet. 4) Not to paint or alter the dwelling without
first obtaining the Owner's written permission. 5) To park their motor

B-3 *Long lease*

vehicle in assigned space and to keep that space clean of oil drippings. 6) Not to repair motor vehicles on the premises, if such repairs will take longer than a single day. 7) To allow Owners to inspect the dwelling, have work done on the dwelling, and show the dwelling to prospective tenants or purchasers at reasonable times, with twenty-four hours notice. 8) Not to keep any liquid-filled furniture in the dwelling without written permission from the owner. 9) To pay rent by check or money order to _____ _____, at the above address. 10) To pay for all repairs or damage, including drain stoppages, they or their guests cause. 11) Tenants shall maintain adequate heat in their dwelling at all times to prevent plumbing from freezing. 12) Tenants shall inform the Owners of any defects or material problems that may cause damage to the property.

Violation of any part of this agreement, or nonpayment of rent, when due, shall be cause for eviction under appropriate sections of the applicable code and law. The Owners reserve the right to seek any legal means to collect monies owed to them. The prevailing party shall recover reasonable attorney's fees incurred to settle disputes.

Special Terms or Conditions

_____

_____

_____

_____

_____

Tenants hereby acknowledge that they have read this agreement, understand the entire agreement, agree to the entire agreement, and have been given a copy of the agreement.

If you do not understand this document, consult an attorney.

This is a legal, binding document.

Owner	Date	Tenant	Date
Owner	Date	Tenant	Date
Witness	Date	Witness	Date

B-3 *Continued*

Rental Agreement

This rental agreement, dated _____, is between _____
_____, tenant, and
_____, landlord, for the rental
unit located at _____.
Under this agreement, the tenant agrees to rent the above-mentioned
dwelling on a month-to-month basis, with a monthly rental amount of
$_____, _____. The monthly rent
will be due and payable on the first day of each month, starting on the
first day of _____, 19_____. A damage deposit is
required at the signing of this rental agreement. The deposit will be
placed in an escrow account. The amount of this deposit shall be
$_____, _____. If the rental unit is
returned to the landlord in a clean and good condition, this deposit will
be refunded to the tenant within _____ days of vacating the
property. An additional deposit of $_____, will be
required when keys are issued to the tenant. This deposit will also be
placed in escrow and returned to the tenant within _____ days from the
date the tenant returns said keys to landlord. Tenant or landlord may
terminate this agreement with a 30-day written notice to the other party.
The attached rental policy shall be made a part of this agreement and
shall be binding on all parties.

Tenant acknowledges reading and understanding this agreement and the
rental policy that is a part of this agreement. Tenant's signature below
indicates acceptance of all terms and conditions of this rental agreement
and the rental policy.

_____   _____

Landlord   Date   Tenant   Date

B-4 *Rental agreement*

Rental Policy

- Tenant shall keep all areas of his rented portion of the property clean.
- Tenant must not disturb other people's peace and quiet.
- Tenant may not alter the dwelling, without landlord's written permission.
- Parking of vehicles must be confined to only those areas designated for the tenant.
- The tenant must keep the parking area assigned to him clean and unsoiled by oil drippings.
- Tenant may not perform major repairs on motor vehicles while the vehicles are parked on the premises.
- Landlord has the right to inspect the dwelling with 24 hours verbal notice given to the tenant.
- Landlord has the right to access the rental unit to have work performed on the property.
- Landlord, or his agent, may show the dwelling to prospective tenants or purchasers at reasonable times, with 24 hours verbal notice to the tenant.
- Tenant must receive written permission from the landlord to use a water bed or other water-filled furniture.
- Tenant shall pay all costs of repairs and or damage, including, but not limited to, drain stoppages, they or their guests cause.
- Tenant shall prevent the plumbing in the rental unit from freezing.
- Tenant shall provide landlord with a completed move-in list, to be furnished by the landlord, within five days of taking occupancy of the rental unit.
- Tenant shall inform landlord of any defects or safety hazards that may cause damage to the property or the occupants.
- Pets are not allowed, without the written permission of the landlord.
- Violation of any part of this rental policy or nonpayment of rent as agreed shall be cause for eviction and all legal actions allowed by law.

B-5 *Rental policy*

Cosigner Addendum

Addendum to rental agreement/lease dated:_____, between
_____ and _____. This addendum
shall become an integral part of the above-mentioned agreement for the
rental unit located at _____.
The undersigned has read and understands the above-mentioned
document and agrees to abide by the agreement in the capacity of a
cosigner. In affixing his signature below, the cosigner may be held
accountable for all terms and conditions of the rental agreement/lease
described above.

_____

Cosigner   Date

B-6 *Cosigner addendum*

Rental Addendum

This rental addendum shall become an integral part of the lease/rental agreement dated _____, between the landlord, _____ _____, and the tenant, _____, for the real estate commonly known as _____. The undersigned parties hereby agree to the following:

_____

_____

_____

_____

_____

_____

_____

_____

_____

_____

_____

_____

_____   _____
Landlord   Date   Tenant   Date

B-7 *Rental addendum*

Pet Addendum

This pet addendum shall become an integral part of the lease/rental agreement dated _____, 19____, between _____ _____, tenant and _____ _____, landlord, for the dwelling located at _____.
Tenant is allowed under the following terms and conditions to keep _____ pet/s described as _____, in the above-mentioned dwelling. Tenant shall maintain control of the pet at all times. Tenant agrees to treat the pet in a humane manner at all times. Tenant agrees to clean up after the pet, both in and out of the rental unit. Tenant may not create a condition where other animals are drawn to the property because of the pet. Tenant agrees to guarantee peace and quiet for other tenants, as it relates to the pet. If complaints are filed by other tenants, tenant will make appropriate arrangements to cure the cause of the complaints of the pet. If pet delivers offspring, tenant will remove the young animals within ten weeks of their birth. Tenant agrees to pay an additional damage deposit of $_____, for damage that may be caused by the pet. This deposit will be held in an escrow account and returned to the tenant within five days of vacating the property, if no damage has been caused by the pet. Tenant agrees to pay an additional monthly rent of $_____ for the privilege of housing the pet. Tenant agrees to remove the pet from the rental unit if any of these terms or conditions are broken.

_____   _____
Landlord   Date   Tenant   Date

B-8 *Pet addendum*

Water Bed Addendum

This addendum shall become an integral part of the lease/rental agreement dated _____, 19_____, between _____ _____, tenant and _____, landlord, for the property located at _____.
Under the terms and conditions of this agreement, tenant may use a water bed in his rental unit. The terms and conditions for the use of a water bed in the above-mentioned dwelling are as follows: Tenant must allow landlord to inspect and approve the quality and installation of the water bed. Tenant shall provide the landlord with proof of insurance naming the landlord as first insured for damages caused in regards to the water bed. The minimum amount of liability coverage acceptable to the landlord is $100,000.00. In addition to the insurance coverage, tenant agrees to make an additional damage deposit in the amount of $_____. This deposit will be held in an escrow account and returned to the tenant within five days of vacating the property, if no damage has been caused in conjunction with the water bed. Tenant agrees to remove his water bed immediately, if any of these terms or conditions are broken.

_____   _____
Landlord   Date   Tenant   Date

B-9 *Waterbed addendum*

Sample of Security Deposit Receipt

Landlord hereby acknowledges the receipt of a security/damage deposit
from the tenant in the amount of $_____.
This deposit will remain in an escrow account during the term of the
lease/rental agreement. Landlord has the right to apply this deposit to the
costs incurred to offset any damages or financial responsibilities incurred,
due to the tenant's lack of performance as agreed upon in the lease/
rental agreement dated _____, between the landlord and tenant.
If the tenant complies with the lease/rental agreement and does not
cause damage to the landlord's property, this deposit will be returned to
the tenant within 48 hours of the tenant's vacating the property. If the
terms of the lease/rental agreement are breached by the tenant, or if the
tenant causes damage to the landlord's property, the landlord may retain
any portion of this deposit necessary to compensate the landlord for
financial burdens caused by the tenant.

B-10 *Security deposit receipt*

Sample of a Lease Renewal Clause

If the tenant is not in default of the existing lease/rental agreement dated
_____, between the landlord and tenant, the tenant may renew
the lease, under the existing, current rental terms, conditions, and rates in
effect at the time of renewal. Tenant's lease renewal is subject to new
rules, regulations, terms, conditions, and rates that may apply at the time
of renewal. Tenant's lease renewal is subject to the review and approval
of the landlord.

B-11 *Lease renewal clause*

Tenancy Change Order

This tenancy change order addendum shall become an integral part of the lease/rental agreement dated _____, 19____, between _____, tenant and _____, landlord, for the dwelling located at_____.
This tenancy change order addendum shall serve to change the original terms of tenancy as dictated by the above-mentioned lease/rental agreement. Tenant and landlord agree to the following changes and amendments to the existing lease/rental agreement for the property located at _____.

Changes in Tenancy

_____

_____

_____

_____

_____

_____

_____

_____

_____

_____

_____

The above-detailed changes are the only changes agreed to and in force. Other than for the above changes, the original lease/rental agreement is in full force. By signing below, both landlord and tenant agree to the detailed changes in the existing written agreement between them.

_____   _____
Landlord   Date   Tenant   Date

B-12 *Tenancy change order*

Phone Checklist for Prospective Tenants

1) How many bedrooms do you need?   _____

2) Do you prefer a ground-level unit?   _____

3) How many people will occupy the property?   _____

4) Do you have pets?   _____

5) How much parking space do you require?   _____

6) Do you work in this area?   _____

7) Do you require laundry facilities?   _____

8) Are you new to the area?   _____

9) Do you have a water bed?   _____

10) When would you like to see the property?   _____

11) Will your spouse be attending the showing?   _____

12) Have you seen the exterior of the property?   _____

13) May I have your name and phone number?   _____

14) Do you have any other questions?   _____

Comments

_____

_____

_____

_____

B-13 *Phone checklist*

Move-Out Checklist

Tenant: _____

Rental unit: _____

Item	*Location of defect*
Walls	_____
Floor coverings	_____
Ceilings	_____
Windows	_____
Screens	_____
Window treatments	_____
Doors	_____
Light fixtures	_____
Cabinets	_____
Countertops	_____
Plumbing	_____
Heating	_____
Air conditioning	_____
Electrical	_____
Trim work	_____
Smoke detectors	_____
Light bulbs	_____
Appliances	_____
Furniture	_____
Fireplace	_____
Hardware	_____

B-14 *Move-out checklist*

Item	*Location of defect*
Closets	_____
Landscaping	_____
Parking area	_____
Storage area	_____
Other	_____
	_____

Comments

_____

_____

_____

_____

Inspection completed by: _____

                    Landlord   Date

B-14 *Continued*

Mutual Termination Agreement

For good and valuable consideration, _____
_____, landlord and
_____, tenant agree to terminate the
lease/rental agreement presently in force and dated _____. Said lease/
rental agreement for the property located at _____
_____, shall become null and void, once consideration
has been given and terms and conditions are complied with, as described
below, and this document is executed by all parties.

Terms of Consideration

_____

_____

_____

In this mutual termination, both landlord and tenant agree to the disposition
of deposits and financial responsibilities in the following manner:

_____

_____

_____

_____

_____

_____.

_____   _____
Landlord   Date   Tenant   Date

B-15 *Mutual termination agreement*

Final Notice to Vacate

Be advised, this is your final notice to vacate these premises. All of my attempts to resolve your breech of our lease have gone unanswered. You have five days to vacate this property. If you have not delivered the property to me within five days, eviction proceedings will be started. Eviction is not an enjoyable experience for anyone. I am giving you this final notice to allow you the opportunity to leave these premises under your own power. If you fail to vacate, I will take all actions available to have you removed from the property.

Date: _____

Time: _____

_____
Landlord

B-16 *Notice to vacate*

Past-Due Rent Notice

Please take notice, your rent, that was due on _____, 19_____, is past due. Unfortunately, you will be assessed a late charge for allowing your rent to become delinquent. If you have already mailed your rent, please disregard this notice. If you have not mailed your rent payment, this is your formal, and final, notice of your past-due rent. If your rent is not received within the next 48 hours, collection and eviction actions will be taken. If you are having trouble paying your rent, I will be happy to talk with you to see if we can come to amicable terms. If you dispute this notice, I will gladly meet with you to discuss the circumstances. If you do not pay your rent or contact me within the next 48 hours, you will be notified by the appropriate legal channels of the upcoming proceedings. I can be reached between _____ a.m. and _____ p.m. at _____.

Date: _____

Time: _____

_____
Landlord   Date

B-17 *Past-due rent notice*

Notice to Perform Covenant

To _____,
tenant in possession:

Please take notice that you have violated the following covenant in your
lease/rental agreement:

_____

_____

You are required to perform the aforesaid covenant or to deliver up
possession of the premises now held and occupied by you, being those
premises situated in the city of _____,
county of _____, state of _____,
commonly known as _____.

If you fail to do so, legal proceedings will be instituted against you to
recover said premises and such damages as the law allows.

This notice is intended to be a _____ notice to perform the aforesaid
covenant. It is not intended to terminate or forfeit the lease/rental
agreement under which you occupy said premises. If after legal
proceedings, said premises are recovered from you, the landlord will
attempt to rent said premises for the highest possible rent, giving you
credit for sums received and holding you liable for any deficiencies
arising during the term of said lease/rental agreement.

Dated this _____ day of _____, 19_____.

_____

Landlord

Proof of Service

I, the undersigned, being of legal age, declare under penalty of perjury that
I served the notice to perform covenant, of which this is a true copy, on
the above-mentioned tenant in possession in the manner indicated below:

On _____, 19_____, I served this notice in the following manner:

_____

_____

Executed on _____, 19_____, at _____.

By: _____

Title: _____

B-18 *Notice to perform covenant*

30-Day Notice to Terminate Tenancy

To _____,
tenant in possession:

Please take notice that you are hereby required within thirty days from
this date to remove from and deliver up possession of the premises now
held and occupied by you, being those premises situated in the city of
_____, county of
_____, state of _____, commonly known as
_____.

This notice is intended for the purpose of terminating the lease or rental
agreement by which you now hold possession of the above-described
premises, and should you fail to comply, legal proceedings will be
instituted against you to recover possession, to declare said lease or
rental agreement forfeited and to recover rents and damages for the
period of the unlawful detention.

Please be advised that your rent on said premises is due and payable up
to and including the date of termination of your tenancy under this notice.

Dated this _____ day of _____, 19_____.

_____

Owner

Proof of Service

I, the undersigned, being of legal age, declare under penalty of perjury
that I served the thirty day notice to terminate tenancy, of which this is a
true copy, on the above-mentioned tenant in possession in the manner
indicated below:

_____ On _____, 19_____, I handed the notice to the tenant.

_____ I posted the notice in a conspicuous place at the tenant's
residence on _____, 19_____.

_____ I sent by certified mail a true copy of the notice to the tenant at
tenant's place of residence on _____, 19_____.

Executed on _____, 19_____, at _____.

By: _____

Title: _____

B-19 *30-day notice to terminate tenancy*

Notice to Pay Rent or Quit

To _____,
tenant in possession:

You are hereby notified that the rent is now due and payable on the premises now held and occupied by you, being those premises situated in the city of _____, county of _____, state of _____. Commonly known as _____.

Your account is delinquent in the amount of $ _____, being the rent for the period from _____ to _____.

You are hereby required to pay said rent in full within _____ days or to remove from and deliver up possession of the above-mentioned premises, or legal proceedings will be instituted against you to recover possession of said premises, to declare the forfeiture of the lease or rental agreement under which you occupy said premises and to recover rents and damages, together with court costs and attorney's fees, according to the terms of your lease or rental agreement.

Dated this _____ day of _____, 19_____.

_____
Owner

Proof of Service

I, the undersigned, being of legal age, declare under penalty of perjury that I served the thirty day notice to pay or quit, of which this is a true copy, on the above-mentioned tenant in possession in the manner indicated below:

_____ On _____, 19_____, I handed the notice to the tenant.

_____ I posted the notice in a conspicuous place at the tenant's residence on _____, 19_____.

_____ I sent by certified mail a true copy of the notice to the tenant at tenant's place of residence on _____, 19_____.

Executed on _____, 19_____, at _____.

By: _____

Title: _____

B-20 *Notice to pay rent or quit*

30-Day Notice to Perform Covenant

To _____,
tenant in possession:

Please take notice that you have violated the following covenant(s) in your lease or rental agreement:

_____

_____

You are hereby required within _____ days to perform the aforesaid covenant(s) or to deliver up possession of the premises now held and occupied by you, being those premises situated in the city of _____, county of _____, state of _____, commonly known as _____.

If you fail to do so, legal proceedings will be instituted against you to recover said premises and such damages as the law allows.

This notice is intended to be a _____ notice to perform the aforesaid covenant(s). It is not intended to terminate or forfeit the lease or rental agreement under which you occupy said premises. If, after legal proceedings, said premises are recovered from you, the Owner will try to rent said premises for the best possible rent, giving you credit for sums received and holding you liable for any deficiencies arising during the term of said lease or rental agreement.

Dated this _____ day of _____, 19_____.

_____
Owner

Proof of Service

I, the undersigned, being of legal age, declare under penalty of perjury that I served the thirty day notice to perform covenant, of which this is a true copy, on the above-mentioned tenant in possession in the manner indicated below:

_____ On _____, 19_____, I handed the notice to the tenant.

_____ I posted the notice in a conspicuous place at the tenant's residence on _____, 19_____.

_____ I sent by certified mail a true copy of the notice to the tenant at tenant's place of residence on _____, 19_____.

Executed on _____, 19_____, at _____.

By: _____

Title: _____

B-21 *30-day notice to perform covenant*

Notice to Terminate Tenancy

To _____,
tenant in possession:

You are hereby required within thirty days from this date to remove from and deliver up possession of the premises now held and occupied by you, being those premises situated in the city of _____
_____, county of _____
_____, state of _____, commonly known as
_____.

This notice is intended for the purpose of terminating the lease/rental agreement by which you now hold possession of the above-described premises, and should you fail to comply, legal proceedings will be instituted against you to recover possession, to declare said lease/rental agreement forfeited and to recover rents and damages for the period of the unlawful detention.

Please be advised that your rent on said premises is due and payable up to and including the date of termination of your tenancy under this notice. This notice complies with the terms and conditions of the lease or rental agreement under which you presently hold said property.

Dated this _____ day of _____, 19_____.

_____
Landlord

Proof of Service

I, the undersigned, being of legal age, declare under penalty of perjury that I served the notice to terminate tenancy, of which this is a true copy, on the above-mentioned tenant in possession, in the manner indicated below:

On _____, 19_____, I served the notice to the tenant in the following manner:

_____

_____

Executed on _____, 19_____, at _____.

By: _____

Title: _____

B-22 *Notice to terminate tenancy*

Final Notice

Be advised, this is your last opportunity to resolve your breach of our lease. You have been mailed many notices. All previous notices have gone unanswered. Other means of communication have failed to produce a response from you. If you do not comply with the terms of your lease within the next 48 hours, legal proceedings will be started to resolve this matter. If in doubt, refer to your lease. You will see that you may be held responsible for the fees incurred in these legal proceedings. If you fail to comply with your lease, all legal actions allowable by law will be used to correct this situation. It is not my desire to proceed legally, but you are leaving me with no options. If I have not been contacted by you within the next 48 hours, the next notifications you receive will be from my attorney. Please contact me immediately to avoid legal action. I can be reached from _____ a.m. to _____ p.m. at _____. A copy of this notice has also been mailed to you at this address.

Date: _____

Time: _____

_____

Landlord

B-23 *Final notice*

Friendly Reminder

I wanted to take this opportunity to remind you that your rent for
_____, 19____ is past due. I trust this is the result of
an oversight. If you have already mailed your rent, please disregard this
notice. If you have not mailed your rent, please do so immediately. If
your rent has not been received by _____, 19____, you
will be assessed a late charge, as allowed by your lease. I don't wish to
charge you for being late, but the late-fee policy must be enforced on all
tenants to be effective. Thank you for your prompt attention to this
matter. If for some reason you are unable to pay your rent, please call
me to discuss your circumstances. I can be reached from _____ a.m. to
_____ p.m. by calling _____.

Date _____

_____

Landlord

B-24 *Friendly reminder*

Prospect Log

Name	Address	Phone	Date

B-25 *Prospect log*

Accounts Receivable

Date	Account description	Amount due	Date due	Date received
	Total due			

B-26 *Accounts receivable list*

Notice
Intent to Access Your Rental Unit

Be advised, your landlord requires access to your rental unit on
_____, at _____ a.m./p.m. As stipulated in
your lease, this notice is your formal notification of the landlord's intent to
enter your dwelling. If you wish to be present during this access, you are
welcome. If you would like to attempt to arrange a more convenient time
for the entry, please contact your landlord by calling _____.
In the event you are unable to be available for this access, your landlord
will be present during the time your rental unit is open. In addition to this
notice, an additional notice has been mailed to your address. Thank you for
your cooperation.

Date _____

Time _____ am./p.m.

Notice posted by _____

B-27 *Notice to access rental unit*

Maintenance Expense Log

Unit number	Building address	Date of expense	Nature of expense	Amount of expense

B-28 *Maintenance expense log*

Lease Renewal Schedule

Unit number	Date leased	Lease expires	Tenant contacted	Will renew	Will not renew

B-29 *Lease renewal schedule*

Record of Deposits

Unit number	Tenant's name	Amount of deposit	Date of deposit	Type of deposit	Deposit returned

B-30 *Record of deposits*

Marketing Memos

Ad number	Ad placed in	Calls received	Number of showings	Number of leases signed

B-31 *Marketing memo list*

Vacancy Rate Data

Unit number	Unoccupied	Month

B-32 *Vacancy rate data*

Monthly Utility Expense Log

Unit number	Building address	Date of expense	Nature of expense	Amount of expense

B-33 *Utility expense log*

Helpful Information

This form is for your convenience. We know it can take awhile to get adjusted to a new home, and we will be happy to help you with questions you may have about the community. Thank you for renting with us.

Phone Numbers

Police (non-emergency) _____

Police (EMERGENCY) _____

Fire department _____

Ambulance _____

Emergency room _____

Hospital _____

Doctor _____

Telephone company _____

Utility company _____

Water & sewer district _____

Resident manager _____

Landlord _____

Notes

_____

_____

_____

_____

_____

_____

B-34 *Information sheet for tenants*

Move-In Checklist

Please inspect all areas of your rental unit carefully. Note any existing deficiencies on the form below. The information on this form will be used in determining the return of your damage deposit. Please be thorough, and complete all applicable items.

Tenant: _____

Rental unit: _____

Item	*Location of Defect*
Walls	_____
Floor coverings	_____
Ceilings	_____
Windows	_____
Screens	_____
Window treatments	_____
Doors	_____
Light fixtures	_____
Cabinets	_____
Countertops	_____
Plumbing	_____
Heating	_____
Air conditioning	_____
Electrical	_____
Trim work	_____
Smoke detectors	_____
Light bulbs	_____
Appliances	_____

B-35 *Move-in checklist*

Item	Location of Defect
Furniture	_____
Fireplace	_____
Hardware	_____
Closets	_____
Landscaping	_____
Parking area	_____
Storage area	_____
Other	_____
	_____

Comments

_____

_____

_____

_____

Inspection completed by: _____

Tenant   Date

B-35 *Continued*

Annual Maintenance Reminder

Item	Date for Attention	Completed
Clean heating system	_____	_____
Clean flue	_____	_____
Clean chimney	_____	_____
Service heating system	_____	_____
Clean air conditioning unit	_____	_____
Service air conditioning unit	_____	_____
Inspect water heater	_____	_____
Inspect toilet tanks	_____	_____
Inspect faucets	_____	_____
Inspect caulking at fixtures	_____	_____
Inspect attic	_____	_____
Inspect basement/crawl space	_____	_____
Inspect safety equipment	_____	_____
Inspect parking area	_____	_____
Inspect lighting	_____	_____
Inspect for fire hazards	_____	_____
Inspect porches	_____	_____
Inspect balconies	_____	_____
Interview tenants	_____	_____

B-36 *Annual maintenance reminder*

Key Log

Unit number	Date key was given	Person given key	Phone number	Key returned

B-37 *Key log*

Purchaser's Quick
Reference Information Sheet

Attorney's name _____

Attorney's address _____

Attorney's phone _____

Inspector's name _____

Inspector's address _____

Inspector's phone _____

Lender's name _____

Lender's address _____

Lender's phone _____

Loan officer's name _____

Escrow agent's name _____

Escrow agent's address _____

Escrow agent's phone _____

Insurance agency's name _____

Insurance agency's address _____

Insurance agency's phone _____

B-38 *Purchaser's information sheet*

Broker Commission Arrangement

If _____, broker of the
_____, agency procures an
acceptable offer for the purchase of my real estate, commonly known as
_____, and the
property is successfully sold, the real estate agency shall receive a
commission equal to _____% of the closed sale price. The listed
price of this property is _____
($_____). This commission agreement will remain in
effect from _____ to _____.
Seller agrees that if the property is sold within six months to anyone the
broker has registered with the seller, as a prospective buyer, the broker
shall be entitled to the above commission. This does not apply if the
seller lists the property with a licensed real estate brokerage on an
exclusive basis.

_____		_____	
Seller	Date	Broker	Date
_____			
Seller	Date		

B-39 *Broker commission arrangement*

Multiple Offer Notification

In response to your offer to purchase the real estate commonly known as
_____, dated
_____, please be advised there are multiple offers for the
purchase of the property at this time. All of the offers are unacceptable,
therefore, new offers are welcome and will be reviewed on
_____, at _____ o'clock, AM/PM. New offers will be
accepted in person with an appointment or by mail. Seller retains the
right to accept any offer or to reject all offers.

_____
Seller   Date

B-40 *Multiple offer notification*

Counteroffer

This counteroffer is in response to the purchase and sale agreement dated_____, between the Purchasers,

_____, and the Sellers,

_____, for the sale of the real estate commonly known as _____.

All other terms shall remain the same, Seller retains the right to accept any other offer prior to written acceptance and delivery of this counteroffer back to the Seller. This counteroffer shall expire at _____ o'clock AM/PM on _____, unless an executed accepted copy is returned to the Seller prior to the above deadline. The following counteroffer is submitted for your review:

_____

_____

_____

_____

_____

_____

_____

_____

_____		_____	
Seller	Date	Purchaser	Date
_____		_____	
Seller	Date	Purchaser	Date

B-41 *Counteroffer*

Comparative Property Data Sheet

Address _____

Style _____   Rents _____

Amenities _____   Number of Rooms _____

Number of Bedrooms _____   Number of Bathrooms _____

Siding _____   Heat Type _____

Type of Hot Water _____   Water (public/private) _____

Sewer (public/private) _____   Basement (yes/no) _____

Utilities paid by landlord _____

Security _____   Storage _____

Laundry facilities _____

Deposit required _____   Pets allowed _____

Parking facilities _____

Proximity to shopping _____

School system _____

General condition of rental units _____

Floor Plan

	1st	2nd	3rd	Basement
Living Room				
Dining Room				
Family Room				
Bedrooms				
Bathrooms				
Kitchen				
Comments				

Other Pertinent Information

_____

_____

B-42 *Comparative property information*

Index

Illustration page numbers are in **boldface**.

About the author

R. Dodge Woodson has nearly 20 years' experience as a homebuilder, contractor, master plumber, and real estate broker. He is also the author of many books, including *Home Plumbing Illustrated*, *Roofing Contractor: Start and Run a Money-Making Business*, *Troubleshooting & Repairing Heat Pumps*, and *The Master Plumber's Licensing Exam Guide*, among others.